EQUAL JUSTICE

EQUAL JUSTICE

FAIR LEGAL SYSTEMS IN AN UNFAIR WORLD

FREDERICK WILMOT-SMITH

Harvard University Press

CAMBRIDGE, MASSACHUSETTS

LONDON, ENGLAND ||| 2019

"The Lonesome Death of Hattie Carroll" by Bob Dylan. Copyright ©
1964, 1966 by Warner Bros. Inc.; renewed 1992, 1994 by Special
Rider Music. All rights reserved. International copyright secured.
Reprinted by permission.

"Long Walk Home" by Bruce Springsteen. Copyright © 2007 by
Bruce Springsteen (Global Music Rights). International copyright
secured. Reprinted by permission. All rights reserved.

Library of Congress Cataloging-in-Publication Data
Names: Wilmot-Smith, Frederick, 1986– author.
Title: Equal justice : fair legal systems in an unfair world /
    Frederick Wilmot-Smith.
Description: Cambridge, Massachusetts : Harvard University Press,
    2019. | Includes bibliographical references and index.
Identifiers: LCCN 2019014639 | ISBN 9780674237568
    (hardcover : alk. paper)
Subjects: LCSH: Justice. | Equity. | Equality before the law.
    | Fairness.
Classification: LCC K247 .W55 2019 | DDC 340/.114—dc23
LC record available at https://lccn.loc.gov/2019014639

For my teachers

CONTENTS

EQUAL JUSTICE

INTRODUCTION

JUST LEGAL SYSTEMS

The Problem

Convicted of corrupting the youth of Athens and not recognising the Polis's gods, Socrates was sentenced to death. Plato's *Crito* finds him presented with the option of escaping Athens. He refuses and is executed.

Socrates's dilemma is often discussed under the aegis of "unjust laws." That is not quite right. When called to explain his reasons to Crito, Socrates imagines the laws of Athens asking him, "Do you think that state can exist and not be overturned, in which the decisions reached by the courts have no force but are made invalid and annulled by private persons?"[1] His dilemma was not whether to obey the law; it was whether to evade a sentence imposed by a legal procedure.[2] This concern is not with the authority of laws; it is with the authority of legal institutions.[3]

Here, at the foundation of Western political thought, a philosopher wrestled with the question of the proper authority of a legal system. One of my aims in this book is to convince you that it is not enough, when answering that question, to think only about the justice of laws. A legal system with a perfect set of laws would be unjust if, for example, it excluded people of certain races or religions from its courts. Financial barriers can operate in largely the same way: an effective court system that is very expensive to use is not much different from an institution open only to the nobility. The effects of the court system also matter. Legal structures that make enforcement of the law practically impossible will leave weaker members of society open to exploitation at the hands of, for example, unscrupulous employers or spouses. Without proper regulation, the government is able to use the legal system as a tool of political oppression. It can do this, most obviously, by inventing offences and running show trials. But it can also do it through selective enforcement of the law, allowing some politicians or corporations to act with impunity. These are matters concerning the just and proper structure of the justice system.

So what is a just justice system? It is easy enough to say, one where victims of injustice get justice and no one suffers injustice at the hands of the system. There is a sense in which that answer is right. But it faces two problems as a practical ideal. First, the benefits of a justice system are scarce. No institutional arrangement will eliminate all forms of domination in society. No structure can ensure that all injustices are repaired, or that all those with legal claims to various goods have those claims enforced. The adoption of a particular arrangement will, therefore, inevitably benefit some at the expense of others. Second, any institutional arrangement will be imperfect. Laws will be misapplied: even unbiased and diligent judges can reach incorrect conclusions on both facts and law. The consequences of these imperfections can be devastating: wrongful convictions can lead to life, even death, in jail; incorrect decisions on civil entitlements can result in unfair dismissal from jobs or homelessness.

So we face a distributional question: some will fail to obtain the benefits they are owed; others will suffer burdens they do not deserve. A justice system must justify itself to those who bear the burdens of these decisions. Which victims of injustice should get reparation, given that not all can? Who should suffer injustices, such as wrongful conviction, given that some will? To answer these questions, we need a theory of a just legal system. I will offer one such theory in this book. Before turning to that, some prefatory remarks are in order: on the special priority justice systems should have in our political thought; their neglect in modern political theory; and the distinction, vital to make in this context, between means and ends.

The Priority of Justice

When a government has money to spend, it has to choose among schools, hospitals, roads, and so on. Any amount spent on legal resources—court fees, legal aid, court buildings—is money that could have been spent on these other things. And, when faced with the choice of a bit more money for the justice system or, say, the healthcare system, many people plump for the latter. Can a claim to repair a breach of contract really be as important as life-saving surgery? As it was once put, "If the issue is a choice between more access to legal aid or more accessible medicare, health comes first. If the choice is between investing in public legal education or job retraining, employment must take precedence. If it is between sheltering the cost of legal services from taxation or sheltering abused spouses, who would see this as a matter for debate and choice?"[4]

This way of thinking regards justice as one matter of state discretionary spending among many. A more radical thought is that justice is an ordinary consumer good. Perhaps few would accept that characterisation. But many suppose that a fair justice system can be established through a free market, with legal services priced and distributed like ordinary marketable commodities. Many legal services are distributed through a market, albeit one with restrictive entry conditions; the problem, it is often thought, is that the market is not free *enough*.

A central theme of this book is that we should resist these thoughts. Justice has a special value. As Thomas Nagel writes, "Justice plays a special role in political argument: to appeal to it is to claim priority over other values. Injustice is not just another cost; it is something that must be avoided, if not at all costs, then at any rate without counting the costs too carefully. If a form of inequity in social arrangements is unjust, it should not be tolerated."[5] This priority is carried through to legal institutions: these must not be treated as ordinary consumer goods; securing justice in our legal institutions should have a priority. I will not summarise all my arguments for these claims here, but some recurrent features are worth stressing at the outset.

Perhaps most important is my focus on matters of systematic design.[6] The justice system is often neglected at the expense of, for example, healthcare because the goods on offer are characterised in one-shot terms. We are asked to compare individual instances of injustice or ill-health: the reparation of a breach of contract versus the reparation of a broken leg. When things are put in that way, resources inevitably go to the reparation of the broken leg. But this way of thinking also occludes the more systemic importance of the justice system.

Very many important distributions in society—from healthcare and welfare to money and property—are ultimately answerable to legal rules. Justice in those myriad realms will be impossible without a just justice system. Two features of the legal system's role in ensuring justice are important to distinguish. These two features undermine a contemporary characterisation of the legal system as a *competing* demand on state resources (competing, for example, with education and healthcare). A just justice system is a necessary precondition of justice in other spheres.

First, when distributions are managed by institutional processes, the way the regulatory institution is set up will affect whether the ultimate distributions are just.[7] A right to be paid wages is not worth much if you cannot get your employer to pay; a right to healthcare or welfare is of scant value if no one can be made to treat your ailments or pay your claim to benefits. This shows a causal priority of the justice of legal institutions over justice in other spheres: these must be just to ensure that the distributions being controlled are just.

Consider one important example in a little more detail. Justice at one point in time does not guarantee justice in the future. Property might be stolen, wrongs might be committed, and inequality of opportunity might be entrenched by persistent material inequality. One way states try to regulate justice over time is through systems of tax and transfer, especially inheritance tax.[8] Whether these measures are effective will depend in part on whether the rules are just. Even if the rules governing the taxation of inheritance are perfectly just, they will do little good if the rich and powerful can evade them at will. Even if the rules governing taxation of corporations are perfectly just, they will be ineffective if corporations are able to secure sweetheart deals. If legal institutions are unjust, that injustice will infect all the domains that the law regulates.

The second feature of the justice system derives from the scarcity of state goods like education, healthcare, and welfare. For example, in the United Kingdom, the National Health Service (NHS) has to formulate guidelines to determine which treatments can and cannot be funded out of public funds. One patient's treatment has resource implications for other patients. Those who miss out on potential treatments—who, for example, fall on the wrong side of the NHS's rules on the treatments it will fund—may well be aggrieved. For it to be justifiable for any patient to receive treatment, it must be justifiable to deny the other patients treatment. The rules used to make the original allocation (to the one patient at the expense of the others) are important in this justification. But they are not a complete answer. The rules might be badly administered: the administrators might grant or deny treatment incorrectly. The structure of the legal system will affect whether and how people challenge those decisions. If, for example, it is impossible to get a lawyer to help you challenge an allocative decision, you may have no way of testing its justice.

Whether the initial scheme is justifiable depends in part on the way in which the scheme is run and the extent to which decisions taken under it are subject to review. It is not enough, when those who lose out object to a distribution, to point to a perfect set of rules. Those who lose out might say that the rules have not been administered correctly. And they might be right. In this way, the justice of the legal institutions is part of what makes the distribution of these other scarce goods—education, healthcare, and welfare—justifiable. A just justice system part constitutes the justice of other distributions.

Philosophical Neglect

Given the central importance of legal systems to a just political order, one might have expected legal and political philosophers to have carried on Socrates and Plato's work on these questions. This might not have resolved all disagreements—philosophers are not always an irenic bunch; even if they were, politicians do not always pay close attention to philosophers' theories—but it would give us some idea of the way to think about the problem. It has not been so. The just design of a legal system has been ignored by almost every moral, legal and political philosopher. The widespread neglect of the problem can be seen through consideration of a few of the most prominent theorists since the early modern age. Thomas Hobbes's *Leviathan* is concerned with the conditions of a justified state. It includes helpful and suggestive remarks about what a legal system should do. But, despite the centrality of legal authority to his own theory of a just state, Hobbes gives no substantial treatment to that topic.[9] John Locke says still less.[10] Immanuel Kant has a complete and systematic discussion of the distinction between law and morality, including quite stringent conditions on the justification of legal norms; nowhere is there any sustained consideration of how the structure of the legal system might affect the justice of laws, or even what a just system of administration of laws would be.[11]

In the modern era, legitimacy and the proper design of political institutions have been central questions. Discussions of gerrymandering and campaign finance, for example, continue to dominate the popular and academic press. But almost nothing has been said about legal procedures' place in a just political system. John Rawls, the most important political philosopher of the past century, considers our duties to obey an unjust law but has nothing to say about our duties to obey an unjust ruling (or what would make a legal system just or unjust).[12] Robert Nozick, Rawls's most famous critic, claims that justice consists in the protection of rights and reparation of rights violations; he tells us very little about how to secure a just system to adjudicate on disputes and enforce judgments.[13] (Should there, for example, be taxation to support a system of legal aid?) Turning to legal philosophers, both H. L. A. Hart and Ronald Dworkin had plenty to say about the nature of law.[14] They also, in their different ways, wrote a lot about the justice of laws.[15] But neither gave much consideration to the question of how a legal system should be designed and structured, or how its instruments should be distributed.[16]

Some of this neglect is quite intelligible. Sceptics about law, like some Marxists, will inevitably regard concern over the just structure of a legal system somewhat like anxious concern over the most humane method of torture: there might be scales of inhumanity, but to think about them is to ask the wrong question. Anarchists, too, can be forgiven for setting these questions to one side. But for those philosophers who regard a legal system as a necessary part of a just political order, the just design of the legal system should be of fundamental importance.

Part of the explanation for the question's recent neglect may concern the intellectual division of labour in philosophical debates of the twentieth century. Following Aristotle's influential discussion, scholars customarily distinguish distributive from corrective justice.[17] The former concerns questions like: what distribution of material resources is justifiable? These questions have been the bailiwick of political philosophers. The latter concerns questions like: how (and why) should wrongs be repaired? Those questions have been appropriated by legal philosophers. Questions of just justice, which concern (inter alia) the distribution of claims to correction, are lost in the gaps between the distinction.[18]

Means and Ends

I have claimed that principles of just justice are crucial if we are to establish a just political order; I have said very little about what those principles are. Even if I fail to convince you that my own principles are correct, I hope that my framework provides resources to structure future discussions. In developing any theory, an important distinction to make is that between means and ends. The distinction is well-known, though, as the examples I will offer may indicate, it is not always easy to pin down.

To bring out the distinction, consider an address of Lyman Abbott, a lawyer turned preacher, given to a New York legal aid society's dinner at the turn of the twentieth century. He spoke on the importance of legal aid, warning that "if ever a time shall come when in this city only the rich man can enjoy law as a doubtful luxury, when the poor who need it most cannot have it, when only a golden key will unlock the door to the courtroom, the seeds of revolution will be sown, the firebrand of revolution will be lighted and put into the hands of men, and they will almost be justified in the revolution which will follow."[19] In similar fashion, Reginald Heber Smith, the godfather of American legal aid, warned that the "denial of justice is the short cut to anarchy."[20] How? Smith adds, "Differences in the ability of classes to use the machinery of the law, if permitted to remain, lead inevitably to disparity between the rights of classes in the law itself. And when the law recognizes and enforces a distinction between classes, revolution ensues or democracy is at an end."[21]

Abbott and Smith are both concerned with the nature of a just regime; they also warn of the risk of revolution if justice is not ensured. This demonstrates the importance of isolating the kind of claim being made. Talk of the risk of revolution moves from the normative to the empirical, requiring us to ask how people will respond to injustice in the legal system. There does not seem to be much evidence that they respond through revolution. There is, in fact, quite some evidence to the contrary. Deborah Rhode claims that "about four-fifths of the civil legal needs of the poor, and two- to three-fifths of the needs of middle-income individuals [in the United States], remain unmet."[22] If she is right—even if she is *more or less* right—most Americans are entirely incapable of vindicating their basic legal rights. The American political scene is certainly eccentric, but the prospect of a Communist revolution seems remote; relatively little political activism seems to be motivated by inequality in legal services (rather than, say, inequality per se). Most people do not care that much about it, compared at least to their objections to the injustice of substantive laws (the tax code, the nature of property rights, and so on).

Warnings of revolution are addressed to privileged elites, stressing all they stand to lose when the revolution comes. The philosophical inquiry should first be into the grounds that those who might rise up in revolution would have *to* rise up. For that reason, many of the arguments I will make in this book are not subject to this kind of empirical refutation because they do not build in causal features. I will make claims, for example, about the importance of liberty, the meaning of the rule of law, and the just distribution of legal systems' benefits and burdens: these concern individuals' entitlements; they are the ends to realise rather than the means to those ends. Such claims concern the grounds people might have *for* political activism, not warnings *of* political activism. I will also, though, make some claims about means. For example, as I will explain shortly, I argue that a proscription on contracting out of the public provision of legal resources will help ensure greater justice. This is a causal claim and depends on whether, in the real world, the consequences of the proscription will be as I predict. I will say something more now about my claims.

JUSTICE IN EQUALITY

The keynote address at the Legal Aid Society's seventy-fifth anniversary celebration was delivered by Learned Hand. "If we are to keep our democracy," he said, "there must be one commandment: Thou shalt not ration justice."[23] This commandment has become a rallying cry of legal aid activists worldwide.[24]

This book is a wholehearted rejection of Hand's claim. Justice is a norm to regulate the distribution of scarce goods. The benefits and burdens of the justice system, as well as its legal instruments, are all scarce. They must be rationed and distributed like any other good. We already ration these things: in a world like ours, we have to. When legal systems do things badly, the problem is not that they are rationing justice. It is that they are rationing it according to unsound norms.

I aim to explain and justify these claims in Chapter 1. The problem is, roughly, how the legal system should be set up and structured. There are a number of intersecting questions worth our attention. For example, how should legal resources—especially courts and lawyers—be distributed? In other words, who should get justice, if not everyone can?

My central claim, which I introduce in Chapter 2, is that there must be a kind of equality in the provision of justice, that a just justice system is an equal justice system. That label, "equal justice," is an umbrella for a number of connected claims: that certain benefits and burdens of a legal system should be shared equally by all in society; and that all divergences from equality must issue from a fair procedure. A procedure will only be fair if certain arbitrary factors—such as class, race, gender, and wealth—do not play a distorting role in determining whether justice is done. If the rich are able to use the legal system to gain advantages simply because they are rich, that is unjust; if the poor stand an increased risk of wrongful conviction or heightened punishment simply because they are poor, that is unjust. These ideas are intuitive, almost uncontroversial: Aristotle said that everyone thinks "the unjust is unequal, the just is equal . . . even apart from argument."[25] But their radical implications, which I develop in subsequent chapters, are rarely grasped. If I am right, legal systems today are profoundly unjust, more so than even their sternest critics seem to recognise.

I turn, next, to the definition of a fair institution. Chapter 3 considers whether it is fair to distribute legal resources through a market. Although the solution is widely condemned and has, for centuries, been subject to interventions, objections to the market are rarely set out in detail. Few have put forward systematic proposals as an alternative. And, perhaps most importantly, many legal resources are still distributed (shorn of distracting complications) through a market. I argue that markets are apt to distribute the goods of justice in an unjust way.

It is always easier to say where others have gone wrong than it is to get things right. My initial proposals for the distribution of legal resources are found in Chapters 4 and 5. I make a series of increasingly controversial claims. Least contentiously, I argue that there is a basic level of legal resources to which everyone is entitled; any polity that fails to secure this distribution will fail to justify the burdens of a legal system to those who bear them. That may seem like an elucidation of the obvious. The demands of fairness are, however, stringent: fairness may require, for example, an equal distribution of lawyers between all in society. I fortify that thought in Chapter 5, which makes a sustained argument for an equal distribution of legal resources across society. In practice, this means that lawyers should not be traded through a private market; contracting out of the public option should be proscribed.

The proposal to equalise legal resources is perhaps the most controversial in this book. An important objection is that the ban would require an unjustifiable interference with liberty. In Chapter 6, I consider a number of liberty-based objections. None are powerful. Equal legal resources is, absent any other suggestion, our best bet of realising a just justice system.

This, though, does not conclude the inquiry. Principles to this point have concerned the distribution of legal resources as well as the benefits and burdens of the legal system. Those are not the only important questions when designing a legal system. We also need to consider, for example, where claims of justice are adjudicated. Chapter 7 considers this question, examining the plurality of dispute resolution fora in contemporary society: from mediation to arbitration to state courts. There are fierce debates today concerning the principles that should be used to assess arrangements of these fora. But it is impossible to make sensible proposals, I claim, without a more general theory of the justice system (such as that set out in Chapters 2 through 5).

A further consideration, when setting up a legal system, is the powers institutional actors should have and how institutions should be designed in virtue of those powers. In Chapter 8, I argue that courts should have the power to make laws; that much is not particularly controversial. More important is the implication of this: it constrains the design of legal systems. If judicial law-making is to be legitimate, for example, certain groups cannot be excluded from the forum of debate where law-making occurs. This shows that various contemporary trends—such as the increased use of online courts or private arbitration—pose democratic concerns for the common law.

The final part of the book considers two more practical questions thrown up by the earlier chapters. First, how should we pay for the justice system? In Chapter 9 I claim that there is relatively little of interest to say in this context: there is simply a general question, to be answered by a more general theory of distributive justice, of who ought to fund the expenses of a state. Although that may sound obvious, it goes against a prominent trend in this context: many people have argued that local considerations (such as who benefits from the justice system) should be used to apportion its costs.

That answer presupposes not only that we have sound principles of distributive justice—to work out who should pay for what—but that a state *conforms with* those principles. This assumption is implausible: distributive injustice is, and has always been, rife. And contemporary societies systematically fail to meet the ideals of just justice. What then? If the state has not got enough money to fund the ideal justice system, what should it do? That is the topic of the last chapter.

1

THE PROBLEMS OF JUSTICE

INTRODUCTION

Legal systems are both a solution and a problem. Unconstrained power can cause great injustice; to constrain it, most societies set up a legal system. This is a good solution but it creates new problems. The laws must be just, of course. But just laws must also be administered justly. Philosophers, statesmen, and citizens have spent a lot of time worrying about what makes laws just; none of us have spent enough time thinking about what makes the administration of those laws just.

This neglect is an intellectual and a political failure. Coherent criticism of legal systems requires knowledge of what makes their design unjust; equally, without some sense of what a just justice system would be, reform proposals are rudderless. The topic is also urgent. One reason is that the stakes can be very high: individual liberty depends on the legal system's arrangements; lives can hang in the balance. Another is that the justice system is in a state of flux. The debate over its proper structure is as contested as with any other feature of the modern state, at least as much as those concerning healthcare and schooling. Policy proposals are legion; many legal systems are in a state of perpetual reform. Thinking more about what makes a legal system just provides a structure for debate. It also shows that contemporary legal systems are seriously deficient.

I have two aims in this chapter. First, I want to bring some coherence to the topic and the questions I want to answer in this book. Second, I want to say something more about how those questions should be answered.

THE CONCERNS OF A LEGAL SYSTEM

Institutions and Lawyers

Many contemporary debates on the justice system revolve around two topics. First, individuals' access to legal institutions (courts, tribunals, and so on); second, the availability of lawyers to help individuals navigate those institutions. Starting with these is a good way of introducing the kind of questions we have to consider—and of bringing out what matters when thinking about the design of a legal system.

The access individuals have to legal institutions depends on a range of factors. Some legal systems have excluded entire groups from their courts. In the mid-nineteenth century, a slave from Missouri, Dred Scott, brought a legal claim for his freedom. Roger Taney, the chief justice of the US Supreme Court, held that "a negro, whose ancestors were imported into this country, and sold as slaves" could not enjoy "the privilege of suing in a court of the United States in the cases specified in the Constitution."[1]

No modern democracy would countenance such status-based exclusion. That said, almost all courts have filing fees. If you do not (or cannot) pay the entrance fee, your claim will not be heard. It has long been recognised that access to legal institutions should not depend entirely on one's wealth. An edict of Constantine the Great, issued in 331 A.D., proclaimed, "Let the ears of the judge be opened to the poorest and to the rich alike."[2] To make that promise a reality, Constantine seems to have banned all fees to access judges.[3] But if ability to pay is not the right criterion for rationing access to courts, what is?

The second major issue is the availability of lawyers. Sometimes lawyers work for free. Aeschylus's *Oresteia*, first dramatized in 458 B.C., ends with the trial of Orestes for the murder of his mother, Clytemnestra. Apollo, an Athenian deity, represents Orestes pro bono. But lawyers usually need an incentive to do this. (Apollo, for example, was scarcely an altruist or disinterested observer: he had, through his Oracle at Delphi, ordered Clytemnestra's murder.) When no lawyer will work for free, what then? Lawyers (especially, though not only, good lawyers) are expensive. If their availability was determined by laissez-faire principles, only the very rich could afford them. Various mechanisms have been used to distribute access more equitably. In 1495, Henry VII of England, concerned to ensure that "indifferent justice" could be obtained "aswell to pou*er* as riche," created the *in forma pauperis* procedure, assigning "lerned Councell and attorneyes" to serve "without any rewarde."[4]

Contemporary societies have diverged in their response to the problem of the distribution of lawyers. In 1949, the United Kingdom created a comprehensive legal aid scheme, designed to ensure that citizens could access lawyers even when they could not afford them. The United States did not follow suit. Its Supreme Court has held that "an indigent litigant has a right to appointed counsel only when, if he loses, he may be deprived of his physical liberty."[5] If the state threatens to take a mother's children from her, whether she has lawyers to help her through the legal process depends on whether she can afford them. It is easy enough to assert that this is unjust. But difficult questions of design remain. If "ability to pay" is not the right method of distributing lawyers, what is? And who, if not the individual represented by the lawyer, should fund these goods?

These are some of the practical questions that arise once a legal system has been set up. How should we think about the problems thrown up? Here is one way. We can regard courts, judges, and lawyers as *legal resources*. They are scarce. There is not enough court time for all to have their day in court; there are not enough lawyers for everyone to have one for every legal problem. And legal resources are valuable. It is natural, therefore, to ask: how should these resources be distributed?

Beyond Legal Resources

That question is well worth asking; we do not ask it enough. But it is not the most fundamental question we should ask about a legal system.

Long before Dick the Butcher's drastic suggestion to "kill all the lawyers," legal systems strove to simplify procedures such that lawyers were unnecessary.[6] The Romans let individuals defend themselves in trials, though orators were also permitted.[7] In England, attempts were made to broaden access to legal procedures in the twelfth and thirteenth centuries, when Henry II set up courts of General Eyre. Litigants almost certainly did not have to pay a fee to present their complaints, which means the records show pleas of very poor people. The bills also had no standard form: individuals could represent themselves. Similar reforms appear periodically, though they are never entirely successful; lawyers remain practically necessary (or, at any rate, valuable) in most situations. But there is a sensible thought behind these reforms: if we can achieve the same outcome without the use of lawyers, that is a good thing.

This is no surprise. Few people want legal resources for their own sake: people want a lawyer or to have access to courts in order to achieve an outcome. The outcome can be noble (where they want justice) or ignoble (where they want to exploit those who cannot afford a lawyer of their own). We set up legal systems in part to promote the noble outcomes; the best design will be best partly in virtue of its promotion of those outcomes (and avoidance of the ignoble ones). If we could achieve the same outcomes without the expensive instruments, legal resources, so much the better. This shows that legal resources are, at least in part, instruments to achieve further goals.

We can throw some light on those goals if we ask: what would be wrong with a world without law? Answering that question gives us some idea of the things legal systems are trying to fix, and, so, the outcomes we should have in mind when we are thinking about distributions of legal resources. In the next section, I set out the problems of a world without law and explain how a legal system is supposed to address them. The benefits of living under a legal system, the good things we get when the system does address these problems, I term the "benefits of legality." The distribution of legal resources matters in part because legal resources affect the amount and distribution of those benefits.

The creation of a legal system is not an unalloyed good. While legal systems do generate various benefits, they also generate a number of burdens. I turn to those—the "burdens of legality"—in the subsequent section. The final section of this chapter sets out the questions we should ask when thinking about the design of the justice system.

THE BENEFITS OF LEGALITY

A legal system is an answer to a particular problem, that of a world without law. Thomas Hobbes gave the worst-case scenario. "The life of man" in a world without law would be "solitary, poore, nasty, brutish, and short."[8] We should, he said, set up a state and legal order to escape that predicament. What, exactly, is the predicament? And why are things better with a legal system?[9]

A legal system offers justice and welfare benefits. It is sometimes helpful enough to group these together as "benefits of legality." But the distinction is important to my claims in subsequent chapters so it is worth setting them out and saying something about each group.

Justice Benefits

David Hume said that "the vast apparatus of government [has] no other object or purpose but the distribution of justice."[10] James Madison was even more succinct: "Justice is the end of government. It is the end of civil society."[11] For these people, the problem of a world without law is that there would be injustice; the alleviation of that injustice is the principal benefit a state brings.[12] What, though, do they mean by "injustice"?

Adam Smith drew a helpful distinction between justice without and within the state. "The first duty of the sovereign," Smith wrote, is to protect people "from the violence and invasion of other independent societies."[13] Providing security from foreign threats is still widely believed to be the primary function of states. Presupposed here is the idea that collective protection is an end of the state, an end worthy of considerable expenditure. Not only is such protection costly, it generates burdens in the risk to life and limb; the distribution of these risks is a matter of justice, as I discuss in more detail in Chapter 2. Important as protection from threats is, it is not achieved via a national legal system.

Smith went on to say that "the second duty of the sovereign [is] of protecting, as far as possible, every member of the society from the injustice or oppression of every other member of it."[14] This is injustice from within. To protect its citizens, Smith reasoned, the state must establish institutions for the "exact administration of justice."[15] This gives us a clearer picture of the injustice that a legal system seeks to thwart. Without law, power relations between members of society can go entirely unchecked; the powerful are able to do what they want, regardless of the morality of their actions. The creation of a legal system can help in three different ways.

A principal aim of legal systems is to prevent wrongs—or to repair them when they occur. Various acts, such as murder and torture, are wrong regardless of whether there is a state. States aim to prevent these wrongs, for it is, as Hobbes stresses, "much more conduceth to Peace to prevent brawles from arising, then to appease them being risen."[16] This is done, for example, through the creation of a criminal law code, a police force, and a criminal justice system. When wrongs do occur, legal systems aim to ameliorate them. If you break my leg, you should apologise, help me get to a hospital and perhaps pay for my treatment. Legal systems should ensure that you conform with duties like these.

Problems of justice arise, as David Hume put it, when "there is not a sufficient quantity of [goods] to supply every one's desires and necessities."[17] In a perfect world, all wrongs would be prevented; in the next-best world, all wrongs would be repaired. Our world is far from either of these: we are yet to design institutions capable of preventing or repairing all wrongdoing. This scarcity (of prevention, of reparation) gives rise to a problem of justice: which wrongs should be prevented, given that not all can? Which wrongs should be repaired, given that not all can be?

The way institutions are arranged will affect the extent of the reduction or repair of wrongs. Here, as in all areas of justice, it is not enough to think only about the extent of the reduction of wrongdoing. To see why, consider Jeremy Bentham's proposal that we should aim, in all our decisions, to achieve "the greatest happiness of the greatest number."[18] That arrangement could generate grave inequality in the distribution of happiness, which can seem unjust. In most spheres of justice, norms of justice do not seek only to maximise. Some say that everyone must receive a basic level of certain resources, such as money or education. Others are more egalitarian, saying that certain goods should be held equally: each person gets one vote, and no more, for example. So we also need to consider the distribution of wrongdoing and repair. Some arrangements are unjust on distributive grounds.

It is unjust, for example, if the policing is confined to the rich area of town: the benefits of reduced wrongdoing are inequitably distributed. Equally, if only the rich are able to secure reparation of wrongs done to them, that is unjust. To design just structures to reduce and repair wrongdoing, we need principles of justice to determine which distributions are fair.

If a politician wins an election because she is able to stuff the ballot box, that is unjust: elections are not supposed to test who is better able to cheat.

If an athlete is selected for her country's Olympic team because she is friends with the coach, that is unjust: sports teams are not supposed to be selected on the basis of friendship networks. These examples show the basic structure of justice in allocation: the outcome of an allocative procedure is unjust when the wrong kind of facts play a determinative role in the outcome of some procedure.[19] Portrayals of Iusticia—justice embodied—often show her with a blindfold and a scale. The blindfold is to show that justice ignores all but the salient facts, those that weigh on her scales. The more an institution allocates goods according to the underlying reasons for the allocation, the more responsive it is to those reasons, the more just that institution is.[20]

Without the rule of law, power arrogates wealth. If there were no legal system, the powerful would be able to ensure that valuable goods were distributed to them, regardless of the justice of that distribution. The existence of the legal system can (and should) prevent distributive arrangements from being upset: the incidence of theft, for example, will be reduced if people cannot get away with it simply because they are rich or powerful. And, again, there are distributive questions here: if the legal system only protects the property of the rich, that is unjust. The reason, I will argue in the next chapter, is that the benefits of a legal system should be shared equally.

If a legal system fails to prevent injustice in allocation, it can help repair any disruption. Suppose that you steal something from me. Your holdings are unjustly increased and mine are unjustly decreased. As Aristotle noticed, there is a particular form of justice, corrective justice, "which plays a rectifying part in transactions between man and man."[21] This is supposed to restore the parties to equality, usually by means of compensatory damages.[22] James Nickel puts this line of thought well when he writes that "compensation protects just distributions . . . by undoing, insofar as possible, actions that disturb such distributions. . . . Justice is a matter of people having those things that they deserve, are entitled to, or otherwise ought to have, and compensation serves justice by preventing and undoing actions that would prevent people from having these things."[23] A legal system should repair these distributive injustices when they occur, ensuring justice in allocation.[24]

Just as with the wrongdoing, there are distributive questions with respect to allocation of resources. Different institutional arrangements will mean that different people are more secure in their holdings than others; different arrangements will make some rather than others more able to get reparation. Any theory of the legal system should say what those distributions should be.

The first two injustices concern things people can do to one another: they can injure them or take their resources, for example. A final problem of injustice that the legal system aims to address is the status of individuals in a world where people have powers to act with impunity. In that world, the factual freedom of the poor would depend on the grace of the rich; they would, for that reason, stand in a relation of dependence and subordination to the rich. A just society should not permit such relations.

A legal system attempts to address this status injustice by the provision of legal rights. These provide entitlements that all are supposed to respect: people are not permitted to exploit or injure others, for example. Exploitation or injury, if it occurs, should be repaired. In this way, legal systems aim to ensure that individuals have a zone of liberty into which no one can encroach. This provides a necessary precondition for individuals to stand in equal relations to one another, itself a precondition of a democratic community. As in previous instances of injustice, the mere provision of rights will not be enough: institutions must be set up to ensure respect for those rights. And, in the event that those institutions must favour some over others, there is a further question of justice about whose interests to favour.

Welfare Benefits

Not all of the benefits of legality concern justice, things that can be claimed as a matter of right. Legal systems can also improve individuals' welfare through the creation and maintenance of rules and institutions. These benefits are distinct in part because, unlike certain basic wrongs (such as enslavement or torture), they do not concern claims individuals have in virtue of their humanity. Instead, these are claims individuals can have only once there are practices, rules, or institutions.

Without law, there would be disagreement about what people ought to do and when they ought to do it. That would be a problem. An important part of the solution, Thomas Hobbes pointed out, is the creation of "a common measure of all things that might fall in controversy."[25] A legal system institutes rules for everyone to follow. It is not up to each individual to decide on basic questions of obligation because the law gives a "common measure" for us all.

There are two principal benefits to this public system of rules. First, their systematic character should help us find out what we ought to do.[26] Individuals are not always in the best position to know what the best thing for a collective body to do is, in part because it can be very difficult to work out what the consequences of one policy or another would be. Well-drafted laws can solve this. In theory, law-makers have the time to work out what actions would lead to the best consequences overall: for example, what policy on car engines or supermarket plastic bags would lead to the greatest reduction in pollution. A law can instruct us how to act better to achieve that collective goal. A legal system can thus help us to achieve together what we would struggle (due to the limits of our knowledge) to achieve alone.

Second, laws make cooperation of a large group possible. The mutual cooperation of a large group can bring great gains for everyone. However, the larger the group, the harder it is to ensure their cooperation. Legal systems can square this circle: laws can fix coordination problems; solving those problems can unlock the gains of cooperation.[27] A familiar illustration is traffic codes. It does not really matter what the content of many of the rules actually is. All that matters is that there is some rule. It does not, for example, matter whether we drive on the left or right hand side of the road; we just need there to be a rule which everyone knows and is able to follow. The legal system can say which side we must drive on. That, in turn, solves a whole host of further coordination problems. For example, car manufacturers could not be sure, prior to the law, which side of the car it would be best to put the steering wheel. Now they know.

Collective schemes can break down if enough people refuse to go along with what is required. Even if the scheme still works, it is unfair to those who do their bit if others simply take the benefit without doing anything to support the scheme. This can reduce the amount of benefits there are to go around. Worse, if some are not assured of others' cooperation, they might not want to participate in the scheme, further reducing the net benefits. Road traffic is again a good example. The value of the rule commanding us to drive on one side of the road would be massively reduced if a sizeable portion of the population decided to disobey and drive on the other side. Legal systems are able to increase compliance with the rules: states can punish those who refuse to comply. This forces the intransigent to cooperate—and, just as important, it removes incentives everyone else has not to comply. When I drive, I am not on edge when I turn a corner; I don't worry that someone will be coming the other way on my side of the road. This provides assurance to everyone in the community.[28] In these ways the legal system can ensure greater compliance and cooperation. This brings about various important benefits. And, as with all other examples, the precise structure of the institutional arrangement will partly determine who receives which benefits.

A legal system can also create valuable institutions that can generate more important benefits. Legal powers can be constituted and distributed; the justification of doing this, and the grounds to praise or criticise any particular arrangement, is the beneficial effect it can have on welfare. Perhaps the most widely considered examples are contract and property. If you and I were marooned on an island we would both have various rights—not to be tortured or enslaved, say—merely in virtue of our humanity. But it is far less clear—political philosophers through the ages have disagreed on the question—that we can acquire contractual and property rights merely in virtue of being human. Such institutions are artificial. We create them, in other words, to unlock the morally significant benefits which flow from having them.[29] Part of the reason to set up a state is to institute a system of property (perhaps, though not necessarily, private property) and contract.

You do not need to agree with this account of contract and property to see that there are enormous potential benefits to the creation of the state. Suppose that it is possible to acquire contractual and property rights without a convention. Morality alone would be indeterminate about the limits of these rights. I cultivated various crops on my land that blew onto yours. Am I allowed to get them back? You cultivated my land by mistake at no cost to me. Are the crops that grow yours or mine? We agreed that you would trade some of your crops in exchange for mine, but your harvest was very poor and the trade would be punishing for you. Are you excused from the deal? Without the clarity a legal order can bring, we risk internecine squabbles, losing the potential benefits of our trade and our farming. A legal system gives determinacy by making concrete what we could not agree upon, or which morality failed to specify with any precision. So even if you believe that there are contractual and property rights pre-existing the state, there are benefits to be reaped from the creation of a legal system.

The prospect of these benefits is part of the reason why we have good reason to create it.

The state should often be thought of in the same way as individuals or companies: they can all violate rights and disrupt holdings unjustly in the manner just described. I will consider some matters of greatest concern, such as wrongful imprisonment, in the next section. But governments' powers to regulate and control institutional arrangements are also an important feature of contemporary states. Public powers can also be used, for example, to regulate structural features of markets (such as which companies are permitted to merge) and environmental controls. The same analysis applicable to property and contract applies (with some revisions) to these institutional arrangements. In all these cases, the design of the legal system affects who receives the benefits in question. So there is a question of justice in the design of the legal system: how does the fact that institutional arrangements will impact on others' welfare affect how the institutions should be structured?

THE BURDENS OF LEGALITY

A legal system can, all this shows, be a good thing. But its creation also generates new problems and new burdens. That these burdens are part and parcel of running a legal system is one reason why setting up a legal system is morally risky and why there is such urgency to questions of justice reform.

We can distinguish, with respect to the burdens, the injustices the state will perpetrate from the restrictions to everyone's liberty which is entailed by a society governed by laws. Let me say something more about each category.

State Injustice

Some things that go on in a legal system, things I term "absolute injustices," are bad regardless of the number of people they happen to. Incorrect legal decisions, such as the wrongful conviction of the innocent, are injustices regardless of the position of others in society.

A criminal justice system means individuals can and will be imprisoned (or even executed) for crimes they did not commit; some punishments will be disproportionate to the crimes committed, as when people in the United States are jailed for life for their third felony. A civil justice system means private disputes can be adjudicated by a public institution with a coercive enforcement mechanism. These institutions will not always get things right. When they get things wrong, the full force of the state is used to enforce the unjust decision. Administrative officials will, at times, misconstrue their powers, depriving individuals of things to which they are entitled. Events like these are inevitable: no human process is perfect.

The structure of legal systems will affect who, amongst all in society, suffers these injustices. When the ability to enlist lawyers' help depends on an individual's race or wealth, for example, those unable to secure legal services will be more likely to incur the injustices. In 1757, Eleanor Eddacres was prosecuted for forging a bond. She protested that "I have not a six penny piece left to pay a porter, much less [enough] to fee counsel. . . . If I must die because I am poor, I can't help it."[30] She was sentenced to death. Those rich enough to hire star lawyers could escape these injustices. In 1788, a prosecutor lamented that two men "got off because a Mr Garrow," a fearsome Old Bailey defence advocate, "was their counsel."[31]

Absolute injustices are inevitable. A theory of the justice system must, therefore, explain how the imposition of absolute injustices is morally permissible; I will argue that the distribution of those injustices is an important part of that story.

Other things that go on in a legal system, things I term "comparative injustices," are bad because people in the same position are treated in different ways. One person's treatment is comparatively unjust only when compared to another person's. (This is one illustration of a general truth, that just laws can be unjust if they are differentially applied.) Comparative injustices can arise in the realm of, for example, conviction or sentences imposed for crimes.

Suppose that a large number of blacks and whites in a particular community deal in illegal drugs—and that all those incarcerated for dealing drugs were actually guilty of the crime.[32] If the only individuals incarcerated for drugs offences are black, that fact is important and suggests an injustice in the system.

Consider now inequality in the sentencing of those rightly convicted of crimes. Bob Dylan sings of the killing of Hattie Carroll, "a maid of the kitchen," by William Zanzinger. Zanzinger has "a tobacco farm of six hundred acres" and "rich wealthy parents who provide and protect him." He is caught and brought before a judge:

> In the courtroom of honor, the judge pounded his gavel
> To show that all's equal and that the courts are on the level . . .
> And that even the nobles get properly handled.

A good start. But then comes the denouement. The judge hands

> out strongly, for penalty and repentance
> William Zanzinger with a six-month sentence.[33]

Zanzinger was rightly convicted of murder; the concern is not that he escaped conviction. But had Carroll killed Zanzinger, she would have gone to jail for much longer. This is a comparative injustice.[34]

Such injustices are possible in any area of law. Given certain institutional arrangements, some might be more likely to have the civil wrongs they suffer repaired than others in the same position, or to get substantial damages for wrongs done to them. The injustice in here is in the different treatment of people in the same position; like cases are not being treated alike.

Liberty Restrictions

In Max Weber's famous definition, the state is an entity that successfully claims a "monopoly of the legitimate use of violence."[35] That monopoly creates the risk of injustices at the hands of the state. It also generates another burden of legality in liberty restrictions, restrictions that apply to all of us equally—albeit restrictions that can be vastly more or less burdensome, depending on the risks we face in society.

To show what I have in mind, suppose again that we are marooned on an island. You think that I stole your crops. I refuse to pay you any compensation: I never touched your crops. (Maybe the birds ate them, maybe they blew into the sea. I don't know.) Do you have a permission to punish me? Certainly not: I never went near them. If there is no legal system, anyone innocent has a permission to resist unjust punishment.[36] So when you come to extract some revenge, I am well within my rights, pitchfork at the ready, to resist your punishment and to fight you off. Things are quite different when there is a legal system. The innocent are not legally entitled to resist wrongful punishment: innocence is no legal excuse to a prison break. Prisoners are expected to get out via the state's appeal process. And, very plausibly, some of those legal obligations are also moral obligations: just as we might have duties to obey minimally unjust laws, we may have duties to obey certain unjust legal orders.

The same is true of civil cases. Consider Alice Knotte. In 1292, in Shropshire, Alice complained that Thomas Champeneys "detaineth from her seven shillings in money and a surcoat of the value of three shillings." "Alice can get no justice at all," she protested, "seeing that she is poor and that this Thomas is rich." She implored the judge, "I have none to help me save God and you."[37] Alice was lucky: she managed to get before a court; one of the problems with contemporary legal systems is that few people can do this. But she was also in one way worse off because of the legal system. Suppose that she was correct, that Thomas did owe her seven shillings, but that there was no legal system.[38] Plausibly, she would have been morally permitted to take the money from Thomas by force. A legal system forecloses that line of action: it would be theft to take Thomas's money, even if Thomas was in the wrong. This is a further burden the creation of a legal system occasions: powers to respond to injustice are taken out of your hands. When we have disagreements with our fellow citizens, we can no longer resort to force; if the disagreement is intractable, we must take our grievances to court to allow a judge to adjudicate on their merits. The conditions through which we can access courts become very important.

THE STRUCTURE OF JUSTICE

Resources and Legality

We now have a picture of the things legal systems aim to regulate and the burdens they can create in so doing. The next question is how we should think about those tasks. Questions of justice generally have two features: an object of distribution and a distributive norm. Aristotle, for example, wrote that "where flute players are similar with respect to the art, aggrandizement in flutes is not granted to those who are better born. They will not play the flute better on this account; but it is to one who is preeminent in the work that preeminence in the instruments should be granted."[39] The object of distribution is flutes. Two rival norms are considered: distribution to "those who are better born"; and distribution to the best flute players.

Such norms vary in their generality or specificity. The more general the norm, the more objects it purports to govern. Aristotle was not proposing a norm solely for the distribution of flutes; the distribution of flutes was used to illustrate a more general distributive principle. Compare, though, Bernard Williams's claim that "the proper ground of distribution of medical care is ill health."[40] This is a specific norm: it purports to govern the distribution of only one good, medical care; it would be unintelligible as a principle for the distribution of flutes.

In our context, there are two objects of distribution: legal resources and the benefits and burdens of legality. One task of this book is to establish the norm or norms we should apply to those spheres. A complicating factor is that the ultimate distribution of the benefits and burdens of legality depends in part on the distribution of legal resources. It is likely, for example, that the lower the quality of legal resources (be they judges or lawyers), the higher the risk of errors taking place. It is also likely that the risk of those errors will be affected by the distribution of the legal resources. (If one side has an excellent lawyer and the other a dullard, the one represented by the dullard is more likely to suffer injustice than the other.) Inequality in the distribution of lawyers might lead to an unequal distribution of the benefits and burdens of legality—and there may be fewer benefits and more burdens if the amount of legal resources is reduced.

A graphic illustration is the US case of *Powell v. Alabama*. Nine young, illiterate black men were sentenced to death for raping two white women. Their trial was conducted without the benefit of defense lawyers. Justice George Sutherland of the US Supreme Court said that "the right to be heard would be, in many cases, of little avail if it did not comprehend the right to be heard by counsel."[41] For this reason, Justice Hugo Black called it "an obvious truth" that "any person haled into court, who is too poor to hire a lawyer, cannot be assured a fair trial unless counsel is provided for him."[42]

The interrelation between these spheres also shows that we can, like Justice Black, reason from one sphere (e.g., the risk of wrongful conviction) to another (e.g., the provision of a lawyer for those accused of crimes). If we can establish justice in the distribution of legal resources, for example, justice in the realm of benefits and burdens might follow. But the distribution of the benefits and burdens of legality should have a priority in our thought: the distribution of legal resources is principally a procedure to ensure justice in that sphere.[43]

The Place of Procedures

The norms I have considered to this point state a distributive outcome to achieve. Not all norms of justice have that form. Others propose a procedure to determine an outcome. To distribute political offices, for example, we often use the procedure of elections.[44] What place should these ideas have in our thought about the justice system?

 The interrelation between procedures and outcomes is complicated. Procedures are sometimes the handmaid of outcome-based norms. When this is so, we must specify the desired outcome and design procedures that will best achieve it: the procedure is better or worse depending only on its accuracy in achieving the desired outcome. This is the main way we should think about legal resources: the just distribution of legal resources is the distribution that best secures justice in the realm of legality.[45] That explains persistent efforts to eliminate lawyers from legal processes; it is also why reforms to the distribution of lawyers are ultimately answerable to their impact on justice and injustice.

At other times, there is no correct outcome except the outcome that results from a fair procedure.[46] The customary example is lottery winnings. No person has a claim to the winnings before the lottery is held: the only person with a claim is the one whose numbers come up. When fair, the procedure clothes the outcome with legitimacy.

These two options are two ends of a spectrum.[47] Between those poles, procedural norms cannot be reduced to outcome-based norms or vice versa. Consider political power. Many societies have thought that certain individuals, such as the children of kings, have a special claim to political office. There is a certain outcome in mind and no separate consideration of the justice of procedure: the procedure should ensure that the ruler's kin rules, nothing more.[48] Democratic communities believe that there is a procedural constraint on the allocation of political power. Democrats have not given up the idea that there are better or worse outcomes to the distribution of political power: they will argue for one candidate or another by pointing to that candidate's characteristics or policies. But ultimate political power must be distributed, the democrat says, to those selected according to the rules of a fair (democratic) procedure.

We cannot eliminate these dual dimensions. Some outcomes are better but procedurally irregular; others are procedurally just but disastrous in outcomes. Consider four possible mechanisms we might use to allocate goods: a vote, a lottery, a queue, or a market. None distribute with a particular outcome in mind.[49] Each of these models might, in certain contexts, be thought procedurally legitimate; and each could, in those same contexts, lead to an unjust outcome.

In later chapters I will argue that there are better and worse distributions of the benefits and burdens of legality. In that respect, procedures are not at the core of justice.[50] But I will also argue that any deviation from equality of those benefits and burdens can only be justified by following a fair procedure. In that respect, my account puts procedures at the core of the practice of justice; and, because a theory of the justice system needs to say what makes a procedure fair, they will be central to my own argument.[51]

WHAT NEXT?

The distributive sphere of principal importance, when thinking about the justice system, is the benefits and burdens of legality. The challenge of the next few chapters is to establish what principles should govern that sphere and how those principles should be pursued through legal institutions. In the next chapter I argue that the justice benefits and burdens of legality should be shared equally: legal systems should aim, as it is sometimes put, to secure equal justice.

2

EQUAL JUSTICE

A PROTEAN VIRTUE

"In the matter of private disputes" in Athens, Pericles claimed in his funeral oration, "everyone is equal before the law."[1] This ideal endures today, but its meaning is protean. Everyone agrees that "equality before the law" is a good thing; the coalition falls apart as soon as concrete proposals are drawn up.

This uneasy alliance is sustained because many quite different ideas can be cloaked in the banner of equality. Equality can refer to both a distribution and a value. Someone might argue that fairness (a value) requires equal shares (a distribution); or they might argue that equality (a value) requires unequal shares (a distribution). This can make it hard to keep track of what is being argued.[2]

So what does equality before the law require? The idea is sometimes thought to consist in laws applying equally to all. Friedrich Hayek talked of an ideal of "general and equal laws" where the rules "are the same for all."[3] A very similar notion counsels judges to apply the laws without regard to individuals' personal characteristics. John Rawls, for example, writes that "if we think of justice as always expressing a kind of equality, then formal justice requires that in their administration laws and institutions should apply equally (that is, in the same way) to those belonging to the classes defined by them."[4]

It is easy to make fun of these interpretations. Anatole France, for example, wrote that "in its majestic equality, the law forbids rich and poor alike to sleep under bridges, beg in the streets, and steal loaves of bread."[5] His point was that the same rules can impose different burdens on different people depending on their personal circumstances. True enough. But we should not be too dismissive of the idea. Formal equality is a virtue of law and adjudication: laws' demands should not depend on arbitrary characteristics (such as an individual's class); legal rules should be applied to the facts without distortion.[6]

This principle does not proscribe the law from drawing any distinctions between people. Hayek, for example, qualifies his own statement: "The requirement that the rules of true law be general does not mean that sometimes special rules may not apply to different classes of people if they refer to properties that only some people possess. There may be rules that can apply only to women or to the blind or to persons above a certain age."[7] Social security provisions might be restricted to the worst off; higher rates of taxation can legitimately be imposed on higher earners. Seen in this way, all the ideal requires is that legal distinctions be justified and that justified laws be applied properly to all. Thus characterised, the formal interpretation escapes France's criticism; it also gives up on the idea that equality is the central notion.

Understood in Rawls's sense, the ideal of formal justice can be used as an instrument of reform: if some distributions of legal resources will mean that adjudicators are likely to fail to respond to the relevant facts, if those distributions will mean that "poverty, and not the judge, may be deciding the case,"[8] it tells us to reform those distributions. But that ideal is, as Anatole France's objection suggests, not the most fundamental claim of equality and the law. What is?

THE IDEA OF EQUAL JUSTICE

Ancient Foundations

Herodotus's *Histories* contains a debate between Persians about the best form of rule. Otanes extols "the rule of the majority" over other systems, such as monarchy.[9] This sounds like a defence of democracy—and Herodotus later describes it as such.[10] But Otanes talks of *isonomia,* not *demokratia:* he defends a system of "equal law."[11]

An important feature of *isonomia* is the notion that "both ruler and ruled are equally bound" by the political norms and regulations of a society.[12] This is a democratic urge; it was used by Cleisthenes to argue for his reforms. As Martin Ostwald explains, *isonomia* "is closely related to democracy but not identical with it; it is a political principle rather than a form of government, and it implies not only an equality of political rights but also the potential exercise of political power."[13] Unlike political principles that focus only on the rights individuals have, *isonomia* is concerned with how those rights are implemented in practice. Equal political rights are not enough in a democratic society if the power individuals can exercise with those equal rights is vastly discordant.

This background helps illuminate an important passage in Euripides's *Suppliant Women,* first dramatised in 420 B.C. The play concerns whether Theseus, the ruler of Athens, will help secure the burial of Oedipus's sons, Eteocles and Polynices. Creon, the king of Thebes, has refused them burial and a Theban herald arrives to order the Athenians not to help. When the herald extols the virtues of one-man rule, Theseus provides a defence of Athens: "When the laws are written, both the powerless and the rich have equal access to justice . . . and the little man, if he has right on his side, defeats the big man."[14] Although the herald is unconvinced—"you hold to your opinions and I shall hold to the opposite"[15]—Theseus is onto something important. He is offering a defence of equal justice.

There are two egalitarian concerns here. First, that the little man succeeds even against the rich and powerful: right defeats might. Second, that the powerless and powerful have no better prospects of securing what is theirs as of right: this is the idea he captures with the reference to "equal access to justice."[16] These two ambitions are separate: the first goal may require only a basic level of legal resources; the second goal requires more radical reforms to legal institutions. I will explain those implications in more detail when, in the next two chapters, I turn to the institutional arrangement of the legal system. Before we can think about that, though, we need to get a better idea of what the equal justice ideal actually is and why it is valuable.

The Basic Idea

Pericles's funeral oration was delivered less than two decades after Euripides's play was first staged. The translation I began the chapter with refers to all being "equal before the law."[17] That sounds like formal equality. Benjamin Jowett's translation of the same passage lends it a different inflection. In his hands, Pericles proclaims that "the law secures equal justice to all in their private disputes."[18] This makes Pericles's oration harmonious with the claims of Theseus and Otanes: they all claim that equal justice is a foundational political ideal central to a democratic community.

Very similar things are said today. The building that houses the Supreme Court of the United States, for example, is engraved with the maxim, "Equal Justice under Law."[19] And Michael Walzer has written that "If justice is to be provided at all, it must be provided equally for all accused citizens without regard to their wealth (or their race, religion, political partisanship, and so on)."[20] These ideas suggest that the amount of *justice* people get should be the same.

It is tempting to dismiss all this as confused. Justice is a norm, not a thing; what would it mean for people to get the same amount of justice or to suffer the same amount of injustice? But there is something vital here. It comes into clearer focus in the hands of Thomas Hobbes. Hobbes claimed that "the safety of the People, requireth further . . . that Justice be equally administred to all degrees of People; that is, that as well the rich, and mighty, as poor and obscure persons, may be righted of the injuries done them; so as the great may have no greater hope of impunity, when they doe violence, dishonour, or any Injury to the meaner sort, than when one of these, does the like to one of them."[21] There is something wrong with a legal system— it fails to live up to the demands of equal justice—if "poor and obscure" people cannot get justice for wrongs done to them; and there is something wrong with the legal system if the rich and powerful can escape the sanction of the law when they "doe violence." The wrong is comparative: the rich and mighty must have *no greater* hope of impunity than the poor and obscure.

The ideal is clarified further if, instead of talking about equality of justice, we talk of the benefits and burdens of legality.[22] The benefits of a justice system are the escape of injustice (the reduction of injustice, the increased amount of justice in allocation and the reparation of injustice) and the increased welfare that comes from legal institutions and rules; the burdens of a justice system are the risk of wrongful conviction and the duty to submit to the state's cumbrous procedures to resolve disputes. It makes perfect sense to talk about the equalisation of these benefits and burdens. Equal justice refers to the ideal that the justice benefits and burdens be shared equally.

If equal justice is an ambition for a legal system, its institutions should be arranged so as to secure it. One question for later chapters is how institutions can best realise that goal. First, though, we need to consider what the grounds of equal justice are. Why might it be thought a good thing?

THE GROUNDS OF EQUAL JUSTICE

Of the 1,317 passengers who set sail for New York on the HMS *Titanic*, 492 survived. There was a strikingly different survival rate amongst First and Third Class passengers: 61 per cent of those in First survived, compared with 24 per cent in Third.[23] Thomas Schelling writes that "there were enough lifeboats for first class; steerage was expected to go down with the ship. We do not tolerate that anymore. Those who want to risk their lives at sea and cannot afford a safe ship should perhaps not be denied the opportunity to entrust themselves to a cheaper ship without lifeboats; but if some people cannot afford the price of passage with lifeboats, and some people can, they should not travel on the same ship."[24]

The moral of Schelling's hypothetical is that some schemes are permissible only if the benefits (e.g., lifeboats) and burdens (e.g., the risk of death on the boat) are shared equally amongst participants in that scheme.[25] The ideal of equal justice makes an analogous claim: a legal system is morally permissible if both the benefits and the burdens of that scheme are shared roughly equally between all members of the political community.[26]

Schelling's story is evocative, but it is not an argument for equal justice; in this section, I give two sets of arguments for the ideal. The first set connects equal justice with democratic value; the second set demonstrates that equal justice is a precondition to justice in other distributive realms.

Democratic Ideals

Equal justice connects with democratic ideals in two distinct ways: democracies grant citizens equal rights and those rights are only equal, in the salient sense, if equal justice holds; a democratic government treats individuals with equal concern, which means the benefits and burdens of democracy should be shared equally.

EQUAL RIGHTS

When Otanes explained his preference for *isonomia* he said, "I wish neither to rule nor to be ruled."[27] This suggests an ideal of political society where no one rules over others. Thus Hannah Arendt writes of *isonomia* as "a form of political organization in which the citizens lived together under conditions of no-rule, without a division between rulers and ruled."[28] An important precondition to realising that ideal in practice is that the law must rule over everyone. If the laws do not bind all equally, or if some may break the law with impunity, members of the society are not one another's equals. A democratic community may not require equality in all dimensions— democracies can, for example, tolerate some income and wealth inequalities— but it cannot countenance inequality of justice.

Any theory of a democratic state will have to prescribe various rights to participation. These might reduce to a right to hold public office and to vote; they might also include a wider range of rights, such as those to freedom of speech, necessary to guarantee the democratic process.[29] The democratic urge of *isonomia* is found, more generally, in arguments that certain rights must be held equally. Rawls's first principle of justice, lexically prior to the second, holds that everyone should have "the most extensive total system of equal basic liberties compatible with a similar system of liberty for all."[30] Very many political theories accept a principle like this, though they may disagree about the nature of those liberties or what it means for them to be equal. Whatever these fundamental liberties are, they should not be traded off for greater welfare. It is not morally permissible to strip an individual of their rights to physical security simply because doing so increases the country's gross domestic product.

The principle of equal rights is highly intuitive and widely recognised as a goal.[31] But it is not enough that rights be equal; they must be equally enforced. Power and outcomes matter. A justice system aims to ensure that law, not power, controls outcomes. If there is no equal justice, those with more power can distort the law (even a law with equal rights) in their favour. The commitment to equal rights can thus be used, with one extra step in reasoning, to underline the importance of equal justice.

This connection is sometimes missed because of a common distinction in political theory between the liberty to do something and the power to exercise that liberty. In one sense, the sense mocked by Anatole France, everyone is free to hire the best lawyer in the land; in another sense they are not, because few have the money to do so.[32] Most people have the liberty but not the power to hire the lawyer. Because individuals' powers to exercise their liberties vary, the same liberty might be more or less valuable to different people, depending on whether they are able to exercise it.[33] This distinction can occlude the centrality of equal rights to equal justice. But, properly understood, the two concepts are intimately connected.

Infringing a liberty of yours is usually worse than reducing the value of your liberty by the same amount. If you run a hairdresser, I might open a rival shop and reduce your income by $1,000 per month. That reduces the value of your liberty to run the shop but does not infringe that liberty.[34] I would infringe your liberty if I stole $1,000 from you every month. The net consequence for you is the same, but only the former action is permissible. The corollary is that it is generally thought more important to protect liberties than to augment their value. That is why most people think that it is more important that liberties be equal—that their rights not be infringed or removed simply because they have less money, for example—than that the value of liberties be equal. When it comes to the value of liberty, it is often thought, equality does not make the same strength of demand.

People's liberties can, however, be more or less valuable for a number of different reasons. Sometimes an individual's liberty is less valuable because of background factors affecting their ability to exercise those liberties. A lack of knowledge or money, for example, might make someone less able to take advantage of their rights. Distributive justice does make claims here, for example concerning how much the state owes to ensure a basic level of education or income. But the lack of knowledge or money affects only the value, not the nature, of the liberty; it is not conceptually linked to the liberty itself.

Other background conditions are different. Some concern the protection and reparation of liberties. Consider Immanuel Kant's claim, that compensation for violation of my legal rights aims to "preserve what is mine undiminished."[35] That is not quite right. Compensation does not always give me back what I have lost: if you break my leg, compensation will not fuse the bone. But the justification of compensation is a desire to put things right, to repair the right violation as much as it is possible to do so. When you break my leg, it is because I had a right to my person that I am entitled to reparative damages.[36] Those damages are supposed to put me in as near a position as possible to a world where no wrong occurred. Such protections are rationally connected to the rights themselves in a way the factors affecting the ability to exercise the rights are not.

This connection explains some common mistakes people make about rights. If two people have rights not to be fired from their jobs on account of their race, but only one of them is entitled to exercise that right in court, the value of these rights is vastly different. This background condition falls into the second class; it is a condition concerned with the protection and reparation of liberties. When people object to a state of affairs like this, they sometimes phrase the objection as a deprivation of the underlying rights.[37] That is a mistake—the rights are still there; that they are there, unprotected, is why we should reform the legal system—but it is an intelligible mistake once the connection between rights and their enforcement mechanisms is revealed.

Most importantly, in our context, the uncoupling of all conditions on the value of liberties reveals an intimate connection between the repair of rights violations and the rights themselves. This is sufficient to distinguish background factors concerned with vindicating rights from those concerned with the exercise of rights. Those factors related to protection and enforcement of liberties are more important than other background factors: they are conceptually connected with the liberty itself. If liberties ought to be equal, the protection of those liberties should be supplied equally, too.

The justice benefits of legality include the reduction of injustice, the increased justice in allocation, and the reparation of injustice. These benefits are concerned, roughly speaking, with the protection from and reparation of injustice. To say that the protection of liberties should be equal is, therefore, another way of saying that the justice benefits of legality should be distributed equally across society. The premise, that liberties should be equal, generates an argument for equal justice.

EQUAL CONCERN

Democratic governments treat their citizens with equal concern.[38] If equal concern means citizens have claims to an equal distribution of the justice benefits and burdens of legality, equal justice connects with this democratic ideal. This can be seen in common objections to situations of inequality as creating "second-class citizens." It is also inherent in the idea that various institutional structures can make it the case that there is "one law for the rich and one for the poor": the law does not, people say, bind equally if institutions are not set up correctly.

To see what there is to these objections, consider first the benefits of legality. If you and I invest equal amounts in a scheme, absent some good reason for a different distribution—such as one of us coming up with the idea for the investment or putting in more labour—we ought to share equally in its outputs. Tim Scanlon proposes a principle that explains that conclusion. Suppose, he writes, "that the members of a group have equal claims to a certain form of benefit, such as the wealth produced by their combined efforts. If a distributive procedure is supposed to be responsive to these claims, then it will be unfair if (absent some special reason) it gives some of these people a higher level of benefit than others. This provides, in schematic form, an argument which leads us to a prima facie case for equality in a certain dimension of benefit."[39] The principle, at its most abstract, suggests that members of a collective scheme have equal claims to the products of that scheme.[40] An inegalitarian distribution by a government suggests a want of democratic concern. If, for example, the quality of hospitals is better in the richer communities than the poorer, those in the poor part of the country are treated as "second-class citizens."

The equal benefit principle applies to the benefits of legality. Entry into a legal system does not entail equal investment of financial resources: some people pay no taxes; some pay a lot. But entry does entail equal loss of freedom to redress injustice on our own: the creation of a legal system means, if we cannot agree on a solution, that we must resolve our disputes through law. We can characterise this as a joint and equal investment in a collective scheme, the legal system. We ought, therefore, to share equally in the fruits of that scheme.

Let's turn now to the burdens of legality. But to motivate the idea that equality matters, consider an analogous situation: national defence. The security of a state is costly and its costs, the most vivid of which is the risk to life, must be borne by someone. How should that burden be allocated? In 1863, the US Congress established the first military draft in its history.[41] All white men between the ages of twenty and forty-five had to register. From those, the preliminary group of soldiers—those who had to bear the burden—was selected through a lottery. But the next clause in the act gave each individual the option of buying their way out of the draft. The option cost $300.[42] The consequence was, as James Tobin writes, that "the power of the purse saved the life of one boy in exchange for the death of another."[43] Given that the cost of the buy-out was 75 per cent of a labourer's annual wage, it is more precise to say that the lives of rich boys were saved in exchange for the lives of poor boys.[44]

The New York City riots broke out in lower Manhattan on the morning of July 13. With a death toll of at least 105 over five days, it remains the bloodiest riot in US history. Like any such event, the motivations were doubtless diffuse. Racial prejudice, inflamed by the exemption of blacks from conscription, was evident: the Colored Orphan Asylum, which housed hundreds of children, was robbed of its supplies, then razed to the ground;[45] William Jones, a black cartman said by the police to have been "returning from a bakery with a loaf of bread under his arm," was beaten, hanged, and burned.[46] But the rioters also objected to the buy-out: the New York *Evening Express* reported that the buy-out was condemned by all, "whether one liked or disliked the Conscription Act" itself.[47] It has never been re-enacted.

Why was the buy-out thought objectionable? There are three possible explanations, of increasing force. The first explanation starts from the view that some burdens can justifiably be imposed on one individual only if they could, in principle, be imposed on any individual.[48] When this permissibility precondition holds, a good litmus test of whether it is permissible to generate a particular burden (say, as part of some optional collective scheme) is to ask whether there would be anything wrong with that risk being distributed by lottery. If a lottery is thought acceptable, it seems permissible to impose those risks on any individual; if it is thought unacceptable, it suggests that we do not believe that those risks may be imposed justifiably on any member of the community.[49] And having a legislative scheme with a lottery and a buy-out might be thought to equivocate on the crucial question, of whether the burdens are justifiably imposed.

This explanation connects closely with the second. Amongst those with full civic rights, or the perceived capacity to fight, the lottery distributed the burden of the draft across all members of society at random.[50] Before the lottery is drawn, all those theoretically eligible bear the same risk of selection. This makes it an ex ante egalitarian method of distribution. Part of the attraction of this method—and, so, part of the objection to the buyout—was the political discipline it imposed. When the rich are able to buy their way out of a burden, they never have to face up to the consequences of that burden. This might make the rich more willing than they should be to impose that risk on others. If the political class is, as a rule, richer than the average person, the lottery system is a good way of ensuring that the politicians imposing the draft genuinely believe that the imposition of the burden on any individual is morally defensible: if a politician's child stands the same risk of bearing the burden as anyone else's, the politician must be willing to subject their child to that risk.

The equal sharing of the risk of death is, on this explanation, an instrument that could be discarded if the same quality of legislation were generated by an unequal distribution of risk. If the equal sharing of risk was of more than instrumental importance, these first two explanations would not explain everything that was objectionable about the buy-out. Intuitively, it seems important that the lottery distributed the risk of death in war equally amongst eligible individuals. Permitting some to buy their way out of the draft disrupts that egalitarian distribution of risks according to a fact, the distribution of money, that is morally arbitrary from the point of view of the risk in question. This explanation is the reflection of the equal benefit principle: the burden, these risks, was permissible only if it was shared equally by all the beneficiaries of the collective scheme that gave rise to the risk.[51]

This sort of principle is most plausible in situations, such as the draft, where a burden arises as a side effect of a collective project. When none deserve to incur the burden, the inegalitarian distribution of the burden, as when it is distributed according to individuals' wealth, undermines the community's claim to democratic virtue. Such a community treats some citizens as second-class members. Consider, for example, the fact that blacks are six times more likely to be murdered than whites in the United States.[52] If this differential distribution is the result of institutional features, the inequality is unjust. When it is said that "Black Lives Matter," the objection is to the structural arrangements that generate figures like these. This is a democratic objection because it claims that certain groups are not being treated with equal concern: the benefits of legality are not being distributed equally to all in society.[53]

The example of the draft also closely relates to the risk of wrongful conviction. Adam Smith distinguished two duties of the sovereign: the protection of people "from the violence and invasion of other independent societies" and "from the injustice or oppression of every other member of it."[54] A legal system's protection against injustice is the counterpoint to an army's protection against violence and invasion. Both collective schemes generate burdens: the army creates the risk of death for anyone fighting in it; the legal system creates the risk of wrongful conviction. These burdens can be shared more or less fairly. It is not enough, to return to a point I have stressed, to seek to minimise the burdens of a legal system (or to maximise its benefits): we must pay attention to the distributions of those benefits and burdens.[55]

One of the burdens of legality is the risk of wrongful conviction. No individual deserves to bear that burden. The risk imposed on an individual will be permissible, therefore, only if that risk might permissibly have been imposed on any individual. And, as the second objection to the buy-out suggested, the equal distribution of the burdens of legality might have salutary effects, encouraging members of the political community to ensure these risks are as low as possible. This suggests a decent rule of thumb to determine whether a society has a fair criminal justice system: we can consider the risks of wrongful conviction each individual bears and ask whether everyone else in the community would rationally be willing to bear that risk; if not, the risk to that individual is indefensible.

These ways of thinking about the risks of wrongful conviction do not capture everything. As with the draft, equality in the distribution of those risks is fairest.[56] No individual could object to equality on the grounds of desert: if no one deserves to suffer the burden, all those who bear the risk of the burden equally cannot say that some other person should suffer more to ensure that they suffer less. It is important to bear this in mind when we turn to objections to the egalitarian principle—and, in particular, the argument that it is unfair to limit individuals' expenditure on their own criminal defence. If that argument is a good one, it is not an argument related to the desert of suffering those burdens.

Another of the burdens of legality is comparative. In Chapter 1, I referred to two such problems: that only certain classes of individuals are convicted of certain kinds of crime; and that certain classes of individual are given higher sentences than others for the same crime. The injustice of this is easiest to see with factors like race or wealth. If members of two different racial groups break the law an equal amount, it is unjust if one group is convicted more often than the other. Black Americans go to jail on drug charges at a rate of between twenty and fifty-seven times that of white Americans; it is not remotely plausible that this is a function of increased crime on the part of black Americans.[57] Once convicted, there is a further comparative injustice: for example, black Americans have been found to receive sentences nearly 14 per cent longer than white Americans for drug-trafficking offences.[58]

A call for equality in this context is a call to eliminate this comparative injustice. Hobbes, once again, expressed it well. He said that "the punishments ordained by the laws for all the citizens who have transgressed them should be inflicted equally on all."[59] Claims like these are still widely accepted. This feature of the equal burden claim is, for that reason, perhaps the least contentious of my claims about equality of benefits and burdens. When people say that the law should apply equally to all—regardless of race, class, gender, or wealth—they often mean that we should strive to eliminate these comparative injustices.

Equal Justice and Welfare

There are two types of benefit and burden: those concerned with justice and those concerned with welfare. The egalitarian impulse applies with greater force to the justice than the welfare domain. Thinking about how the two come apart also shows a further argument for equal justice: it is a precondition for justice in the distribution of welfare over time.

The welfare benefits created by a justice system are not distinctive qua welfare benefits. On the model outlined in Chapter 1, the institutions of private property and contract are welfare-enhancing; they do not codify rights antecedent to the creation of a legal system. If that model is correct, the welfare advance those systems make is no different from other welfare-enhancing institutions. That is an obvious point, perhaps. But it is important because there is a vast literature on the best way for welfare to be distributed in society: some favour equality; others demur. That literature is the best place to start thinking about welfare; it is not my concern in this book. There is, though, one recurrent theme to the discussion of welfare that does connect to equal justice.

Many believe that it would require too great an interference with individual liberty to guarantee a particular pattern of welfare (or distribution of material resources). It seems that it would, for example, require strict controls on what people can do with their own resources. Consider, for example, what would happen if a community sought to ensure equality in holdings. Suppose that everyone wants to watch the two best athletes play tennis, but they will only play if they are paid a fee. Everyone buys their tickets and the athletes have their game.[60] If transactions like these are to be permitted—and banning them would seem draconian—some will acquire more money than others. This creates its own problems.

It is important to consider the consequences over time of certain individuals acquiring more money than everyone else. The rich can (absent complications I consider next) advance their own interests and the interests of their friends and family. They can buy all the newspapers in town, suppressing stories about their own corruption. This would be a bad position for any community to find itself in. Another problem of inequality in holdings is its effect on equality of opportunity for the next generation.[61] A common concern is that those who end up succeeding in particular fields are overwhelmingly from privileged (usually wealthy) backgrounds: wealthy parents can purchase the goods that help their children get ahead; poor parents cannot.

We have two powerful, apparently conflicting, intuitions in the realm of welfare. On the one hand is the idea that contractual transactions can be perfectly fair without preserving equality of distribution. People ought to have a domain of liberty to structure their own lives: we do not want to outlaw all transactions or transfers between individuals. On the other hand, a distributive state of affairs might be unjust even if every individual transaction that led to the state of affairs was itself just.[62] The particular type of injustice that can result from just transactions is a distribution of resources that undermines other political ideals, such as fair equality of opportunity.

To manage this conflict, we should regulate not only justice in individual transactions, such as individual contracts, but also what John Rawls called "background justice."[63] As he writes, "The role of the institutions that belong to the basic structure is to secure just background conditions against which the actions of individuals and associations take place. Unless this structure is appropriately regulated and adjusted, an initially just social process will eventually cease to be just, however free and fair particular transactions may look when viewed by themselves."[64] Justice cannot be established by the examination of individual transactions alone. We must also examine what the (perhaps unforeseen) consequences of those transactions will be: whether, for example, anyone has accrued enough money to disrupt equality of opportunity. The impact of inequality of holdings on other political ideals depends upon the characteristics of the individual polity. A society without private schooling, for example, will find there is less of an interference with equality of opportunity through unequal distributions of wealth than one where the quality of education children receive depends upon their parents' wealth.

It is not enough to ensure that individual transactions are just; there must also be a set of conditions that ensure justice in the long run. Only if the conditions of background justice are achieved is it plausible that individuals may pursue their own self-interest through private transacting. This reveals a normative priority to those conditions over the justice of individual transfers. These background conditions would include, most obviously, rules on taxation and the prohibition of fraud in transactions.[65] Perhaps less obviously, they must also include the rules constituting the legal system itself.[66] There is no point having rules on taxation if they are not enforced properly. There is no point prohibiting fraud if the defrauded cannot prove that advantage has been taken of them. Having a just justice system is a condition that must be met if background justice is to be achieved.

If the gains and losses of market transactions are to be justifiable to those who lose out, the legal structure must comply with equal justice. This ensures that those who accrue wealth through these transactions are not able to control the instruments regulating those distributions: might cannot control right.

THE PRINCIPLE IN PRACTICE

An old tradition holds, with Cicero, that justice consists in "in allocating each person their due."[67] None are more entitled to justice or deserving of injustice than others. In our context, therefore, Cicero's proposal would be: all those entitled to justice should get it; no one should suffer injustices.

Although that proposal is somewhat facile, it contains an important truth: it does describe the ideal state. Our question is the principle that governs the distribution of justice and injustice given that not everyone can get justice and someone must suffer injustice. The equal justice ideal is the most promising principle we have. But there are two practical objections to it, both of which derive from the apparent impossibility of the ideal: it is simply not possible for all to get justice and none to suffer injustices. So what sense can we make of the principle of equal justice?

Equality and Arbitrariness

This equal benefit principle applies whenever all potential beneficiaries have an equal claim on some resource. That principle does not entail brute equality in outcomes; it only means that divergences from equality must be justified.[68] A state might spend more money on roads in a poorer part of the country, for example, because those citizens in that area are more in need than others. This suggests a natural proposal to escape from the apparent impossibility of equal justice: any movement from a situation where all get justice and none suffer injustice must not be arbitrary.

This cannot be a complete answer, for reasons I will soon explore. But there are scales of arbitrariness and injustice in how deviations from perfection come about. Equal justice proscribes some disruptive factors more forcefully than others. For any person, whether they get justice for some individual wrong, or whether they are wrongfully convicted, will depend on a number of factors: their wealth, their spare time, their tenacity, their luck, and so on. The principle of equal justice makes a rather general claim, of inequalities being unjust. Sometimes inequalities are unjust. It is a mark of societal injustice if an individual's access to the benefits of a legal system depends upon their status. If, for example, only the nobility (or the political class) could bring claims in a country's courts, that would be unjust—and it would be unjust even if the decisions of the courts did not unjustly favour the nobles or the politicians. The injustice is in the distribution of the benefits of legality. The same applies to race, class, gender, or wealth: it would be unjust if distributions depended on those factors. In a corrupt legal system, the judiciary might select cases based on whether the litigants are their friends or foes, or whether they are upper- or lower-class. Yet we are not equal in our escape from injustice if your connections or class enable you to get reparation while I am unable to get it. This inequality seems unjust.

Antecedent wealth is no different from class or connections, from race or gender: inequalities in who gets justice should not be a function of different financial circumstances. This point is fundamental to the formulations of equal justice I have already quoted. Another evocative example is Mr. Crawley in Anthony Trollope's *The Last Chronicle of Barset*. Crawley is accused of stealing a cheque. When he refuses to employ a lawyer, he reasons, "I will have no one there paid by me to obstruct the course of justice or to hoodwink a jury. . . . If I am dragged before that tribunal, an innocent man, and am falsely declared to be guilty, because I lack money to bribe a lawyer to speak for me, then the laws of this country deserve but little of that reverence which we are accustomed to pay to them."[69] Crawley's objection is not to wrongful conviction. It is to wrongful conviction *because of* his poverty. His objection is to a legal system where the risk of wrongful conviction depends on an individual's wealth. Wealth is, like race, class, and gender, an arbitrary factor on which the distribution of benefits and burdens of legality should not depend.

Other inequalities seem different. If some people do better in the justice system merely because they are willing to stick to their guns, dedicate the time required to succeed, and so on, that seems less objectionable. That gives us a strong reason to equalise justice benefits and burdens relative to money; inequality caused by individual tenacity in pursuing justice seems permissible.

Or so it seems in theory. It is a complicated and difficult issue in practice. The complicating factor is that the time people have can be a function of their own career choices: some people pursue time-intensive jobs, which endows them with greater financial resources; others prefer to have more free time and less money. If allowing inequalities in opportunities for justice to result from different investments of personal time is permissible, but inequalities from different investment of money is not, this gives rise to a seeming paradox: those who value free time more than money are able to leverage that preference to do better in terms of justice; those who value money over free time are not equally permitted to leverage that preference in the justice context. How can this paradox be resolved? It only arises, notice, if there's a reasonably fair system for the distribution of money through wage labour. In real life, many people work extremely long hours for very low pay; many of those in high-paying jobs do not work anything like as hard, or suffer from anything like the stress, as those in low-paying jobs. The paradox trades on the idea that financial outcomes are explained only by individual responsibility—and that is not true.

Perhaps the ideal state is not brute equality in the justice benefits and burdens of legality. Instead we want equality to hold between those of, for example, equal tenacity. Preventing people from working on their own cases would be an interference with their liberty: it prevents them from doing something they seem, on the face of things, to have a moral permission to do. The more important point, though, is the scale of arbitrariness inherent in the principle of equal justice: that ideal drives us to eliminate the control of certain factors—in particular race, class, and wealth—on legal outcomes. This scale helps when it comes to formulating institutional proposals.

Limits to Liberty

The attempt to equalise the benefits and burdens of legality relative to various arbitrary factors—such as race, wealth, and class—is important to the proper arrangements of institutions. But isolating this scale of factors, where some factors are more arbitrary than others, does not resolve all the puzzles thrown up by equal justice. Any deviation from perfection is in one sense arbitrary: some individuals will no longer get their due. Even if a community could achieve equal justice relative to individual tenacity (and it is doubtful that it can), they would still have to impose extraordinary burdens upon certain individuals: someone will be denied justice when they deserve it; someone will suffer injustices they do not deserve. This raises a problem for equal justice in practice: how are these burdens to be justified to the citizens in question?

To set this problem up, we should recall the position in a state of nature. Each individual would have a moral permission to do various actions, a permission they are denied in civil society. There are two limits of importance that it is worth recalling.

Just as people are both morally and legally obligated to comply with just laws, they are, and should be, bound to comply with correct and just orders of tribunals. More counterintuitive, perhaps, is that they are also, and (usually) should be, bound to comply with incorrect and unjust orders of tribunals. Think again of Socrates. He had no legal permission to escape his execution. More striking still, he reasoned that it would be morally wrong to escape even if the conviction was itself unjust.[70] This is a striking asymmetry with the pre-legal position: if there is no legal order, an individual is entitled to resist any unjust aggressive action, such as an attempt to punish her for something she did not do. This is a heavy burden.

Although this burden falls primarily on the subjects of a legal system, it also has implications for officials. Some, such as judges, jailers, and executioners, are tasked with carrying out the laws or legal orders. These officials are supposed to follow what the law directs rather than considering what justice requires.[71] There is a related question about how these duties, duties to apply, at times, unjust laws or to mete out unjust orders, can be justified.

Think again of Alice Knotte, who complained that Thomas Champeneys "detaineth from her seven shillings in money." The legal system made her, in one sense, worse off. If Thomas did owe her seven shillings but there was no legal system, she might justifiably have taken the money from him. Once there is a legal system, that would be theft.

There is a quite general point here. If there were no legal system, any wronged individual would be morally entitled to seek redress. But part of the point of a legal system is to make everyone settle their disputes through law. One of the burdens of legality arises because the state claims a monopoly power to settle disputes: the legal system has the final say on any matter of disagreement. That imposes a burden on the wronged party.

The Need for Fair Procedures

These limits are not voluntarily imposed: we have to live up to the law whether or not we consent to it. And they are coercively enforced: individuals do not get to choose whether to comply with the law. How can these burdens be justified?

There are three stages to my argument. The first task is to show that it is valuable for individuals' liberty to be limited in these ways: without these burdens, a legal system could not work. Socrates saw this. He imagined the laws of Athens asking him, "Do you think that state can exist and not be overturned, in which the decisions reached by the courts have no force but are made invalid and annulled by private persons?"[72] He had no answer. Neither legislation nor adjudication would work if individuals did not comply with the laws or accord legal decisions a substantial degree of deference. If individuals were to decide for themselves what to do at any moment, or whether they have suffered an injustice, the advantages that laws can bring would be lost.

There is a more fundamental point here. People disagree about what justice requires. Alice and Thomas might legitimately disagree about whether he owes her the money. Those accused of crimes might reasonably believe themselves innocent of wrongdoing. The law would achieve nothing if Alice and Thomas were able to decide for themselves who was right; the problem arises because they disagree. Equally, a criminal justice system that allowed individuals to decide upon their own guilt would be somewhat ineffective. If individuals were not bound by the laws or decisions they disliked, there would be no legal system at all. It would be a return to a state of anarchy.[73]

If individuals were not bound in these ways, the legal system could not achieve its ends. But that alone does not justify calling on any particular individual to obey; it does not justify the burdens to those individuals. This is clearest when the decisions in question are unjust. When an individual is found guilty of a crime they did not commit, the individual is bound to pay whatever fine is ordered and even to go to jail if so directed. When a civil claim should succeed but is denied by a court, it is impermissible to extract reparation from the wrongdoer by force. When a civil claim should fail and yet the court finds that it succeeds, one must still pay the compensation the court finds is due. These are extraordinary burdens; few would, if such injustices befell them, feel anything other than aggrieved. How can they be justifiable? How, more precisely, can these burdens be justified to the individuals on whom they fall: the wrongfully convicted, the unjustly obliged, and so on?

The problem, at its most general, is this: how can the fact that some system generally works to the benefit of some (or even all) make a token decision—which might be unjust—binding on an individual? Part of the answer is to repeat the account just given, that the legal system would not work if these obligations did not exist. If the collective scheme—the scheme that creates the burdens—did not have good aspects, such as those outlined in Chapter 1, the burdens would obviously be unjustifiable. But this cannot be the whole story. We should not impose burdens upon people simply because doing so has good consequences. Consider the execution of Admiral John Byng following the Battle of Minorca, in 1756. The British and the French fought a naval battle. The French won. Byng, the British commander, was convicted of "failing to do his utmost to take or destroy the enemy's ships." He was sentenced to death and shot.[74]

Voltaire satirised this in *Candide,* saying the British killed an admiral now and then "pour encourager les autres"—to give courage to, or to encourage, the others.[75] The execution may have done the trick: it is said to have entrenched a culture of "aggressive determination" on the part of British naval officers.[76] But, ethically speaking, this is neither here nor there. One may not impose burdens like death on a person simply because it benefits others. It would be very helpful for those on the organ donor register if I were to be murdered in a hospital, but murdering me would still be wrong. Similarly, a judge might sometimes conclude that the conviction of an innocent person would prevent other crimes, but it would be wrong to convict for that reason.[77]

This shows that the story about preserving the legal system does not quite go far enough. Some will have to suffer injustices; others will not get the justice they are owed. We also need to offer a justification to these people if these burdens are to be justifiable. The justification cannot be desert-based: by hypothesis, the burden (wrongful conviction, an unjust decision) is not one the burden-bearer deserves, so there is no pattern of inequality that tracks desert criteria better than others. And yet, if we are to have a legal system, we have to distribute these burdens somehow. Where there is no correct distribution of the good in question, the only legitimate outcome is one resulting from a fair procedure.[78] We might generate obligations to obey the decisions of legal procedures, even incorrect or unjust decisions, if these burdens result from a fair process.[79]

It follows that everyone must have a right to a sufficient level of legal resources to make these burdens, and legal procedures generally, fair.[80] But this does not tell us much. The question becomes: what procedure is fair? That is the topic of the next two chapters.

THE CHALLENGE

In 1912 a legislative committee in the United Kingdom suggested that "whatever remedies for legal wrongs are within the reach of the well-to-do should be placed by the State within the reach of the poorest in the land, so far as is reasonably possible to do so."[81] It is not enough, the committee supposes, that people have access to law; the poorest should not be *worse off* than the "well-to-do" in their access to remedies for wrongs. This proposal is grounded in equal justice.

Perfect equality is impossible to achieve in the real world. There are two implications for institutions. First, some disruptive factors are more arbitrary than others: legal systems should strive to reduce the control factors such as race, class and wealth have on outcomes. Second, the ultimate distribution of benefits and burdens must issue from a fair procedure. The challenge is to design institutions in such a way as to minimise the control of these arbitrary factors and to ensure procedures are fair. The next two chapters consider the fairness of procedures; Chapter 5 considers how, beyond a fair procedure, the control of arbitrary factors might be limited.

3

A MARKET IN LEGAL RESOURCES

EX ANTE EQUALITY

Late one evening in April 1841, the *William Brown*, an American ship bound for Philadelphia from Liverpool, struck an iceberg. Of the eighty-two aboard, half—nine crew and thirty two passengers—made it onto the ship's longboat; ten more, including the captain and the second mate, escaped on the jolly boat. The rest went down with the ship. The longboat had not been serviced properly and leaked water. Some had to die that others might live. How should that burden be allocated? One member of the crew said, "If we are to die, let us die fair—let us cast lots."[1] The rest of the crew had different ideas: they threw sixteen passengers, fourteen men and two women, overboard.

A year later, a Philadelphia jury was asked whether Alexander Holmes, one of the crew, was guilty of manslaughter on the high seas. In his remarks to the jury, Circuit Justice Baldwin reasoned that it might have been just to select victims by lot: that is "the fairest mode" to distribute the burden because it would ensure that "those in equal relations may have equal chance for their life."[2] Whatever their reasons, the jury agreed that Holmes was guilty of the crime: he was sentenced to six months' solitary hard labour.[3]

The judge's reasoning recalls the equal burden principle, the idea that the social imposition of certain risks is permissible only if those risks are shared equally. The challenge is to find a way to ensure that kind of equality in the realm of justice. Someone might, following the judge, suggest a lottery. All those in equal relations would thus (it might be said) have ex ante equal chances of obtaining the benefits and burdens of legality.

A lottery system would select at random from a group of possible beneficiaries of legal resources. A random distribution ensures that legal resources are not distributed according to arbitrary factors, such as wealth or class. It also means that resources are not distributed according to factors such as individual need. In this way, the lottery's virtue is also the lottery's vice. The vice is partly one of inefficiency: it would dramatically reduce the benefits and increase the burdens of legality.

The normative attraction of markets may derive from a sense that they seem to square this circle, maintaining the virtues of a lottery without the attendant vices. Markets are a procedure for the distribution of goods. No particular distributive outcome is sought directly; the distribution is arrived at as a consequence of the intersection of supply and demand curves. Markets are, for that reason, similar to lotteries: they can be said to institute a kind of ex ante equality without seeking a specific distribution ex post. This might make markets a tempting proposal for those who seek a fair procedure for the distribution of legal resources. In this chapter, I assess—and reject—that proposal. Markets, I will argue, do not secure the virtues of a lottery: distributions of legal resources through a market lead to inegalitarian consequences. And they may not secure the efficiencies customarily associated with markets.

My arguments connect with a prominent recent trend in political philosophy, one concerning whether there are moral limits to markets—whether, that is, there are certain things (friendship? sex? bodily organs?) that ought not to be traded through markets. The objection is not to markets *sans phrase;* it is to the use of markets for the distribution of certain things. After all, as Debra Satz points out, "People do tend to react quite differently to inequalities in access to medical care or to legal assistance than they do to inequalities in automobiles, clothes, and yachts."[4] But legal services, although largely ignored by philosophers, are in some ways the most important of these: the very idea of a free market, I will argue, presupposes a just distribution of legal resources. Before we can think about markets in anything, therefore, we need to think about justice in legal resources.

A MARKET IN LEGAL RESOURCES

Assessing Markets

People sometimes talk as if markets are a natural or presumptive regulative principle. When formulating principles for the distribution of goods, the thought goes, it makes sense to start with a laissez-faire distribution and to proceed with choice interventions where appropriate. This is no argument at all; it merely asserts the normative priority of a certain kind of market. And talk of "naturalness" is rarely a helpful way of thinking about things. In the legal context, for example, if any arrangement is natural, it is a state without a legal system, a world where people can lie, cheat, and extort so long as they can get away with it. Few would defend that arrangement.

It is also sometimes thought that economists are unthinking believers in markets' virtues, blind to their contingent value. True enough, some have argued that markets should be used to distribute a very wide range of goods.[5] But few now make that claim in an unqualified form. It is widely accepted, for example, that the just distribution of public goods depends on governmental intervention.[6] Economists have spent the last few decades undermining various assumptions made by neo-classical models.[7] Today, most economists' commitments to markets are measured and sensitive to context; they afford markets no presumptive priority.

Perhaps the motivation to talk of markets as "natural" stems from a belief that there is an intrinsic value realised through their use.[8] Markets may sometimes serve the ends of justice when compared to status-based exclusions. Markets offer, as I explain next, a kind of equality of access: this link to lotteries is sometimes thought to reconcile markets with egalitarian ideals. Nevertheless, the principal advantage of markets is not the realisation of any intrinsic value. Their value—when they have value—comes from the consequences of their use.

This was Adam Smith's view. "Commerce," he said, "gradually introduced order and good government, and with them the liberty and security of individuals, among the inhabitants of the country, who had before lived almost in a continual state of war with their neighbours, and of servile dependency upon their superiors. This, though it has been the least observed, is by far the most important of all their effects."[9] The "most important" effect of market exchange, Smith reasoned, was the ability to bring about liberty and to free people from dependence on others. If a laissez-faire market undermined those goals, Smith was perfectly happy to regulate it: "When the regulation . . . is in favour of the workmen, it is always just and equitable; but it is sometimes otherwise when in favour of the masters."[10] Markets stand or fall as a means of distribution depending on the consequence of their use: as liberty- or welfare-enhancing, for example.[11] In our context, the principal consequence markets should serve is the realisation of equal justice. Insofar as they fail to do so, they should at least provide a fair procedure for the distribution of justice and injustice.

Two Clarifications

Before assessing markets in legal resources, we should bring slightly more focus to the proposal. In contemporary societies, particularly the United States, markets are used to distribute very many goods: not only luxury items, such as champagne and tickets to popular events (such as sporting or artistic occasions), but also healthcare, schooling, and citizenship.[12] In our context, the proposal is to distribute legal resources through a market, where resources are traded by willing buyers and sellers according to principles of supply and demand.

A related proposal would hold that a market distribution is the presumptive approach, albeit that it should be subject to certain regulations. These regulations might include the provision of government vouchers, a legal aid regime, or the recognition of voluntary service requirements in the professional standards of lawyers. Many of the objections I will raise to markets apply to their centrality as a distributive mechanism in this context and, therefore, would apply as much to a market-plus-regulations scheme. But not all: some of the objections I raise can be met by the provision of a basic level of legal services (that could, in principle, be achieved via vouchers, legal aid, or the imposition of professional obligations).[13] My main concern in this chapter is to establish why the use of a market in legal resources is a bad distributive principle; the question of whether a market-lite measure or some planned distribution is preferable is largely deferred until Chapters 4 and 5.

The proposal to use markets to distribute legal resources is, in many respects, not reformist. Markets are used to distribute very many legal resources. To appreciate a complication to that basic point, two features of the proposal should be distinguished. First is the question of who should pay for the use of some good. The distribution of legal resources to "willing buyers" means that the user of that good is the one who should pay.[14] Second is the question of how the price for that good is set. Markets set prices through the interaction of supply and demand. When thinking about legal resources, these two features must sometimes be distinguished: some legal resources have fixed prices that must be borne by individual buyers.

Both features are represented in contemporary procedures for distributing lawyers. Although it is a regulated market—to sell your services as a lawyer, you need to acquire professional qualifications—shorn of complications, the best lawyers go to those willing and able to pay the most. Legal aid regimes introduce something like a sufficiency criterion into the system, such that an individual who cannot afford a lawyer but needs one is (in some systems, for some claims) given one. (The cost is carried either by the lawyer or the state, depending on the system.) But these reforms, which I consider next, are an intervention in the market rather than a challenge to market distributions.[15]

The position of courts is a little more complicated. In general, individual users must pay to access courts; in that respect, courts fit the first element of the market proposal. Although courts have been (and are) sometimes used to make profits for the state—that was part of the objection the barons had to King John's courts—the price is not set by a competitive market. The cost is (like judicial salaries) set by the state. There are also, beyond this point about price, other substantial restrictions on a free market in access to courts. Judges are allocated to cases based on time and expertise; litigants cannot pay more for their judge of choice.

It would be wrong to overplay the extent to which market norms govern legal resources. That said, there are indirect pressures that lead to the allocation of court time to those able and willing to pay most for it, an implication of a market distribution. This means that the second element of the market definition applies indirectly even for the distribution of courts. Let me give one example.[16] In England, victorious litigants are in principle entitled to claim their court costs from the losing party. Litigants whose claims are worth less than £250,000 and who refuse to mediate—to attempt to settle their dispute rather than have it resolved on the merits—"may be required to justify to the Court of Appeal their decision not to attempt mediation at subsequent court hearings."[17] Rules like these inevitably channel cases with a very high financial value into court; and these claims are usually brought by individuals or companies with very high net worth. The effect is that the richest in society are the ones who end up getting the bulk of that resource.

The Arguments Ahead

Markets have various virtues, ones we should not ignore. An attraction in this context is that some legal resources are also people: lawyers and judges. People and their talents are not proper objects of justice; they are not up for distribution, and any inequalities in that realm cannot be unjust. As John Rawls puts this point, "The natural distribution [of talents] is neither just nor unjust; nor is it unjust that persons are born into society at some particular position. These are simply natural facts."[18] However, Rawls adds, "the way that institutions deal with these facts" can be just or unjust.[19] In our context, the reference to legal resources is a shorthand: the site of justice is the institutional arrangement generating legal powers and distributing lawyers; this will be clearest in Chapter 6, where liberty-based objections to my proposals are considered.

Another virtue of markets is that they can unlock a form of motivation, self-interest, which can be very powerful in fuelling productivity. The argument in this context would be: permitting lawyers to trade their services on an open market unlocks productivity in the realm of justice; this leads to more justice overall than there would be on any other plausible distributive arrangement. I will respond to this argument in Chapter 5, where I consider the possible consequences of a proscription on contracting out.

In the next three sections I offer three arguments against using markets as a means of distributing legal resources. The "primacy" argument points to a logical problem the proposal faces: a just distribution of legal resources is a constitutive feature of a just market, so justice in that distribution must come prior to the market. The "justice" arguments claim that markets will fail to secure equal justice: they make the distribution of benefits and burdens turn on an arbitrary fact, antecedent wealth; and they threaten to undermine the core goal of a legal system, which is to govern distributions by right, not might.[20] Finally I highlight some features of legal resources that make it, like healthcare, peculiarly difficult to distribute efficiently through a market.

THE PRIMACY OF JUSTICE

Some distributive injustices in certain goods are mere reflections of underlying injustices in material holdings. Perhaps, this thought goes, it is in principle permissible for one person to sell their kidney to another; but when the vendor is extremely poor and the buyer extremely rich, a market in kidneys will tend to have bad effects.[21] When, as in contemporary societies, there is grave injustice in the distribution of material holdings, we may have good reasons to regulate some markets (such as those in kidneys) more than others (such as those in champagne). But the grounds of the injustice remain the underlying injustice in distribution. Other injustices are different. Even when they supervene on material inequality, there is an extra disvalue in unequal distributions in certain goods. If there were a market in votes, for example, the resultant injustice would supervene on the underlying inequality in money. But the basic objection to the market would not concern that underlying inequality: the objection would be that votes are not the sorts of things that should be distributed in that way.

Legal resources are not like champagne or plovers' eggs and should not be distributed as if they were; objections to the use of a market in legal resources are more like objections to a market in votes. One reason is that the justice system has a conceptual priority in a market economy. The problem arises because, as Claudius points out in *Hamlet,*

> In the corrupted currents of this world
> Offence's gilded hand may shove by justice;
> And oft tis seen the wicked prize itself
> Buys out the law.[22]

This highlights a striking fact about market distributions of legal resources: ill-gotten gains can be defended *with* those ill-gotten gains. The priority argument begins with this fact—and the sense that permitting this is unjust.

The civil legal system is the way we adjudicate who is entitled to what. An individual should not be able to defend their entitlement to their resources by *spending* those resources; this is particularly the case if the more resources they have, the better their chance of defending those resources. But that is the system a market in legal resources permits.

What, though, is the precise objection? A problem Claudius identifies is that the use of a market to distribute the instruments of justice undermines the whole point of instituting a justice system. That is a form of a later argument I make, which I call the argument from justice. But there is another point. The idea that markets have normative priority—such that the legal system should be arranged through a market—has things backwards. Markets require defined and protected property and contractual rights.[23] But a market requires more than the mere legal rights: it also requires a mechanism to enforce and protect those rights. If contractual and property rights can be expropriated without cost, for example, the creation of those rights will be insufficient to create a functioning market.

The point can be put with more force if we talk about *fair* markets. It is not a fair market if one side has a gun during negotiations. Likewise, it is not a fair market if the court that adjudicates on any ultimate dispute is partisan.[24] Just as legal rights are analytically prior to the market, a fair method of dispute resolution is analytically prior to a fair market.

If a just legal framework is required for a market to operate properly, we need principles independent of a market system to determine the just arrangement of legal frameworks. Otherwise we would be in an argumentative circle: we need a just distribution of legal resources before any market is instituted for the market to be fair; but a fair legal system, if a market is to be used, depends on a fair market to distribute legal resources.

This does not show that it is illegitimate to use a market to distribute legal resources. But it does show that, if a market is the best method of distribution, it must be in virtue of some feature independent of markets' value. When I make more concrete proposals for a fair distribution of legal resources, I will invoke a number of further values of a legal system. In the remainder of this chapter, it is enough to show that a market in legal resources would lead to arbitrariness in the distribution of the benefits and burdens of legality.

MARKETS AND EQUAL JUSTICE

Unjust and Unequal

Statements that people should be treated equally are always indexed to particular abilities or circumstances. Consider John Rawls's principle of fair equality of opportunity: "Those who are at the same level of talent and ability, and have the same willingness to use them, should have the same prospects of success regardless of their initial place in the social system."[25] Rawls wants two people to have an equal chance of success only if they have the same talent and tenacity; those with greater ability can, the principle suggests, justifiably have greater opportunities. Not everyone will agree with that particular proposal. But any egalitarian principle will be relative to a certain set of characteristics or circumstances.[26]

Similarly, any distributive mechanism that seeks to secure ex ante equality will secure it relative only to certain characteristics. Lotteries secure ex ante equal chances, but only for those entered into the lottery. Markets, too, offer a kind of ex ante equality. Because they do not allocate goods according to a pre-planned distribution, they can eliminate the direct control of arbitrary factors on access to various goods and institutions. Compared with a distribution to "whites only," the introduction of a market can be a genuine advance of justice: no longer are distributions directly governed by an arbitrary factor, race.[27] As will become apparent (if it is not obvious already), this egalitarian advance is highly contingent: markets, absent regulation, have no method to prevent the same arbitrary characteristics coming to govern distributions indirectly.[28]

The goal of a market distribution in legal resources is set by the principle of equal justice. Individuals should have an equal chance of obtaining justice and incur an equal risk of being treated unjustly; and any inequality in practice should issue from a fair procedure. Various arbitrary facts should not govern distributions, in particular race, class, and wealth. How does the market measure up against that benchmark?

For justice to be done in individual cases, institutions—courts, tribunals, and so on—must be responsive to the right kind of facts. They must respond to the kind of facts that justify distributions (like facts about individual desert) rather than facts that merely explain them (like facts about power). We can ask whether things are being distributed to the right people and for the right reasons. If you have a legal structure determining who is entitled to welfare payments, welfare should go to those who have an entitlement under that system and not to those who do not. If some person is entitled to welfare and does not get it—say, because she does not realise that she is entitled to it—that is as much a problem as if she claims the entitlement and a court denies her.

We can assume that the better a lawyer is, the greater is the chance of winning a case.[29] The market distribution of legal resources means that, roughly speaking, the richer someone is, the better their lawyers are likely to be. In the civil context, as I will develop next, the adversarial system means that this is particularly problematic. In the criminal context, an individual's chance of being convicted—rightly or wrongly—of some crime will depend in part upon her wealth. The use of a market in legal resources is consistent with there being no floor to legal resources whatsoever: in theory, no one would get legal representation unless they could pay for it (or a charitable donor provided it). That is the position in the United States today with respect to civil justice.[30]

All this suggests an obvious problem. The market distribution of legal resources makes outcomes depend in part upon antecedent wealth. Wealth buys influence; influence affects outcomes. As King Lear put this point,

> Plate sin with gold,
> And the strong lance of justice hurtless breaks;
> Arm it in rags, a pygmy's straw does pierce it.[31]

Antecedent wealth—"gold"—is an arbitrary fact: the point of having a justice system is to make right, not might, the determining factor in distributions. But a market in legal resources enables rich individuals to control outcomes indirectly by stacking the procedural deck.

This suggests that a market in legal resources will lead to a greater incidence of incorrect decisions than alternative regimes.[32] At the very least, it suggests the need for interventions in the market. Are *interventions* all that is needed? A market in legal resources, someone might say, is not doomed to failure; we just need to be more precise in our design of the market. How so? The legal system's rules of procedure might be used to counterbalance how the cases in court are decided. Even if richer people are able to hire better lawyers, legal procedure should be set up to ensure that everyone is treated equally. Does the objection to the use of a market fade away? No.

To see why, we need to consider the distributive implications of using markets.

Sometimes it is better to distribute less in a more equitable fashion. On John Rawls's influential account, for example, an arrangement of resources that produces greater net benefits for society as a whole is ruled out if those benefits accrue to the best-off, with no improvement in the welfare of the least-advantaged.[33] In our context, some individuals are bound to suffer from injustice and not everyone with a sound claim in justice will have it vindicated. That is so regardless of the arrangement of legal resources. The distributive question arises: who should bear these burdens and get these benefits? Any distribution of legal resources might make up for a deficiency in decision making—the decreased justice and increased injustice it seems to entail, relative to other possible arrangements—if it gives a good answer to the distributive question. A market in legal resources may lead, for the reasons just canvassed, to inaccuracy in decision-making; but, a defender might say, if it secures the equality of equal justice, it may yet be vindicated.

The form of this argument is quite familiar and acceptable. But the claim is risible with respect to markets in legal resources. Although markets do not seek a particular pattern of distribution, the ultimate distributions are predictable. Very roughly, goods end up in the hands of those who value them most *and* who are willing and able to pay for them. That is why Friedrich Engels objected that "the proceeds" of market distributions are divided by a "fortuitous standard," "competition, the slick right of the stronger."[34] This feature of markets means that the distribution of the benefits and burdens of legality will be controlled by arbitrary factors: in particular, antecedent wealth. A market system means, in other words, that those with more wealth benefit more and suffer less than those with fewer resources.

This is clearest with respect to lawyers. Once a market is instituted for lawyers' services, the best lawyers become accessible only to those who are able to pay the lawyers' fees. The scarce benefit (justice) ends up going to the wealthier segments of society while the scarce burden (injustice) rebounds more upon the poor. So a market in legal resources not only risks less justice and more injustice, it also means that the rich will get justice and the poor will suffer injustice. This is impossible to defend in good faith.

The use of markets will affect not only how cases are decided in court—this is the area that the earlier argument about procedure purports to answer—but also which cases are *brought* to court. A market system means that those with more money will be able to bring their cases to court while those with less money will not. From a class of possible cases to resolve, in other words, the market in legal resources will pick the litigants with the most money and adjudicate on those—it will not pick the disputes whose litigants would benefit the most from court time. This much is clear even when a more measured approach, such as fixed fees, is used. Court fees, which are centrally fixed, do not make decisions less likely to be just: if courts have a relatively fixed capacity to hear cases, a fee scheme will not affect the rate of injustice done in court. Nevertheless, fees are an indirect method of controlling access to courts: only those who can afford the fees can get into court. They prejudice the opportunities of those earning lower incomes. One effect of court fees is, therefore, that those with money have a better chance of getting justice than those without.

Suppose, to illustrate this point, that court fees were prohibitively high and there were no other ways of forcing wrongdoers to account: this could lead to greater levels of injustice outside courts (as the unscrupulous know they can act with impunity); it would also mean that only the rich would get justice. This suggests an objection to using a market to control access to courts: its effect is that, when only some victims of injustice can get justice, those able to pay more for it will be more likely to get it. That is the situation mocked in the old aphorism that "in England, justice is open to all, like the Ritz hotel."[35]

What If Wealth Was Equal?

These arguments have, for the most part, assumed inequality of holdings. But what if everyone had a fair income—or if wealth was equal? Suppose, to develop a thought experiment proposed by Ronald Dworkin, that a number of individuals are shipwrecked on an island. If they are to start a society with private property, they have to decide how to divide up the island's resources. Dworkin suggested giving each member a number of clam shells, which act as currency, and having them bid for the resources in an auction. The idea is, as Dworkin writes, that "when the auction finally ends, and everyone is satisfied that he has used his clamshells most efficiently . . .

no one will want to trade his bundle of resources for anyone else's bundle, because he could have had that other bundle in place of his own if he had so wanted."[36] There would then be a kind of equality of resources: no islander would prefer another's resources to her own.

Would there be anything wrong with the islanders implementing a market in legal resources as their method of distributing legal resources? The result would be, you might think, that any inequality in the distribution of the benefits and burdens of the legal system would be the result of each individual's choice.[37] People could, if the islanders' society is sophisticated, purchase legal expenses insurance against the risk of future injustices—and if they fail to purchase insurance, someone might say, it is their lookout if they are unable to afford to employ lawyers when they want to go to court.

This misses the point. Permitting a market in legal resources to determine what happens in disputes undermines the reasons why we set up a legal system in the first place. Suppose that a market in legal resources is created on the island. Some people will purchase insurance (or make enough money that they can buy legal resources at cost). Some will not. Legal disputes will arise where some can afford lawyers and some cannot: this will affect each individual's prospects of success in their dispute.[38] But the decision to purchase insurance is irrelevant, as a matter of justice, to the litigants' dispute. One individual's decision not to purchase legal insurance does not make them more deserving of suffering an injustice, or less deserving of the benefits of legality. Part of the point of setting up a legal system is to make such arbitrary facts irrelevant to questions of distribution or reparation, and that point is undermined by the market system. In this way, a market in legal resources tends to undermine justice in outcomes *even if* there is equality at the start of the story: it undermines the very reason we set up justice systems.

The criminal law is no different. We should not be wrongfully convicted of crimes regardless of whether we get a fair income; it is still an injustice for someone making a fair wage to be wrongfully convicted of a crime. If someone chooses not to buy legal expenses insurance and has no money to hire a lawyer, they will face a much larger risk of wrongful conviction than someone with such insurance. The advocate of the market system might defend this by reference to the individual's choice not to purchase insurance. Yet, as I argued in Chapter 2, the creation of a criminal justice system, and the risk of wrongful conviction it entails, is only justifiable if these risks are equally shared. Therefore, the advocate's claim is false. A market in legal resources undermines one of the things that makes it permissible to institute a legal system.

Markets sometimes have value in their evasion of certain vices. Some defend markets as a means of distribution, not on the basis that market distributions are a panacea but because any other means of distribution will be subject to political corruption and regulatory capture; and, therefore, that these methods will be even worse.[39] These are not trivial concerns. But the risk of capture by special interests should be turned on its head: the use of a market in legal resources enables those who are supposed to be governed by law to capture the means of that regulation. This will prevent the justice system from making right, not might, govern distributions.[40]

As inequalities in wealth emerge, the use of the market to distribute legal resources enables those with wealth to purchase yet more and better resources. If the system itself is a market good, the rich can take control of it simply because they are rich. Once they own the legal system, they can set the terms of use, including the exclusion of anyone they choose from the system. That is the risk of capture in a market system. The problem can be illustrated by considering Dworkin's island again. If everything were subject to auctioning, sooner or later someone would buy the auction house. The house—or, more specifically, its owner—would get to set the terms of all future auctions.[41]

This doomsday scenario is not only the stuff of a philosopher's thought experiment. In practice, the problem arises when powerful groups—those the law should aim to constrain—control the institutions (or access to the institutions) designed to hold them to account. When those groups are not able to mould the law to their whim, they can control its enforcement. They are able to renege on their legal obligations without risk of sanction, rendering any general rights that are granted a dead letter.

Consider, to illustrate, judicial appointments and the law on arbitration in the United States. After the death of Justice Antonin Scalia in 2016, President Barack Obama nominated Judge Merrick Garland to the Supreme Court. Nominations require the consent of the Senate to take their place as a justice—but Senate Republicans refused to give Garland a hearing or a vote; his nomination expired when Donald Trump became president.[42] One organisation, Judicial Crisis Network, spent $7 million to fund a campaign to block Garland's appointment. The same organisation then pledged to spend "at least $10 million" in support of Trump's ultimate nominee, Neil Gorsuch.[43]

The nomination had inevitable effects on the decisions of the court. The most salient example for our purposes concerns arbitration. Arbitration is a form of privatised dispute resolution where individuals must pay, not only for the lawyers they use, but also for the judges. So long as public courts are pliable, corporations can require that (for example) their employees' claims of justice are resolved in arbitration. Once the door to public courts is closed, corporations can exclude various procedural rights: to discovery of the other side's documents, for example, or to participate in class actions.[44]

Class actions can make it worthwhile to litigate collectively where individual suits are inefficient: as Judge Richard Posner has remarked, "Only a lunatic or a fanatic sues for $30."[45] For this reason, employers sought to proscribe class actions in arbitration. The US Supreme Court was asked to consider whether that was legally permissible. In a 5-4 decision authored by Justice Gorsuch, the conservative wing of the court found that employers were permitted to control employees' procedural rights in this way.[46] Dissenting, Justice Ruth Bader Ginsburg warned that "employers, aware that employees will be disinclined to pursue small-value claims when confined to proceeding one-by-one, will no doubt perceive that the cost-benefit balance of underpaying workers tips heavily in favor of skirting legal obligations."[47]

This illustrates the risks of a market in legal resources. The market can place even courts under the control of those with most money. The legal system can then no longer serve its functions; might wins out over right.

MARKETS AND ECONOMICS

These arguments give us strong reason to reject markets as a method for distributing the instruments of justice. Someone may still respond that markets are the best distributive mechanism of a bad bunch. That may be so, though we would have to have other possible mechanisms on the table to be sure. Before making some proposals, a note of caution should be sounded about markets' potential to operate efficiently in the legal context.

Markets and Efficiency

Markets are often thought peculiarly effective as a means of ensuring a kind of efficiency. They may, in particular, be especially good at securing Pareto optimality of welfare. That is not the goal of a legal system; legal systems are supposed to do justice.[48] Even if it were, though, there are serious doubts about whether a market in legal resources could be economically efficient. A great deal of economists' work in the past half-century has concerned the various ways in which markets fail. A market in legal resources exhibits a range of familiar market failures; I will outline three.[49]

Market Failures

When things go well, the police and the army make everyone in the community safer. My neighbour's increased security does not undermine my security: it is a benefit bestowed on the community as a whole, so we are not rivals for security. Further, short of forcing me into exile, there is no way to exclude me from the benefit of living in a safer community. In this way, the security is both non-rivalrous and non-excludable. Security is a public good.[50]

These concepts, of non-exclusion and non-rivalry, are scalar. Some police protection is easy enough to exclude people from: the police can simply refuse to come to certain houses or to help certain people. And some police resources are rivalrous: police are a scarce resource and they have to be allocated to various deserving causes. Nevertheless, the more public a good is, the more likely a market for its distribution is to fail.

It is uncontroversial that public goods are not efficiently provided by a market.[51] Adam Smith, for example, said that the "third and last duty of the sovereign" was "that of erecting and maintaining those public institutions and those public works, which though they may be in the highest degree advantageous to a great society, are, however, of such a nature, that the profit could never repay the expense to any individual, or small number of individuals; and which it, therefore, cannot be expected that any individual, or small number of individuals, should erect or maintain."[52] Recall, though, Smith's first two duties of the sovereign: defence against both external invasion and internal threats. The need to protect from injustice within the state was the reason why (on Smith's account) governments should create a legal system. This is simply another way of saying that a market in legal resources would be inefficient: because many aspects of law exhibit the character of public goods, it is inefficient to distribute those resources through a market.

I will explore the sense in which the provision of a legal system is a public good in greater detail later in the book; it is, I argue, incautious to characterise legal resources as pure public goods. For now, it is enough to note that the general security and assurance provided by a legal system is non-rivalrous and non-excludable; further, most of the welfare benefits unlocked by the provision of a system of contract and property are similarly public. Given this high degree of publicity, market failures would be inevitable if a market in legal resources were the regulative norm. This does not tell us what a superior method of distribution would be; it does give us grounds to doubt that a market provision is the best procedure.

For any market to work well, buyers and sellers have to know what they are buying and selling.[53] There is a lot of publicly available information regarding the quality of many commodities, such as consumer goods. That is why these things can be efficiently traded through a market. When markets display substantial informational asymmetries between buyers and sellers, market efficiency can break down.

Kenneth Arrow highlighted various features of healthcare that made it different from the "usual commodity of economics textbooks."[54] One important distinction between healthcare and many consumer products is that in the former context there is "uncertainty as to the quality of the product."[55] It is very difficult for consumers to become well-informed about individual healthcare products; there is an asymmetry between the knowledge of patients and doctors. This feature, amongst others, meant that "the *laissez-faire* solution for medicine is intolerable."[56]

Arrow's arguments can be transposed to any context in which there is a similar informational asymmetry. There is a very close analogy between the markets for healthcare and the markets for legal services.[57] Experts struggle to define what makes a lawyer a good one, so how do laymen have a chance? It is also very hard to predict what the marginal effect of a particular lawyer is on the outcome of a particular case. For some major commercial cases, lawyers seem to be either drastically overpaid (because the result would be the same regardless of whoever is presenting the case) or massively underpaid (because they make a difference to which party gets the billions in dispute).

Even if there were a perfectly just distribution of initial resources, a perfectly competitive market in legal services could not be formed. This undermines the premise of the market measure: legal resources are not an appropriate object of market distributions.

Arrow's third point was that demand for healthcare services is "irregular and unpredictable."[58] You only need healthcare in the event that you get sick. Similarly, you only need a lawyer if you suffer a wrong or are charged with a crime.

This alone is not enough to set legal resources (or healthcare) apart from various private goods. My need for cough medicine is unpredictable and irregular, but the market works perfectly well for its provision. But there is a further point of importance: both healthcare and legal services can be extremely expensive in the event that they are required. Some lawyers charge thousands of dollars a day; it can cost millions to pay for a case.

The consequence of these two features is that a market in legal resources could only plausibly work through the mechanism of insurance, with individuals insuring against the risk of injustices in the future. However, an important feature of human psychology makes the use of an insurance market in this context (where demand is unpredictable and rare) problematic. Humans are systematically optimistic about the future. In Shakespeare's *The Merchant of Venice,* Antonio guarantees a bond; if he fails to pay, Shylock is permitted to take a pound of his flesh. Antonio believes that he will be able to pay the bond because his ships, out at sea, will bring in "thrice three times the value of [the] bond."[59] On the date the bond falls due, none have arrived.[60] We all share Antonio's optimism. Few expect to have their rights violated or to be prosecuted for crimes they did not commit. Yet these things happen. The risk of an insurance market in legal services is that people would underinsure.[61]

LESSONS

The market in legal resources has long been subject to regulation and intervention. Most modern legal systems have legal aid schemes of varying generosity and court fee waivers in certain circumstances. This recognises a point I have laboured to make: that a market in legal resources is a bad way of distributing legal resources. It fails even to approximate to the ideal of equal justice, making outcomes turn on antecedent wealth rather than the merits of the claim. And the process it instantiates is unfair: not only may results be incorrect and the distribution of benefits and burdens inegalitarian, the wealthy will ultimately gain control of the legal institutions. The powerful can then proceed with impunity.

At their weakest, these arguments suggest a need for greater market regulation. I have also given arguments that seek to rule out even a *regulated* market distribution. Either way, the challenge ahead is now clear. Interventions into a market system should not be made on an ad hoc basis. To justify any intervention and to know whether it is working, we need to know the reason *for* the intervention; once we know that reason, we can ask whether its rationale extends to yet further reforms. The guiding ideal is the principle of equal justice. But how is that to be realised? Do we need to provide some individuals with state-funded lawyers? If so, why not provide *more*? To answer questions like these, we need to think about how our legal system should be structured so as to achieve the equal justice ideal. I turn to that question in the next chapter.

4

A FAIRNESS FLOOR

THE IDEA OF A FLOOR

Many people believe that there should be a minimum level of provision of certain goods available to anyone. There are now few societies, for example, that do not provide a basic level of education and healthcare. Even in the United States, where healthcare is a point of particular controversy, emergency services are provided to all free of charge; people should not be left to die in the streets. Numerous countries provide social security payments to those without jobs. Some people argue that every citizen should be entitled to a basic income.[1] All these measures suggest widespread support for a "floor": a basic level beneath which no one should fall.

This chapter concerns whether there should be a floor in legal resources, and what such a floor would be. Consideration of the market in legal resources in the previous chapter suggested that a situation with no guaranteed distribution would fail to secure equal justice. That conclusion is reinforced in this chapter by consideration of two values, liberty and the rule of law. These values suggest that a floor is necessary for a legal process to be fair, a precondition of realising equal justice. A basic level of legal resources must be granted to everyone subject to the legal system's demands; only then will the ideals of liberty and rule of law be met. There is an important implication: if individuals cannot afford a basic level of legal resources, the failure to grant them one renders the law's demands of them illegitimate.

The next question is what a floor in legal resources actually requires. It is sometimes thought that the level of basic provision should be invariant to others' resources. Regardless of the truth of that thought as a general matter, it is mistaken in the legal context. What counts as "enough" legal resources depends on the amount others have. In this chapter I suggest that we have enough legal resources only if we have roughly the same amount as those with whom we are in dispute. In this way, my arguments for sufficiency ultimately shade, in this chapter and the next, into arguments for equality.

LIBERTY

The Danger

Writing of the subjection of women to their husbands, John Stuart Mill notes "the wife's entire dependence on the husband, every privilege or pleasure she has being either his gift, or depending entirely on his will."[2] This would be objectionable even if the husband treated her very well: the problem is her dependence upon his will. That dependence means that she lacks a certain form of freedom; in lacking that freedom, she does not stand in a relation of equality with her husband. All societies should strive to eliminate such relations of servility. It is a condition of democratic communities that citizens stand (at least in certain contexts and in certain ways) as one another's equal and, as Elizabeth Anderson puts it, "Equals are not dominated by others; they do not live at the mercy of others' wills."[3]

Mill's example concerns two individuals. A further problem in political society arises where some few individuals have this kind of control over many others. Where a few accumulate a large number of resources, they enjoy numerous further powers to control the lives of others. As Tim Scanlon writes, "Those who have vastly greater resources than anyone else not only enjoy greater leisure and higher levels of consumption but also can often determine what gets produced, what kinds of employment are offered, what the environment of a town or state is like, and what kind of life one can live there. In addition, economic advantage can be translated into great political power."[4] It is worth pausing to say precisely why this would be objectionable. Part of the problem is that the rich would be able to violate the moral rights of others—rights to physical integrity, for example—with impunity. They would also be able to disrupt distributions of resources unjustly. These are some of the things a legal system should prevent. But that is not the only thing that would be objectionable. The freedom of the many would depend on the grace of the few. This is objectionable even if those powers are never exercised so as to infringe rights or disrupt distributions. It concerns individuals' status and standing to one another, rather than the distributions that might result from any inequality.[5]

Many of the lofty ideals of civic states are concerned not with distributive unfairness but with this kind of liberty. Thus John Locke wrote that "freedom of men under government is, to have a standing rule to live by, common to every one of that society, and made by the legislative power erected in it; a liberty to follow my own will in all things, where the rule prescribes not; and not to be subject to the inconstant, uncertain, unknown, arbitrary will of another man."[6] These ideals are often translated, in practice, into the grant of legal rights: legislators thus aim to ameliorate such relations of domination.

The mere grant of rights will not eliminate the risk.[7] In Demosthenes's speech against Meidias, he notes that "many of his victims are not willing to testify about all the wrongs that they suffered because they dread . . . the resources, which make [Meidias] strong and intimidating."[8] These victims had legal rights, but Meidias's power meant that they did not enjoy the protection those rights were supposed to offer.

At least three further conditions must hold; together these help to establish what a fair process would be.[9] First, legal systems must be accessible to right-holders. Sir William Blackstone pointed out that our rights would be a "dead letter" if there were no method to "secure their actual enjoyment."[10] For that reason, he said, there is a right "of applying to the courts of justice for redress of injuries. Since the law is in England supreme arbiter of every man's life, liberty, and property, courts of justice must at all times be open to the subject, and the law be duly administered therein."[11] Again, the mere grant of the right is not enough: its exercise must be practically possible. It is no good granting me a power to take Meidias to court if I cannot afford the filing fee to issue the claim: empty rights merely cast a veneer of legitimacy over illegitimate regimes.

Second, legal systems must have more power than private individuals or corporations. If an individual or corporation is able to control the application of the law, not only would they be able to evade its strictures, they can (threaten to) impose certain burdens on certain groups. The democratic concern here is brought out by Demosthenes's entreaty: "let no one be spared or put to death just because a particular person wishes it, but depending on whether a man's deeds warrant sparing him or not, you should cast the vote that he deserves. That's how it should be in a democracy."[12]

To ensure that no particular person is above the law, legal and political institutions must have considerable powers. That, though, creates the risk of domination at the hands of the state. Quite a lot of politics and political philosophy has concerned itself with that risk, of state domination, so we do not need to explore all its implications here. Various measures have emerged to manage it, including the imposition of duties and conditions on officials' powers.[13] But one further condition is worth mentioning: the need to control the state's legal resources. This is the third concern arising out of Meidias's story.

If Meidias is able to bribe the judge, the existence of the legal system is scarcely an advantage to me. Locke puts this point colourfully: "Where an appeal to the law, and constituted judges, lies open, but the remedy is denied by a manifest perverting of justice . . . there it is hard to imagine any thing but *a state of war*."[14] Less widely recognised is that the distribution of lawyers must be regulated. If Meidias can purchase the finest lawyers in town and I can afford none, the creation of the legal system puts me in an even worse position: inequality in legal resources will reinstitute relations of domination via the law's coercive institutions. The creation of a legal order can help to reduce the oppression of those like Meidias, but unless its procedures are carefully structured it can, instead, operate to assist such people in their actions. If a strong and effective legal order is instituted, but only those with wealth can use its procedures effectively, the injustice of domination can be compounded. Further, individuals must have sufficient access to legal resources to ensure they do not stand in this relation of domination to the state. This is clearest in criminal cases, where the risk of domination is greatest. But it can also be required in public law, where state decisions can exert enormous power over individuals' lives. Given its importance to the justice of legal institutions, let's explore this third concern in more detail.

Liberty and Equal Resources

The risk of domination through the legal process shows that a fair process is one where legal arms are roughly equal. We can think of two lawyers as equal where they have roughly similar competence. (Competence is a function, not only of the lawyers' intelligence and industry, but also their available time: many public defenders might be perfectly good lawyers if they had the time to work their cases.) To clarify the argument, we should begin with a distinction between equality of lawyers for litigants locked in an individual suit and equality for litigants across a legal system.

There is equality in an individual suit when both adversaries have roughly equal amounts of legal resources (or, a more permissive standard, equal opportunities to acquire legal resources). If McDonald's were to bring a suit against a homeless individual in a regime with no legal aid, there would likely be great inequality in the individual suit: McDonald's could buy the best lawyers around; the homeless person could acquire none.[15] Such inequality can be cured by levelling McDonald's resources down, to ensure they get no better representation than the homeless person, or the homeless individual's up, to ensure that they get the same quality of representation as McDonald's.

No such problems arise when McDonald's sues Burger King or one indigent sues another. Yet these possible lawsuits suggest a different kind of inequality. There might be inequality across a legal system if the level of legal resources in each suit is different. McDonald's and Burger King might have the finest lawyers on the planet for their suit; others might make do with two incompetent (but affordable) lawyers at the helm. This is the second kind of equality, equality across the legal system.[16]

Although I have illustrated these two types of equality with civil cases, the same distinction can be applied to any area of the justice system. Consider the criminal domain. If a defendant can employ the finest lawyers in the land, that results in inequality in the individual case: given budgetary constraints, the government's resources, and consequent ability to mount a prosecution, are limited. And there is undoubtedly inequality across a legal system where one person can purchase an army of lawyers and others are left with a very rudimentary defence counsel (or none at all). The same points could be made of administrative litigation against the government: if the finest lawyers in the land sue the government, there may be inequality in the suit; if most individuals have to bring cases without legal aid, there will be inequality between those litigants and others in the legal system.

Critics of any equal distribution sometimes hold, with Harry Frankfurt, that "what is important from the moral point of view is not that everyone should have *the same* but that each should have *enough*. If everyone had enough, it would be of no moral consequence whether some had more than others."[17] This criticism does not apply here. Even if it matters that everyone has enough, the nature of legal resources is such that "enough" means "roughly equal."

To see why, we need to consider the value of legal resources. In the adversarial context, the effectiveness of my lawyer depends on the effectiveness of yours.[18] So long as your lawyer is not much better or more resourced than mine, the process of adjudication may be fair: there is no risk of domination at the hands of another, because the other does not have greater powers. This argument applies to all legal disputes. It shows how a process can be unfair if one party can buy the best lawyers in the world and the other can afford none: such a situation threatens to reinstitute the domination a legal system is supposed to escape.

Some legal disputes are zero sum.[19] If you and I are in a legal dispute, any success that you have comes at my expense, and vice versa. The level of legal resources an individual has is likely to affect their chances of winning the ultimate dispute. This means that the quality of the lawyer I need in my dispute with you depends in part upon the quality of your lawyer.[20] If you have an army of lawyers and I am left to prepare my case on my own, my level of legal resources is insufficient for fairness. It follows, Scanlon points out, that when a poor litigant is in a suit with a rich litigant, "the state is obligated to provide representation for poor litigants that is as good as whatever the rich can provide for themselves. The obligation is to provide effective representation, and what is effective is measured in part by what opposing litigants can do."[21]

This is a radical proposal. It shows that fairness makes quite stringent demands on legal procedures, ones that are rarely fulfilled in practice. But the argument is limited in this respect: it requires equal resources only in an individual suit, not across a legal system.

Inequality in an individual suit might matter principally because it makes it less likely that the outcome will be correct: the party with the better lawyer might increase their chances of winning simply by spending more money on the suit. This is a fairness argument for equality of legal resources (or against inequality of legal resources) in an individual suit. That argument derives from the fact I have just stressed, that the value of one's lawyer is partly comparative: if we are in a legal dispute, whether my lawyer is good enough depends in part upon how good your lawyer is.

That argument does not make any demands for systemic equality of legal resources. It seems permissible for McDonald's and Burger King to hire the best lawyers to sue one another so long as they do not use that legal team to sue you or me. Similarly, systemic inequality in the criminal law seems permissible, so long as the public option, available to everyone, meets the conditions of the fairness floor. After all, the value of my legal aid lawyer in a criminal case is not (it might seem) reduced by virtue of the fact that you have Atticus Finch as your lawyer in an entirely different case. Thus Scanlon writes that

> in order for a system of criminal law to be just, poor people accused of crimes must have adequate representation by defense counsel, and the state therefore has an obligation to provide this. But . . . there is no re-quirement that this representation be as good as what richer defendants can provide for themselves. If rich defendants can afford higher-powered counsel than poorer defendants, and this makes them more likely to es-cape conviction, even if they are guilty, this is a serious defect in the system of criminal law. But . . . if poor defendants are provided with *adequate* legal representation, such that their chances of being wrongly convicted are sufficiently low, then the only objection to the system is that it is sub-ject to manipulation by rich defendants. If, on the other hand, poor de-fendants do not have adequate representation, and so face an unaccept-ably high chance of wrongful conviction, then this fact itself is objectionable, independent of any comparison with what happens to richer defendants.[22]

The argument is this. When I sue you in a civil case, either you win or I lose; where the state prosecutes us both, we can both be acquitted. Your having a better chance of winning in a criminal case (being acquitted) does not necessarily reduce my chances; it necessarily does in the civil case. There-fore (the argument goes) fairness in civil cases requires equality of legal resources on both sides; it does not require equality between different crim-inal defendants' lawyers. In some cases there is what we might call "scarcity of success": your success is my failure, and vice versa. There is no such scarcity of success, Scanlon claims, in the criminal domain.

This argument misses an important point. Once that point is seen, the fairness argument can be seen to demand that all in the legal system have equal resources (a proposal I examine in more detail in the next chapter). We should begin with a distinction between individual and institutional perspectives. An individual perspective looks only at one case and asks whether success or failure of the litigant affects another individual. In the civil realm, it does: you win and I lose, or vice versa. In the criminal realm it does not: I can be acquitted without affecting your chances of conviction. An institutional perspective, by contrast, examines, not the particular case, but the framework in which the case operates. Your power to pay for a private advocate presupposes a particular system of private advocacy. That framework does affect others' chances when compared with other possible frameworks. The permission to contract for private lawyers affects the supply of lawyers available to those unable to afford the best; it may render the system of lawyering unfair. It can do this if the quality of lawyers available to those unable to pay for lawyers is poor in consequence of that permission.

Suppose, to illustrate, that we have to decide what system of lawyers to set up; our options are a pure-public model, ensuring equality across the legal system, or a private system, where the market is unregulated and no individuals receive government subsidies. Now consider the position of the worst off in society under the two regimes: they would almost certainly be better off under the former regime than the latter. The success of rich individuals in some criminal cases under a private system of lawyers' services will indirectly lead to the wrongful conviction of poor individuals: the creation of a system permitting rich individuals to contract out makes the poor individuals worse off than they would be under some alternative arrangement. This argument applies writ large: the choice of legal institutions indirectly affects the chances all in society have to obtain justice and the risks of injustice they bear. Once the institutional perspective is adopted, the scarcity of success in criminal cases is apparent.

This suggests a more radical implication of the liberty argument, imposing very stringent conditions on a fair procedure. Any institutional arrangement adopted for legal resources must be justifiable. It should be justifiable to all in society, especially the worst off. The standard of legal services many in society will obtain under a model built on the market distribution of lawyers (with choice interventions, for legal aid or even for equality in individual suits) is likely to be worse than under some alternative arrangements. Those alternative arrangements are, therefore, more justifiable.

The worst off can argue that the present regime does not take their liberty interests seriously. The risk of wrongful conviction, for example, is raised relative to alternative possible institutional arrangements. Those individuals become subject to oppression at the hands of the government, which can force them to accept guilty pleas rather than face trials with inadequate resources to defend themselves.[23] Taking seriously the demands of a fair process suggests, for this reason, that it may be necessary to proscribe contracting out of legal resources. I will explore that proposal in more detail in the next chapter. First we need to explore the second ground of a fairness floor: the rule of law. This, too, is ultimately shown to militate in favour of equal resources across the legal system.

THE RULE OF LAW

The Ideal

Aristotle asked whether "it is preferable for the best law to rule or the best man."[24] In Plato's *Laws,* the Athenian Stranger gives this answer: "Where [the law] is despot over the rulers and the rulers are slaves of the law, there I foresee safety and all the good things which the gods have given to cities."[25] These passages bequeath us the ideal of the rule of law or "legality."[26] Although scholars do not always agree about its content, legality is generally accepted to be one of the most important political values in any liberal democracy.

What, though, is its value? Only when we have a surer grasp can we think about the demands it makes of our institutions.[27] There are two intertwined goals; both justify the provision of a basic set of legal resources to individuals.[28] The first feature of a society governed by law is the ability of citizens to obey and be guided by the law.[29] It is impossible to be guided by secret rules; thus the rule of law condemns secret laws. We can call this the "guidance condition."

A second feature is the idea that there should be congruence between the content of laws and their application. If the things done in court have no relation to the laws as promulgated, there is clearly a defect in the rule of law.[30] That is one reason why it is a rule of law problem if there are show trials or if dissidents are convicted on spurious charges; less evocatively, though often of greater practical concern, it is also a problem if there are too many laws and too few resources to ensure compliance. We can call this the "congruence condition" of the rule of law.

The rule of law is, Jeremy Waldron reminds us, "one star in a constellation of ideals that dominate our political morality."[31] It is, in particular, not the same as democracy. But the congruence condition is a reason why the two ideals can march in step with one another. Democracies should allow some kind of equal input into law-making. In systems like ours, we try to realise that ideal by giving each person one vote to elect representative lawmakers. In a just society, no one should be able to rule over all others; the history of modern democracies is a move from regal authority to Parliamentary power. Adult citizens are endowed with equal rights to elect representatives to try to try to ensure a kind of ex ante equality—ex ante, that is, to law-making. But if the application of laws did not meet the congruence condition, something other than law would be governing distributions and outcomes. Outcomes would, instead, probably be a consequence of the factual powers that law aims to control. When a legal system fails to satisfy the congruence condition, the central ideal of the rule of law—that laws, not men, should govern—is probably not met.

Congruence between legal norms and their application is a separate ideal from the guidance condition; it motivates an overlapping but distinct set of requirements for a legal system. In a corrupt regime, it might be perfectly possible to predict how judges will misapply the law—excusing the politician's crimes, extorting the political activist, and so on. There would be a failure of the congruence condition. But individuals could be guided either by the exercise of judicial power (for that power is predictable) or by the law, so long as the law itself is clear.

Guidance

The Emperor Caligula was said to have written laws "in exceedingly small letters on a tablet which he then hung up in a high place, so that it should be read by as few as possible."[32] This is a plain violation of the rule of law. Before you can be guided by a law, you have to first know that there is a law and what it requires: the public availability of the content of law is vital.

I will devote most of my remarks to legal resources, but, as we saw in Chapter 1 and as Caligula's example shows, that is too blinkered a perspective. Perhaps the most basic demand the rule of law makes of legal systems is that laws be published and available to all. Most modern states do this. Legal codes for many countries are available online. Few states live up to the strictest demands of the rule of law, though. The United Kingdom puts the text of most laws it enacts online, but it is very slow to update the text as it is amended: sometimes it takes more than six years for amendments to be made to the online text.[33] It is easy to find out what changes have been made if you have access to an (expensive) legal database. You should not have to subscribe to legal databases to know what laws govern your behaviour.

Even when the text of laws is publicly available, it can still be very difficult to know what the content of law is. There are three reasons for this. First, the laws in question can be very complicated. The Affordable Care Act—the legislation creating the healthcare regime known as "Obamacare"—is 2,700 pages long. When the Supreme Court was asked to determine whether the law was constitutional, a number of the justices admitted that even they had not read the entire legislation; Justice Scalia protested that to ask them to do so would be "cruel and unusual punishment."[34] In the United Kingdom, the Criminal Justice Act of 2003, a mere 476 pages, has 339 sections and thirty-eight schedules. The act was described as "labyrinthine" and "astonishingly complex" by an experienced judge.[35] Even when the text of the law is short, it can be hard to understand.

Second, not only are the texts themselves complicated, the text of laws, even their meaning, is not the same as their legal content. If the enaction of a text is to make law, there have to be some rules making it so. Those rules will determine what the law actually is, and they can divorce the meaning of the text from the ultimate content of the law.[36] For example, the Fifth Amendment to the US Constitution holds that no one "shall be compelled in any criminal case to be a witness against himself." This has been held to create a right against self-incrimination; and that right has been extended to require police officers to tell criminal suspects that they have a right to remain silent and to an attorney.[37] No one doubts that this is the law in the United States—but the right is not explicit in the text of the Constitution.

Finally, statutes are but one feature of legal systems. Courts interpret statutes, a process which inevitably changes the content of the law. The Affordable Care Act is one example: the text of the law refers to an "exchange established by the State"; when interpreted in context, however, the law actually refers to an exchange established by the state *or the federal government*.[38] One English case concerned whether an unmarried man in a homosexual partnership could be said to be living "as his [partner's] husband." It was held that he could: an individual fell within the clause if they were living *as if* they were married.[39] On one reading of these cases, the courts' interpretation of the statutes changed their content. More generally, many legal systems recognise that one source of both criminal and civil law is the decisions of judges. These decisions are not always readily available—and, even when they are, it can be very difficult to work out what the law created by the decisions actually is. (That is why people have to study law for years—and one reason why lawyers are able to command high salaries for their labour.) These various features, which make the law obscure to the average person, mean we have not progressed as far as we might have liked since Caligula: the content of the law is out of reach of anyone without legal advice.

Any legal system that aims to comply with the rule of law must ensure that people are able to be guided by law. Given this, any complex legal system—a system that is structured in such a way as to make legal content inaccessible to those without legal training—must ensure that individuals have sufficient access to legal advice.[40] This can, of course, be achieved in other ways. The internet has made legal knowledge easier to come by. On-line fora, where individuals explain to each other how to get justice in individual cases, can lead to a proliferation of busybodies; they also help to ensure that a legal system complies with the rule of law.

I will examine the precise scope of this argument later, once my other arguments are on the table—and a great deal of its demands are contingent upon various contextual factors, such as the complexity of the legal system. For now, the crucial point to notice is that the complexity of modern legal systems constrains the pursuit of maximum justice. Before we can aim to maximise the justice or minimise the injustice in a legal system, we must first ensure that everyone in society has sufficient access to legal resources to satisfy the demands of the rule of law, that is, to be guided by the content of the law.

Congruence

The promulgation of laws is necessary for the rule of law. But mere promulgation guarantees almost nothing. First of all, to secure congruence between norms and application, law-applying officials (such as police officers and administrative officials) must be created and law-applying organs (such as courts) established. Without these, there could (by definition) be no congruence between norms and application: there would be no norm application. At this point I will limit my remarks to the demands the congruence condition makes on the court system: it applies, I go on to show, well beyond that domain.

The creation of legal institutions will only go so far. Those institutions must also be accessible: I looked at that requirement previously. Further, the institutions must have a certain form. A legal system with excellent laws that are systematically misapplied fails by the lights of the rule of law; there is no congruence between the norms and their application. The congruence condition makes demands of all law-applying officials and institutions.[41] Legal processes must also aim to be truth-tracking. If criminal trials did not even purport to search for the truth, for example, they would be unfair. Individual features of criminal process are explicable in these terms: those accused of crimes are afforded the right to hear the case against them partly because it helps courts reach the right decisions about their culpability. If access to legal resources increases the chance of an individual getting justice, as we have good reason to think it does, that is another reason why citizens should be granted a right to lawyers.

Courts must be staffed with independent judges, able to apply the law rather than the desires of politicians. If the judiciary is not independent of the executive or Parliament, pressure can be put upon them to do as politicians require. This may spare the political wing of the state from enacting laws (and the consequential scrutiny this would occasion); it also allows politicians to mete out injustice in individual cases without having to draft relevant laws. If, for example, a businesswoman falls out of favour with an autocrat, the autocrat might wish to imprison the businesswoman without actually criminalising anything she did. A compliant judiciary would be very useful to the autocrat. This is the case in certain states today. In the past, some nations had codes with numerous valuable rights, none of which were realised; courts had show trials where enemies were strung up on invented charges. This violates the rule of law. And the congruence condition explains why.

Independent judges may not suffice to ensure congruence if the judges get no assistance from the litigants or their lawyers. Judges can need help to figure out what the law requires in an individual case. If only one side of an argument is given, or only one side is given well, the judges will have a skewed impression of what the law is. There is a greater risk of the wrong decision being reached. This is one way in which the congruence condition makes a demand for the provision of lawyers to litigants: so they can, when in court, explain their grievances to the court. This is recognised in a number of legal codes. Article 6 of the European Convention of Human Rights, for example, provides that "in the determination of his civil rights and obligations, or of any criminal charge against him, everyone is entitled to a fair and public hearing within a reasonable time by an independent and impartial tribunal established by law." The European Court of Human Rights has interpreted Article 6 to require the provision of a lawyer in criminal cases and, in certain situations, civil cases.[42]

When people talk about the congruence condition of the rule of law, their focus is sometimes too narrow, on congruence between norms and the decisions of courts. If this was all there was to the rule of law, a dictator could comply with the ideal by abolishing all the courts and ruling only through his secret police: there would be no incongruity between norms and their application by courts: there would be no application *by* courts. Blackstone had a slightly wider focus: he said that there must be some way to secure the "actual enjoyment" of rights if a system is to comply with the rule of law. But this, again, is too narrow. It focuses only on application by courts, whereas the "actual enjoyment" of rights depends on more general features of institutions.

When thinking about the congruence condition, we need a wider scope. A society conforms with the ideal of the rule of law only if actions in the community are sufficiently governed by law. Outcomes in society must relate sufficiently to the underlying laws governing those outcomes. Conforming with that requires much more than the provision of lawyers to those who come to court. It also requires the regulation of access to lawyers of those who never come to court. Most obviously, citizens must have the ability to govern their own lives by law. Whether this requires lawyers depends on the complexity and number of the laws. But when lawyers are necessary to understand laws more generally—contractual rights or tax codes, for example—they must be provided. Somewhat less obviously, and certainly more controversially, rich individuals' access to lawyers can pose problems. It should not be possible for people to buy out the law indirectly. I examine one way this might be achieved in the next chapter.

The congruence condition also requires that all law-applying officials, not only courts, apply the law correctly. Administrative agencies are an example. These have come to occupy a central role in law enforcement and application. It will lead to a rule of law problem if these agencies are insufficiently resourced: they may fail to bring enforcement actions; when they do, they may get the law wrong. The risks can be demonstrated by considering the Ronald Reagan administration's treatment of the Environmental Protection Agency (EPA), which is dedicated partly to the enforcement of environmental laws. President Reagan's transition team asked potential appointees to head the EPA whether they were willing to bring the "E.P.A. to its knees."[43] Anne Gorsuch was willing; she took over as the EPA's administrator. Less than two years later, a *New York Times* editorial said that "Mrs. Gorsuch has undermined the E.P.A. by halving its budget when its responsibilities are doubling. She has induced many of its best professional staff to quit, and has sabotaged the agency's enforcement effort by continual reorganizations and cutbacks."[44] A similar pattern was established in the early era of the Trump administration. The EPA's budget was cut by 30 per cent; it sought only 40 per cent of the civil penalties the Obama administration sought in the same period.[45]

During the Reagan administration, some individuals brought lawsuits to enforce environmental laws: an apparently public function was discharged by private individuals. This led to greater compliance with the congruence condition. But was it consistent with the rule of law? Some think that there are limits to the extent governmental duties can be privatised. I will consider that concern in more detail in Chapter 7. It is simplest for our purposes to say that institutions must be arranged so as to guarantee conformity with the congruence condition, whether through the courts, administrative agencies, or private litigants. Whether there are more stringent conditions on how that condition can be satisfied can be considered later.

A feature of the rule of law, nascent in the congruence condition, is the idea that like cases should be treated alike.[46] The principle is, in one sense, trivial: controversy concerns not the principle, but which cases are alike (and what makes them so). But there are deeply egalitarian roots to the principle, ones with profound implications for legal institutions.

Consider, to draw out those implications, Alan Wertheimer's question: "Why should we allow the use of radically unequal legal resources to make the difference between a meager recovery and an adequate award, between liability and a favorable verdict?"[47] Someone does not deserve more money in a legal settlement simply because they have more money to spend on lawyers: antecedent wealth is, as a matter of justice, an arbitrary fact. In recognition of this, most procedural law is designed to increase the probability that a tribunal hearing a case will reach the right decision (or to decrease the risk of it reaching the wrong decision). Rules of evidence, for example, are tailored to reduce the risk of wrongful conviction or to maximise the probability that the correct outcome will be reached in a trial. But, as Wertheimer points out, it would be "inconsistent and self-defeating to allow the use of grossly unequal legal resources to bring similarly irrelevant factors back into play."[48]

Recall the distinction drawn between equality of legal resources in an individual suit and equality of legal resources across a legal system. Wertheimer's concern is that inequality in an individual suit may make legal procedures less likely to get the right answer in that case.[49] True enough. But inequality across a legal system is also a rule of law problem. Two people might be injured in precisely the same fashion by the same person. If one has a first-rate lawyer and the other a duffer, the first may get an adequate remedy and the second may get nothing. This would, the congruence condition shows, be a violation of the rule of law.

The congruence condition, which helps to define fair procedures, can thus be seen to connect with the broader ideal of equal justice. A legal system would be unfair if it did not meet the requirement that like cases be treated alike. That demand also requires us to seek to equalise the justice benefits and burdens of legality. In the next chapter, we turn to the question of how that might be achieved.

FROM FAIRNESS TO EQUALITY

Legal systems should strive to conform with the principle of equal justice. A precondition of securing equal justice is that legal procedures be fair. This, I have argued in this chapter, is a demanding requirement. Legal institutions should be structured to ensure that no one can dominate anyone else; they should also be structured to ensure compliance with the rule of law. These claims can be understood as demanding quite radical interventions in the legal industry. Both were developed to suggest that equality of legal resources across the entire legal system may be required. The next chapter considers that interpretation in detail, explaining its content and its further grounds for the requirement.

5

EQUAL RESOURCES

EQUAL JUSTICE AND INSTITUTIONS

Equal justice is an ideal for a legal system. It makes two demands: first, that the justice benefits and burdens of legality be, so far as possible, equally shared; second, that inequalities in the distribution of justice in the real world result from a fair procedure. The previous chapter considered a number of requirements legal systems must meet for procedures to be fair. This chapter considers how things might be arranged so as to equalise the justice benefits and burdens of legality.

All institutions that affect the justice benefits and burdens of legality should be arranged to ensure equality. The most controversial institution, in this respect, is the legal industry itself. I will consider that in the two main sections of this chapter. Let's first consider the application of the principle of equal justice beyond the legal industry itself. This shows that equal justice can make stringent demands of our institutions, which is important to remember when we consider the case of courts and lawyers; it also shows the breadth of acceptance of the principle of equal justice.

Beyond Laws and Legal Resources

The ideal of equal justice is often used to make demands of our political community, as where there are calls to eliminate racial- and gender-based oppression. The dynamics of power in a society—for example, racism and sexism amongst employers or in the police force—will affect both the benefits and burdens people suffer through the legal system. In my own case, for example, companies may be more likely to settle claims I might have against them when they realise that I have a legal education; but the fact I have a legal education does not make me more deserving of justice than anyone else. More generally, some individuals are less likely than others to suffer discriminatory treatment—at the hands of employers or the state—because of their race. These are arbitrary characteristics from the perspective of justice.

One prominent domain where the ideal of equal justice is often invoked is the distribution and practice of policing. There are limits to how much the state can equalise the risks individuals face of suffering wrongs. But the approach taken to the reduction of those risks across society can violate equal justice. If, for example, the police only protect wealthy property owners (or only property owners), that is a naked violation of the principle of equal justice. The police can also, if they are racist, prejudiced or simply incompetent, undermine the principle when they carry out their duties. Part of the impetus of the "Black Lives Matter" movement in the United States was the belief that black people were being treated differently from white people. That is a local example of a broader phenomenon: the methods of policing should be kept under scrutiny in part to ensure that the police are not undermining equal justice through their own practices.

The principle of equal justice also makes demands on the regulation and protection of non-state entities, such as the press. The rich and powerful are sometimes brought to justice by investigative journalism. This furthers the goal of equal justice because it increases compliance with norms of the legal system (that those who commit crimes should answer for them) and reduces the comparative injustice of the system (that those in positions of power and influence are able to evade criminal sanctions). A free press is important partly for this reason: if powers were concentrated in the hands of very few, those few could be able to evade scrutiny and accountability; their crimes would come to light only very rarely. The proper design of the institution raises difficult normative and empirical questions, ones far beyond the scope of this book. But the example demonstrates the salience of the principle and its broad acceptance.

Law-Making

Moving closer to our central topic, equal justice also makes demands on the ways our laws are enacted, the way those laws are expressed, and the content of those laws. I will outline each of these ideas in turn.

Equal justice might be promoted by making laws publicly available. That was Theseus's defence of written laws in Euripides's *Suppliant Women:* he argued that writing the laws down would ensure that "both the powerless and the rich have equal access to justice . . . and the little man, if he has right on his side, defeats the big man."[1] I will return, in Chapter 8, to the question of whether judges should be permitted to make law, and the demands that any such permission makes on the design of the legal system. For now, notice only that the distribution of legislative authority should be structured in part to ensure equal justice: if certain methods of legislation make the benefits or burdens of laws more likely to accrue to some than others, that is a mark against those methods.

Not only might equal justice counsel written laws, it also suggests that those laws should be written as clearly as possible.[2] There is a tension here between the quality of the laws made and the ease with which individuals might understand them. And laws have different audiences: some are meant to be understood by citizens, some by lawyers, and some by judges. Pursuing these complications would be a distraction from the main point, which is that laws should, all else being equal, be expressed in a way that furthers equal justice.[3] Once enacted, it should be as easy as possible to ascertain the content of laws. It should not, for example, cost money to access statutory provisions or legal judgments. The reason is that this makes access to legal information depend on an arbitrary factor: wealth.

The impact of a particular law will depend on the context of its enactment. In particular, it will depend on the understanding of those to whom it is addressed. Consider laws against driving under the influence of alcohol. In principle, the best law would set the proper limit of consumption according to the abilities and constitution of each individual: some people are more affected by alcohol than others, and the point of the law is to ensure that no individual falls below an absolute level of competence. Such a law would be unworkable: individuals would not be able to be guided by it; it might lead to more people quite innocently falling below the absolute level because they misunderstand the demands the law makes of them. A hard and fast rule is second-best, in one respect, but best overall at achieving the law's goals.[4]

Just as we consider the ability of the law to guide when we assess the quality of the law, we should consider the ability of the law to result in equal justice. A more complicated tax code, for example, might draw appropriate distinctions between all classes of individuals but be more susceptible to exploitation by the rich. When considering how good a law is, we should continue to ask the questions we normally ask: whether it draws salient distinctions between individuals, whether it discriminates unjustifiably, and so on. But we should also ask whether the law will lead to equal justice.[5]

THE IDEA OF EQUAL RESOURCES

Refining the Idea

In the previous chapter I distinguished between two types of equality in legal resources: equality in an individual suit and equality across a legal system. Equality in an individual suit is easy enough to understand: it requires two opposing litigants to have roughly the same quality of legal services. Equality across a legal system is harder to understand. Attractive as the idea might be in the abstract, what would it be for there to be equality of legal resources? Consider an absurd proposal. Suppose that everyone were granted a determinate amount of time before a judge each year. There is a sense in which the judicial resource would then be shared equally throughout the population. But no one would support the proposal. Legal problems arise contingently and most people get through the year without needing the help of a judge. It would be a waste for everyone to be allotted judicial time.[6]

The proposal cannot be that everyone should have the same amount (say, of judicial time), regardless of their circumstances. Claims that some good should be shared equally are always relativised to certain attributes. In this context, the proposal must be that everyone should have the same amount of legal resources *given certain circumstances*. Everyone would accept, for example, that race is an illegitimate ground upon which to distribute legal resources. The question becomes: which circumstances are relevant (or irrelevant) to the distribution?

It is harder to offer a definition of relevance than it is to rule out irrelevant factors. Most plausible is that legal resources should be allocated to those who need them most. This, doubtless, is a contestable standard. But some progress can be made if we consider which factors are irrelevant. Given that the primary goal of legal resources is to vindicate equal justice, it is most plausible that the irrelevant factors in the realm of equal justice are also irrelevant in the realm of legal resources. One of the most urgent demands in the realm of legal resources is to equalise outcomes relative to individuals' wealth.

A proposal that legal resources be equalised across a legal system can thus be understood to be a proposal that the level of legal resources any individual has should not be a function of (among other things) their antecedent wealth. How might that be achieved?

Contracting Out

When benefits should be distributed equally, or risks should be shared equally, permitting people to buy their way out of an equal distribution is objectionable. The power to contract out changes the distribution: the risks fall on those unable to buy their way out. This was seen most prominently in Chapter 2 with respect to the draft. A natural proposal is to proscribe people from buying their way out of a distribution arrived at in some other way.

Consider, by way of analogy, healthcare. In the United Kingdom the National Health Service (NHS) provides a basic level of healthcare to everyone: the public option. Those with money are entitled to purchase healthcare privately; they can "contract out" of the public option. This regime does not, for that reason, secure equality of medical resources: it builds a fairness floor and then permits deviation from it through private contracting. To achieve equality of distribution, the state might proscribe private contracting in healthcare.[7] Similarly, someone could argue that to achieve equality of legal resources we should have a public option (making legal resources available through state institutions) and proscribe contracting out.

The analogy is intuitive and useful to give some notion of what the proposal is. But the legal context is in some respects more complicated. To develop a system through which we might realise equal resources, we should first distinguish between dispute resolution fora and lawyers; within those different spheres, different considerations arise.

There is a range of different dispute resolution fora.[8] Some, such as courts and tribunals, are set up and run by the state; others, such as arbitration, are set up by private parties (though their enforcement mechanisms depend on the state). This complication means that we need to distinguish between two proposals: a proscription on contracting out within state-supplied institutions and a proscription on contracting out of state institutions.

Within state institutions, the permission to contract out would allow private parties to pay more for a better judge (or a judge they favoured). This could happen directly or indirectly. A direct distribution would be one where the time and energy of state judges is distributed on the free market. People would bid for their judges, meaning the best judges could bring in the most money for the state. To proscribe contracting out is to proscribe this. An indirect distribution is one where procedural rules ensure that the best judges go to those who pay the most. For example, if those with low-value disputes are funnelled into small claims courts, and the best-resourced courts are guarded with high access fees, this can have the same effect as a market distribution: the allocation of the best judges to those best able to pay for them.

Proscribing the direct or indirect permission to contract out does not entail any particular arrangement of legal fora. But the proscription does rule out certain methods of disrupting a presumptive arrangement, most obviously a free market in legal resources. It is harder to prevent indirect contracting out: the disruption is, after all, indirect. A further complication, beyond that simple point, is that various approaches seem permissible without undermining the egalitarian ethos, and some inegalitarian approaches might be dressed as forms of these. For example, just as equality in the provision of healthcare permits specialisation of doctors, judges in an egalitarian system could still be allocated to disputes based on their expertise. This, though, must not be allowed to morph into the proposal that more specialised judges should command higher fees.[9]

The second proposal is a proscription on contracting out of the public option: a permission to use an alternative and private system of dispute resolution, instead of the state-supplied court. Consider arbitration; the same distinctions could be considered for any dispute resolution forum. Courts of arbitration are privately established: parties nominate arbitrators and set up the architecture of the dispute resolution system through contractual agreements. For example, an employment contract might require all disputes between employer and employee to be submitted to an arbitral panel of three specialists in the industry, with the company hosting the hearing in its own offices.

In theory, as that example shows, arbitration is a quite different beast from public adjudication. Judith Resnik explains, "Judges are agents of the state, charged with implementing its law through public decision making; arbitrators are creatures of contracts, obliged to effectuate the intent of the parties."[10] Arbitrators owe their duties to the contracting parties; their obligations are set by their terms of reference.

Arbitration is doubly inegalitarian. Arbitrators trade their services on the open market. If that market works with any efficiency, better arbitrators cost more. This means that the quality of justice individuals get in arbitration is partly a function of their wealth. Further, the availability of arbitration means that an additional dispute resolution forum is available—beyond the public option—to those who can afford it.

With respect to arbitration, options range from facilitation to proscription. Arbitration contracts can be made enforceable in state courts. Historically, at least some arbitral decisions have been given state support in this manner. For example, the Arbitration Act of 1698, drafted by John Locke, made it an obligation to comply with decisions of arbitral panels. Noncompliance was punishable by imprisonment for contempt.[11] In the United States, a string of Supreme Court decisions has confirmed the rigidity of this obligation in that jurisdiction: parties are bound by their arbitration clauses even when those contracts exclude the parties from state courts and proscribe class action suits.[12] This provides public support for the private regime.

A state could, instead, take a more moderate approach and refuse to facilitate the private regime. This would be achieved if arbitration agreements or arbitral awards were unenforceable in public courts.[13] The decisions of an arbitral panel are, without laws on the matter, no more legally binding than a parent's directive to their child: all depends on what laws the state sets up to permit enforcement. If the state were to withdraw its support, this would not eliminate arbitration as a regime; it would make it voluntary, ensuring that anyone who did not want to comply with an arbitral decision could refuse to do so.

The most extreme measure would be to make it illegal to contract for arbitration. I know of no regime that has done this. It might be thought appropriate if the refusal to enforce arbitral decisions did not function to eliminate power inequalities: if, for example, individuals felt compelled to comply, notwithstanding the fact that the state would not enforce them.

There is only so much we can say in the abstract about these different regimes; which regime is best depends in part upon contingent, empirical facts: on what, exactly, the effects of one regime or another would be. One matter does deserve attention: the grounds of assessment to choose between these different regimes. I will offer two reasons to favour proscriptions on contracting out: that it will further equal justice; and that legal resources are a state-created resource that ought, therefore, to be shared equally by members of the community. These reasons help structure thought on which regulatory approach is best. The first approach, enforcing arbitration agreements, poses particular threats to equal justice: those individuals who would otherwise be in the public system are able to secure a superior quality of legal resource simply because of their wealth.[14] The permission to contract out of state institutions makes it less likely that equal justice will be realised.

The second argument for equality, the equal benefit principle, does not make any direct demands on the structure of legal regimes: arbitration systems are not a public resource, so they are not caught by the principle. The choice between the second and third regimes is less easy to make in the abstract. It depends on a question of empirical fact: which system will better contribute to equal justice. Absent strong reasons to favour one over the other, we should presumptively prefer the second regime over the third: we should be leery of creating crimes. The state, in other words, should refuse to lend its hand to the enforcement of private dispute resolution mechanisms; it should not ban them.

The main distinction with respect to lawyers concerns equality in an individual suit and equality across a legal system. To ensure equality across a legal system, we may need to proscribe contracting out in all cases (rather than simply regulating legal resources in individual suits).

The proposal to prevent contracting out should be distinguished from an alternative proposal, which relates closely to my own: the regulation of lawyers' fees. This is an old idea. The Emperor Claudius, for example, implemented a fee cap at 10,000 sesterces.[15] Some contemporary societies, such as Germany, place some controls on the amount of fees that lawyers can charge. Whether this is a good policy is an empirical matter: the question is whether the fee regime brings the system closer to equal justice. We also might favour the proscription of contracting out over fee regulations if there is (as I will argue) an independent reason to favour equality of lawyers.

ARGUMENTS FOR EQUAL RESOURCES

Equal Justice

Formal equality is a virtue of laws and judges: laws should be justified; judges should apply the laws properly. But what if some people are unable to get into court to have the law applied (equally or otherwise) to them? That would be a problem; the formal equality of the laws would be hollowed out by the system of enforcement. Legal resources should, therefore, be distributed in whatever manner would best secure equal justice. This does not entail any particular distribution of legal resources: all will depend on contingent facts about each particular society. We might want, for example, to distribute more legal resources to disadvantaged groups than to others who have more. We have some reason to believe, however, that equality of legal resources is a promising distribution as a method of achieving equal justice. This point can be made by considering the effect of inequality of legal resources in the domains of fora and lawyers in turn.

In the United States, arbitration clauses are prevalent in numerous everyday contracts, such as those for the provision of mobile phones or credit cards. Parties who agree to such clauses may not, given certain conditions, pursue their claims in state courts. This means that individuals tend to lose various procedural rights they would otherwise have: to discovery of the other side's documents, to bring class actions against companies, and so on.[16] These features make it harder for individuals to vindicate their rights; they impact differentially on poorer individuals, who are less likely to have high-value claims justifying the expense of arbitration proceedings.[17]

The consequence is that most disputes between companies and individuals will be conducted by companies' complaints departments. This further exacerbates inequality of treatment: companies are more willing to settle on favourable terms with rich parties (who will bring repeat business) than poor parties (who will not). Bank of America, for example, has developed software that considers how rich a customer's family members are when deciding whether to waive the customer's fee.[18]

Proscribing contracting out would eliminate or ameliorate these pernicious effects. It would mean that individuals' abilities to access courts would not depend on their wealth. And that, it is plausible to suppose, would bring the institutional arrangement closer to one of equal justice.

A permission to contract out of the supply of lawyers can have similarly pernicious effects on the distribution of the justice benefits and the burdens of legality. With respect to the benefits, part of the point of purchasing a lawyer is to improve one's chance of winning an individual dispute. It is very difficult to trace the effect of an individual lawyer on a particular case, but it is plausible—certainly, if one has any faith in the market as a method of distributing resources—that those lawyers who can command the highest fees are more likely to improve a client's position. A tenant who can afford a lawyer is less likely to be evicted unlawfully than one without a lawyer; an employee dismissed unlawfully is more likely to bring a successful compensation claim if they have access to a lawyer than if they act alone.

With respect to the burdens, the risk of wrongful conviction is almost certainly increased if one has no lawyer; the sentence a convicted criminal gets for their offence will vary based on the lawyer they have. A vivid illustration is Supreme Court justice Ruth Bader Ginsberg's claim that she is "yet to see a death case . . . in which the defendant was well represented at trial."[19] Even if the death penalty is unjust and unjustifiable, it is a further injustice that only poor people suffer that burden. It is an injustice—the kind of injustice people objected to when they objected to the buy-out of the draft—if rich people can escape the burdens of a collective scheme simply because they are rich. That thought is best understood as an urge to equalise the justice burdens of legality; and the grossly inegalitarian distribution of criminal defence lawyers makes any prospect of equal burdens remote.[20]

The permission to contract out of public courts and lawyers can allow distributions to be disrupted by an arbitrary factor, antecedent wealth. It also allows the distribution of who gets the benefits and incurs the burdens of legality to be affected by that wealth. Legal resources are not the only factor controlling these outcomes, but they are a very important one.

Any reform to the distribution of legal resources will be justified by this argument only if it improves things in the domain of benefits and burdens of legality. Reforms might, for example, be undermined by private parties finding a way to circumvent the proposed regime. In 204 B.C., the Roman lex Cincia prohibited orators from taking fees.[21] This indicates that people were taking fees before that time. They probably continued to do so: Juvenal quipped that advocates in the late Roman Republic were remunerated indirectly, with "some ancient onions . . . or five flagons of wine brought from up-river."[22] It is always tempting to seek arguments that circumvent this kind of contingency. But the temptation should, here anyway, be resisted: this justification of equal resources depends on the consequences of that reform; any reform must ultimately answer to those consequences.

Whether the proscription on contracting out will further these goals depends on questions beyond the scope of this book. But I have already offered some reasons to think that it will. And I suggest reasons, in the next section, to think that it would also lead to more justice and less injustice. This places the burden on those who seek to reject the proposal.

Equal Benefit

Judges are not traded on an open market. This proscription on markets is probably economically inefficient.[23] Yet no legal system of which I am aware has ever used markets to distribute judges.[24] Why not?

The explanation cannot be the fairness floor: we could ensure that a basic level of judicial services is provided to everyone, with luxury items (for example, the best judges) being sold on the market. The equal benefit principle suggests a more plausible answer. That principle, introduced in Chapter 2, holds that members of a collective scheme have equal claims to the products of that scheme. Judges are employed by the state (although they should be independent of that state) to adjudicate on the disputes that arise in society, according to the society's laws. They can be thought of as a shared resource. This resource only comes into existence because the community institutes a legal system. They are, in that sense, a co-created benefit, one that should be shared equally. This explains and justifies the proscription on using money to disrupt the distribution of judges.

It is an open question whether lawyers should be thought of in the same way. It is certainly possible to argue that they should: lawyers only exist if licensed by the state. This gives an additional reason to proscribe contracting out in the legal context. Further, if this proscription is thought (for reasons discussed in later chapters) too burdensome, the equal benefit argument might be used to justify greater demands of lawyers in other spheres. Just as doctors are thought to have special responsibilities to the public at large, so, perhaps, do lawyers. This runs contrary to the instinctive assumption of many (certainly, of many lawyers), that lawyers are entitled to sell their labour as they see fit. Even if it is best, for practical reasons, to permit a market in lawyers to continue, the argument would warrant increased taxation of lawyers to fund a just justice system.[25]

Quantum

A possible policy proposal is to prevent contracting out. In practice this might mean the distribution of legal resources according to the particular case and the needs of the litigant rather than the litigant's antecedent wealth. The most obvious rejoinder is that this proposal would, over time, impact on the amount and quality of the legal resources. Proscribing a market in legal resources may stifle innovation and thus reduce the amount and quality, overall, of legal services available to everyone. The general concern is expressed well by Arthur Okun when he says that "any insistence on carving the pie into equal slices would shrink the size of the pie."[26] Any pattern of distribution might reduce the amount of the distribuendum.

Given my assumptions about the interrelation of legal resources and the benefits and burdens of legality, that could mean fewer benefits and more burdens. This leads to a further problem: the attempt to achieve a pattern of legal resources necessary to secure equal justice might mean a reduced amount of resources available for distribution. I cannot draw firm conclusions on this topic here; too much depends on empirical evidence. But I want to sound a cautionary note against the assumption that proscribing contracting out would reduce the quality of legal resources. Permitting contracting out will tend to make things worse for some people, worse, that is, than when compared with a similar system where there is no power to contract out. This can be demonstrated by considering the likely consequences of, first, the bare permission to contract out; and, second, the choice of individuals to contract out. A system of equal resources, where contracting out is proscribed, can in this way be justified by its effects for those worst off under the present model of distribution of legal resources. Their position will be improved; there may even be more justice under the new regime.

To get a grasp of the argument here, let us start with an analogous question: how to arrange political institutions. John Locke argued that it would be better to place legislative power "in collective Bodies of Men" than in the hands of an individual autocrat, for it would ensure that "every single person became subject . . . to those Laws, which he himself, as part of the Legislative had established: nor could any one, by his own Authority, avoid the force of the Law, when once made, nor by any pretence of Superiority, plead exemption, thereby to License his own, or the Miscarriages of any of his Dependents."[27] Why might that matter, though? Why is it important that legislators be bound by the rules they enact? Locke claims that if "the legislative power is put into the hands of divers persons who, duly assembled, have . . . a power to make laws, which when they have done, being separated again, they are themselves subject to the laws they have made; which is a new and near tie upon them to take care that they make them for the public good."[28] Locke's insight is that subjecting legislators to the laws they enact ensures a kind of political discipline, the kind of discipline legislators could evade if they are able to escape the law's strictures.

If individuals are bound by laws, they will be more likely to make them "for the public good." The same point can be made about any public good. If individuals must use public goods, they are more likely to help make them work well. This idea can be expressed in the language of permissions and choices. When there are permissions to contract out, those able to use the permission have less incentive to ensure there is sufficient investment in the public option: these permissions are pernicious because they tend to reduce the quality of the public option over time. Individuals' choices to contract out corrode the public option by draining it of resources. These arguments suggest that the proscription on contracting out may not have the bad consequences predicted above. Let me explain these points in a little more detail.

When faced with a decline in the quality of any good, Albert Hirschman pointed out, individuals face a choice of "exit" or "voice."[29] Consumers can choose to stop purchasing the good in question or to purchase a competitor's good; faced with political oppression, some citizens can emigrate. These are examples of "exit." Consumers might, instead, complain about the quality of the good; citizens can speak out against the political oppression. These are examples of "voice." Economists tend to stress the importance of exit: competition will, they say, discipline firms to improve the quality of their goods. If one supermarket is inefficient, another might begin trading next door: consumers might "exit" to shop at the new store. Part of Hirschman's point was that we should not privilege exit: either exit or voice might improve the situation; which it is best to pursue will depend on the context.

Many modern states provide a public option for schools, hospitals, and legal services. These are often conjoined with a permission to contract out of the public option, to purchase education, healthcare of legal services on a private market. The economist's model might suggest that the availability of exit will discipline the public option, keeping it at a certain level of efficiency. However, whether the availability of this permission does improve the public option is a contingent and empirical question. When the availability of that permission leads to the degradation of the public option, we can call the permission to contract out pernicious.

Why might a permission be pernicious? A permission to contract out of the supply of a particular resource offers "exit" to those able to exercise the option. Those able to exit have less incentive to exercise their voice: if the quality of the public option falls below what they deem acceptable, they can go private. Even if those able to go private use the public option, they have less incentive to support and maintain it.

Consider two examples to illustrate this idea. Rich individuals might live in a state and enjoy the benefits its stable government brings. If they have enough money, they can do this safe in the knowledge that they can leave should the government deteriorate. This means they have less incentive to participate in democratic governance: to run for office, to shoulder the burdens of democratic participation. The availability of exit deprives the polity of these rich individuals' voice. Similar remarks apply to public healthcare. If individuals have the ability to purchase private healthcare, their incentive to lobby to improve the public option is reduced by a permission to contract out. Their incentive is reduced even if they use the public option: it is the permission alone (regardless of the choice to use it) which is pernicious. The availability of exit lowers the stakes: those with the power to contract out can let others work to improve the public option, safe in the knowledge that if these other people fail to maintain an acceptable quality of public health-care, they can take their money to the private hospital.

The permission can make things worse even if it is never exercised. What happens when individuals do avail themselves of this option and choose to contract out? The choice might look costless or even beneficial to others in society. Parents do not stop paying taxes when they send their children to private schools, but the children do not take up any of the state's educative resources. A place is freed up in the state's schools at no cost to the state. This rosy picture is a forgery. The choice to contract out can degrade the public option; when it does, it is corrosive. There are two ways in which the choice might corrode the public option: depriving it of the voice of those who leave and removing workers who would otherwise be in the public realm.

Think again of those rich individuals who are able to exit a state if things get bad. Suppose that things do get bad and those people leave. This can make things worse for those left behind: the powerful voices, who might otherwise have worked for reform, fall silent.[30] Or consider schools. If in-dividuals are not permitted to contract out, the only way for an individual parent to improve the quality of their child's education is to exercise voice (or to help out at the school; the point is the same). If the parent does so, the school gets better, not only for their child, but for everyone's. If a pri-vate school opens and these parents choose to send their children to it, that deprives the state school of the voice of those parents. Not only are the rich parents often those with the loudest voice, their voices could be especially valuable: those who choose the private option thereby demonstrate that they care about the quality of their children's education. The quality of the public school will suffer as a result. The choice of these parents to exercise their permission corrodes the quality of the public good.

So far, with respect to choice, I have only stressed the fact that voices might fall silent. Another important effect of the choice to contract out, one that also corrodes the public option, is the way the private option sucks the public option's resources. This is easiest to see if we assume that the supply of the good is fixed. When this is so, the choice to contract out gen-erates an incentive on any service provider to sell their products in the pri-vate market. There is a brain drain. Those who sell their services privately will often be remunerated more than they would be in the public sector. If a doctor has the option of working in a public hospital or a private hospital, a number of factors may make the latter a more attractive option. The pay is often better, for one thing.[31] The quality of life might be better, for another. Hospitals with more paying patients might be better run, have fewer problems of scarcity, and so on. The consequence of people exercising the choice to contract out is that many of the best service providers will drift from the public to the private sphere.

I have developed these points in quite abstract terms, considering public goods analogous to legal resources. In the remainder of this chapter, I will explain how these points can be applied to the specific case of legal resources: both to adjudicators and to lawyers. I use the term "adjudicators" as an umbrella to capture both judges (those employed by the state, working in public courts) and arbitrators (those employed by the parties, working in arbitral tribunals). For both adjudicators and lawyers it is plausible that the availability of the private option corrodes the public option.

When thinking about adjudicators, we should recall the distinction between contracting out within the system and contracting out of the system. Most legal systems prohibit the former but permit the latter. As I explain in Chapter 7, the court system is fragmented into numerous fora. This can have the functional effect of segregating court users: rich companies rarely use the small claims courts, for they have the glitz of the commercial court that will hear their cases. This is a worry—but it is a worry I will defer until we can discuss the topic in earnest. Even so, the basic position in every legal system is equality within the court system: there is no power to contract out within the court system (to pay for a better judge, for example, or a swifter procedure). By contrast, arbitration provides the option of partially contracting out of the public system. It is partial in this respect: arbitral awards are usually enforceable in public courts, meaning people who use arbitration are free-riding on the state's edifice.

There are some reasons to worry that this power reduces the quality of the court service available to other litigants—and, in turn, undermines equal justice. Those are the reasons just canvassed: the decrease in the incentive for voice and the potential brain drain. Consider voice first. When arbitration is available, those who can afford it have a decreased incentive to exercise political voice, to ensure that the court system is adequately funded. So long as the private option remains, therefore, the incentive on those who can afford it to invest in a good justice system is almost non-existent.

We can hypothesise, by contrast, that if contracting out were not permitted, then potential litigators would have an incentive to campaign for a well-funded and efficient judicial system. This is clearest in the civil sphere. One judicial error can cost a company billions of dollars, so the potential costs of having to participate in a substandard justice system are quite high. And the costs of lobbying for a good system are low: good judges are often, when compared with good lawyers, very cheap; and any individual activist company would not have to fund the judge, only to exercise political pressure for the government to invest in the justice system.

The existence of a market in private judges, arbitrators, can also affect the number and quality of public judges. The availability of private practice as an arbitrator—a job without the scrutiny, strictures, or pay restrictions of working in a court—is a powerful pull on prospective and existent judges.[32] Some people become arbitrators rather than judges because they like doing judicial work but prefer to maintain the pay and freedom that private practice involves; some of these people would have applied to be judges were there not the availability of a private market. In the United Kingdom, some judges quit before retirement age to become arbitrators. Corrosive choice makes this a predictable consequence of a market in legal resources: good judges are taken out of the public pool because of the lure of arbitration. If people were not permitted to work as arbitrators, the quality of the judiciary in the public option might therefore improve.

These two points suggest that the availability of a permission to contract out can degrade the quality of the public option. A separate question is what the consequence of that degradation on equal justice will be. Plausibly, it would reduce the amount of justice done and adjust the distribution of it. Resources may be sucked up into complex commercial cases. This may mean justice is done there, but there may be many fewer cases processed overall than there would be under a public system—and that might mean fewer benefits of legality. Further, if good judges leave the system, that can mean worse decisions in individual cases (and, as I develop in Chapter 8, worse law being created); there can, in other words, be fewer benefits and more burdens of legality. And finally, if the private judges are better than the public judges, this can mean an inegalitarian distribution of the benefits and burdens of legality: those able to pay for the private option do best; those unable to do so do not.

Turning now to lawyers, if the wealthy can purchase superb lawyers, their interest in ensuring a functioning legal aid regime is diminished. This applies across both the criminal and civil sphere. The point is most acute in the civil sphere, though, because it is the part of the justice system most often used by the wealthy. If contracting out were proscribed, some litigants would be repeat players, litigants who often sue in the same courts.[33] These litigants would have, and would know that they have, an incentive to improve the quality of legal services for everyone: this would be the only way of improving it for themselves. That incentive is not present where they have the permission to contract out. That suggests that the permission to contract out might undermine the quality of the public option by reducing investment in it.

The proscription on contracting out would also prevent the brain drain of lawyers to the private option. If contracting out were proscribed, the worst off would have a chance of acquiring the best lawyers: they would get them if their dispute warranted the best legal services, rather than if they could afford them. The rich would no longer be able to siphon off the good lawyers for their disputes. This is obviously the case if the contrast category (that is, the system we use to compare the fully public model, with a proscription on contracting out) is a fully private model. On a fully private model, those unable to afford lawyers do not get them. But it is also the case if the contrast category is an intermediate system, where some lawyers are public (i.e., funded by the state) and some are private. If the market works efficiently, the incentives to leave public service will be highest for those who would be the best lawyers. On the intermediate system, the effect of the market is such that a large number of the best lawyers end up working in the private sector—meaning that the pool of public lawyers is not as good as it could be. If these lawyers were not permitted to work in the private sector, they would (in theory) be available for allocation to the worst off. And that could improve things for them.

Despite these optimistic claims, that equal resources would make things better overall, there are some reasons for concern. For one thing, even if the public-private split degrades the public option and undermines equal justice, it is difficult to see how arbitration could be prevented. Preventing arbitration in one country will not prevent it in another: judges could quit the London courts to work in Hong Kong.[34] The same point can be made about lawyers' services: wealthy litigants often have a choice of where to sue and they might decide, if the public option is the only option, to take their case elsewhere. This is unlikely to deprive the public option of voice, when compared with any contemporary system: wealthy litigants, especially corporations, are rarely advocates for improvements to the public option. It would, however, take money (from taxation and spending) out of the system, money that could be spent on legal aid. Absent a dramatic improvement in the quality of trans-national government, these concerns suggest, there may be no way to achieve a public-only system of legal adjudication.

Another reason for concern is that proscribing exit may not, in fact, improve the quality of "voice." Access to legal services is a contingent good. People only need lawyers intermittently, as difficulties arise. This means that even those who stand to lose out through legal aid reforms might happily vote to cut spending.[35] More worrying still, rich individuals could simply evade the public option by hiring in-house "non-lawyers," who would do functionally the same things as the state-supplied lawyers. This would mean that the proscription on contracting out would not, in reality, incentivise them to improve the public option. If so, equality of legal resources would not move us closer to equal justice: wealth would continue to play a large part in determining outcomes.

All this might suggest a counsel of despair. But the argument does suggest a bit more than that. It shows why users of the private system might be called upon to cross-subsidise the public system: they are free-riding upon its resources (in the enforcement proceedings) and degrading its quality (through the pull of arbitration). These are costs that they should internalise. A state could, for example, impose a tax of 1 per cent on all arbitral awards, to be shared with the jurisdictions that would otherwise have been the natural forum for hearing a dispute. This policy proposal is only rational if there is some connection between the private option and the public option; that the private option corrodes the public gives us just such a connection.[36]

SUMMING UP

It is opportune at this point to recapitulate the claims I have made. I argued, in Chapter 2, that the ideal that should structure legal institutions is that of equal justice. That ideal is a label for a number of different requirements.

The justice benefits and burdens of legality should be equally shared, so far as that is possible. Not all disruptions to equality should be thought of in the same way. Built into the ideal of equal justice is an abhorrence of certain factors—in particular, race, class, gender, and wealth—disrupting an equal distribution. These factors must not control distributions if a legal system is to say that right, not might, is the ultimate ground of distributions.

In practice, equal justice is impossible: some will suffer injustice; some will not be able to have their claims of justice recognised. To make this inequality justifiable to those who lose out, the inequality must issue from a fair procedure. Chapters 3, 4, and 5 considered what fairness in procedures required. I began with the suggestion that a basic level of resources—a fairness floor—must be provided; a laissez-faire distribution would be unfair. But as the grounds of the fairness floor were excavated, it became clear that the implications were more far-reaching than is normally accepted. In particular, arguments for a basic level of resources soon shift into arguments for an equal level of resources: equal in an individual suit and, in some cases, equal across a legal system. This chapter took up that suggestion, developing an interpretation of equal resources and offering more arguments for it.

With these claims in place, a quite radical reform agenda is suggested. It seems illegitimate for legal systems to permit contracting out of the public option of legal services. That is in stark contrast with contemporary institutional arrangements. Although there is widespread antipathy to the consequences of our contemporary estate—antipathy I have sought to capitalise on in earlier discussions—few have proposed reforms as radical as mine. Why? One reason is empirical. Some will say that my empirical hypotheses—such as the cheerful prediction that the proscription on contracting out will lead to an increased awareness amongst the wealthy of the value of legal systems—are false. That is not an argument we can pursue here. Another reason is normative. Some people might say that my proposed arrangements have some value but that it would be unjust to implement them. These arguments are most likely to be phrased as concerned with liberty interests. Would it not interfere with liberty to too great an extent if my own regime was set up? It would not, I argue in the next chapter.

6

THREE OBJECTIONS

States have not always permitted those skilled in rhetoric to forge those talents into money or power. In classical Athens, payments to advocates were forbidden as akin to bribery and litigants were expected to speak for themselves (though advocates sometimes wrote the speeches).[1] The 1669 constitution of the state of Carolina, in outlawing professional lawyering, said that "to plead for money or reward" was a "base and vile thing."[2] For centuries, those accused of committing even very serious crimes in England were prohibited from employing lawyers to aid their defence.[3]

These scattered examples show that we should not be too blinkered when proposing policy interventions. They also suggest a number of possible objections to any proposed principles. I have proposed, for example, that we should strive to achieve equal justice, and that this may require an equal distribution of legal resources; I have also said that deviations from equal justice can only be justified if there is a fair procedure. Those proposals may require far more centralised control of the legal profession and individuals' choices than current arrangements. This, it might seem, entails an impermissible interference with individuals' liberty or autonomy. And that, many people will think, is unjustifiable. In this chapter, I will consider three such objections.

The first objection arises if, as is possible, compliance would require the proscription of individuals from contracting out of the public provision of legal professionals. Would-be lawyers, judges, and arbitrators, as well as would-be litigants, might object that this—or limits on the amount they can charge or pay for legal services—is an interference with their freedom to contract.

The second objection arises if compliance with the principles requires that state money be spent on legal services even if individuals would prefer that it be spent on other things. This, people might say, is paternalistic.

The final objection points to an apparent dilemma. Any attempt to satisfy the principles of justice seems to require centralised state control of labour; the state might have to take over the distribution of lawyers. This could (the objection goes) be unjust. When there is a market in legal services, individuals' choice of lawyers is not controlled by the government; this is a bulwark against governmental interference with liberty that would be lost by a centralised system.

Each objection is mistaken. There are no autonomy-based objections to the proposed scheme. Nevertheless, some of the objections can be avoided only if the principles are complied with in particular ways. These objections must be borne in mind, therefore, when designing a particular arrangement of legal resources.

FREEDOM OF CONTRACT

Preliminary Clarifications

Insofar as instituting the principles of justice requires a government to prevent or regulate a market in legal professionals, that might be said to be an interference with freedom of contract. It is not easy to know whether this objection would be made in good faith or taken seriously; every legal system places limits on individuals' abilities to sell their services as lawyers. It is, though, a possible objection that might gain some currency. For that reason, it is worth treating in detail. There are a number of distinct objections beneath the bald statement that any restriction interferes with freedom of contract. To get a grip of their shape, it is worth making two distinctions.

First, we should distinguish who the objection is made by. It can be made either by prospective litigants or by would-be legal professionals (i.e., prospective lawyers and judges) and any objection has a different form depending on who makes it. Roughly, prospective litigants would no longer be able to contract for lawyers' services; lawyers would no longer be able to sell their own services for a price set by a market.

Second, we should distinguish two kinds of claim that might be made under this banner. The litigants or the lawyers might object to one of two interferences: with their freedom to contract itself; or with the interests the power to contract is usually thought valuable to protect. The distinction here is this. Under a laissez-faire regime, individuals have powers to contract with whomever they wish, and those contracts will be enforced in courts. Under a regulated system, they lose that power, and they might object to the mere loss of that power. We can call this the "mere liberty" objection as it objects simply to the loss of the liberty. Often, though, we want the freedom to contract to secure various goals—for example, to ensure that we get the goods we most desire. The litigants' and lawyers' objection might be not to the loss of the power simpliciter but rather to the interests the provision of the power was supposed to satisfy. Their objection, roughly, is that things go worse for them (in the realm of justice, job satisfaction, or wealth) when they lose their power to contract.

I will examine these two kinds of claim in turn. I begin with the mere liberty formulation. There is no objection of any force here: if there is a substantial objection, it must concern the goods people want to secure through freedom of contract. The bulk of this section is concerned with that argument from the perspective of would-be lawyers and litigants. Although there is a close resemblance between the objections of the lawyers and the litigants, as well as the answer to those objections, it takes a little work to see this. It is crucial to explain the structure of the objections in some detail: the bald assertion of an interference with individual freedom can lend the objections force they do not, on analysis, have. So I will discuss the two groups separately. The objection is not powerful: that people are prevented from doing what they would like to do is not, without more, much of an argument; there may be very good reasons to prevent them. The assertion of an interference with freedom ultimately does little more that reassert some rival distributive principle, one that must be defended on its merits as a distributive principle.

The Mere Liberty Objection

The first objection is to the mere deprivation of the liberty to contract that more centralised control of the legal profession might require. What is wrong with that? This is sometimes talked about as an interference with "freedom of contract." Objections are raised in this form so often that it is easy to forget how peculiar it is to invoke the value of freedom in this context. The refusal to recognise and enforce contracts is not an interference with anyone's freedom. People are simply denied a state-granted power. In fact, the normal approach has things backwards. It is much more natural to regard the creation of a contract as an interference with liberty: that is what makes it the case that people come under obligations that can be enforced coercively by the state.

If freedom is not a fruitful line of inquiry, what is? Two possible options are: that the loss of the liberty will make things go worse for some people; and that the government's taking decisions about how people structure their own lives is paternalistic. These two options are promising lines for an objection to take. But they do not actually focus on the loss of the liberty. As I will explain when I consider each objection in detail, they have a quite different form.

We should understand the objection to the loss of the liberty as concerned with individual autonomy. The deprivation of the power to contract for legal services reduces the scope of autonomous choice for individuals. Thus put, the mere liberty objection does not seem to have great force. Notice, first, the limit to the deprivation. Would-be lawyers are still able to choose to be lawyers; what they lose is the ability to charge what they wish for their legal services.[4] (They retain the ability to charge what they wish for any other service they might provide.) Would-be litigants do not lose the ability to go to law; depending on how the system is structured, they may not even lose the ability to choose their lawyer.[5]

These limits stated, some would-be litigants and lawyers do lose the ability to make a choice that would be available to them under a laissez-faire system. Part of the value of autonomy is in individuals' abilities to make such choices, sculpting their lives as they see fit. But loss of this option is not a cause for concern. A state does not need to provide individuals with the maximal possible range of choices if it is to respect individual autonomy. All that matters is that individuals have a sufficient number of choices to develop their lives in the way they see fit. This might mean that the state should not eliminate all bad options: part of living an autonomous life is the ability to make the wrong choices. But the deprivation of the power to contract on privately chosen terms does not deprive individuals of a sufficient range of choices: as I have already said, the limits to individual choices are quite minimal.

These remarks might seem drastically to undermine the force of the objection. The idea that compliance with the demands of equal justice will undermine individual liberty is likely to be the most forceful objection raised in practice. Insofar as there is an objection to the interference with freedom of contract, though, it is more naturally read as concerning the interests individuals have in having the liberty to contract. That is, it is not so much the deprivation of the mere liberty that matters, but the loss of the benefits individuals were able to acquire through the exercise of that liberty. This is a more powerful objection; I consider it now, first from the perspective of would-be lawyers, then from the perspective of would-be litigants.

Would-Be Lawyers

So far, we have only considered the deprivation of the liberty to contract. That liberty is valuable not only for the autonomy interests it can promote but also for the outcomes it might secure. This distinction is visible in Adam Smith's initial defence of laissez-faire principles. Smith was concerned to establish freedom of contract, not for the mere liberty it might secure, but for the interests that liberty would serve: he wrote that free markets were a method of ensuring "the liberty and security of individuals": the "most important" effect of free markets was their ability to free people from "servile dependency."[6] Whether any particular liberty serves individuals' interests is a contingent question; Smith's assessment can look rose-tinted today.[7] But the important point is that the liberty and the consequences of the liberty should be assessed separately.

To clarify what the possible consequences of a particular arrangement would be, we should now distinguish an approach that seeks to realise equal justice by forcing individuals to labour from one that places preconditions on their pursuit of various courses of action. It is possible that some distributive arrangements can only be realised if individuals are forced into certain labour relations. Most people would baulk at the suggestion that we should force certain people into certain jobs so as to achieve justice. Whether we need to do so to comply with my proposed principles depends on whether there are sufficient numbers of able citizens willing to work as

lawyers on the terms available. Experience indicates that systems of socialised medicine are able to find enough people willing to be doctors,
though this is a controversial and difficult topic.

If forced labour is not required, what is? What, in other words, is achieved
by the deprivation of the liberty to contract? People would be allowed to
work in certain roles, such as lawyers and judges, only on certain conditions. To secure compliance with equal justice, rights to work as a lawyer
could be made conditional upon each individual fitting into a scheme of
labour that is most likely to comply with the best principles of justice.
Everyone would retain their freedom to decide in what job they work and
how hard they work; they would not have the same earning potential as
under a laissez-faire system. This would not be structurally different from
the system already in place. One cannot, for example, practice law or work
as a doctor simply because one wants to; you have to train in an accred-
ited school and keep up educational requirements to maintain the licence.
The right to work is already conditional; the question is what conditions
are justified.

Suppose, to simplify the discussion, that the only condition imposed is
a limit to the price individuals can charge for legal services. There are three
increasingly intrusive ways by which that condition could be enforced. First,
a state could say that any contracts in legal services where the price is set
by a market are invalid. The state would not prevent lawyers from selling
their service on a market but would refuse to provide its enforcement mechanisms to assist in that sale. This is the "contractual invalidity incentive"
approach. Second, a state could make professional status (as a lawyer or
as a judge) conditional upon working on a certain wage structure; anyone
who did contract in the private market could then lose their licence to practice law. This is the "professional licence incentive" approach. Finally, a
state could make contracting for legal services illegal (either for litigants,
lawyers, or both), perhaps punishable with a prison sentence. That is the
"sanction incentive" approach.

Would-be lawyers might object either to the condition placed on their
labouring as lawyers or the mechanism by which the condition is enforced.
If the condition on their labouring is justifiable, the first two approaches,
suggested in the previous paragraph, are unlikely to meet with any sensible
resistance: there is no infringement of the lawyers' liberties through those

conditions. The sanction incentive approach is more intrusive. Whether it is justifiable depends, as with many such possible conditions, on how important compliance with the principles of a just justice system are thought to be. So long as people accept the fundamental importance of compliance with the principles of just justice, it is not objectionable.

So what is the objection to the deprivation of the liberty to contract? The most likely objection is simply that lawyers are less able to make as much money through their labour as they are under a laissez-faire system. How powerful is that objection, thus clarified?

Our question is: on what conditions may we permissibly condition the grant of legal licences? In particular, is it permissible to grant the licence only on condition that the lawyer's fees be set by some method other than a market? To answer that question, we should distinguish between an institutional and an individual perspective. The institutional perspective asks, as I have in the last few chapters, what arrangement of legal resources would satisfy the demands of justice. The individual perspective asks whether it is justifiable to implement that institutional arrangement. That these two perspectives might reach apparently conflicting conclusions is shown by the example of forced labour: we might think both that justice demands a universal supply of doctors or teachers through a country and that no one should be coerced into such labour; given further contingent facts about people's preferences, we might have to choose between institutional and individual justice.[8]

The example of forced labour clarifies how such a conflict can arise. There would be an interference with individual liberty if someone is forced to work because people have an interest in determining what jobs to pursue. For an analogous argument to arise in our context, people must have an entitlement to receive money from their labour as lawyers.

No one is entitled to all the possible income their labour might give them: income earned through exploitation and racketeering is not permitted on any view of justice. Instead, individuals are entitled only to those wages that would be earned under a system of just labour relations.[9] No one is entitled, therefore, to the surplus wage earned through the exploitation of an unjust labour relation. This is clearest when considered bilaterally: if I demand "protection" money, I am not entitled to anything because all the money is earned through exploitation. Where an individual transaction takes place against a background of unjust labour relations, the same point applies. If the distribution of lawyers via a market is unjust, a lawyer does not have a moral entitlement to a fee determined by a market; her only moral entitlement is to the fee she would have earned had the relation been just.[10] That is so even if the lawyer is not exploiting her client in the individual case: the fact she was able to make that wage presupposes an unjust system; that is enough to undermine her moral entitlement to the wage.[11]

Some will want to resist this line of argument. If wages are determined in some manner other than a market, are not lawyers deprived of some measure of the wage they deserve? That, perhaps, is an ingrained instinct of many—those who benefit from the market's pricing of their labour, anyway.[12] But it is not easy to fashion any principle of desert that can justify this conclusion. One intuition people have is that individuals deserve what they can acquire with their own abilities. If you and I have an equal plot of land and I work to cultivate the land while you laze in the sun, I, not you, deserve the crops that result. This kind of principle relies upon the output (here, the crops) being sufficiently determined by inputs we deserve (here, the land). These claims rely upon a distinction between those inputs upon which it is just for outcomes to depend and those it is not: it is just for outcomes to depend on our acuity and assiduity; it is unjust for them to depend on our class, connections or wealth.

Can such a principle apply to the market in legal professionals? Perhaps, we might say, prospective lawyers deserve their natural abilities—innate talent, capacity for graft, and so on. We could go further, saying that would-be lawyers deserve their upbringing (good parenting, schooling, and so on). Both of these claims are, to say the least, contentious.[13] Yet there are two further inputs that determine the market price of legal services: the scarcity of individuals with legal abilities and the prevalence of injustice. These conditions, collectively, make lawyers' services financially valuable on an open market.[14] No lawyer would want to claim credit for them for they are, on any view, a bad thing.

A lawyer's complaint that they will be worse off than under a market system is not powerful. It is justified only if they are entitled to the institution of a market in legal professionals. And, as the previous chapters have shown, that is not a justifiable position as a matter of distributive justice.

Would-Be Litigants

The removal of the liberty to contract might also undermine certain citizens' interests and that might look objectionable. It isn't. But to see why not, we need to state the supposed objection as clearly as possible.

The Sixth Amendment to the US Constitution establishes a right to "have the Assistance of Counsel"; this has been described as including a right "to choose who will represent" you.[15] It might seem like the abolition of a market in legal professionals would interfere with this right, the right to choose counsel. That is not so. Even if a market in legal professionals were proscribed, it is a separate question how legal services are to be distributed. Individuals could choose from available lawyers, even if they themselves were not paying those lawyers

In practice, the Sixth Amendment right is, as Justice Byron White put it, "the right to be represented by an otherwise qualified attorney whom that defendant can afford to hire, or who is willing to represent the defendant even though he is without funds."[16] This is a right to exercise a choice in a very particular way, via a competitive market; it is a right to participate in a market in legal professionals.[17] Anatole France's objection to equality before the law reminds us that the value of such rights is highly contingent on individual circumstances. And it is this right that would be lost under my proposed approach. What, if anything, might be wrong with that?[18]

We are not concerned, I have argued, with the mere loss of the liberty to contract. Our concern is with the consequences of the loss of that liberty. The objection can be clarified if we examine the value of that freedom for some participants in the market and the consequences for them of its abolition. The principal value of the freedom is that it enables individuals to secure the service of lawyers whom they think will best represent their interests. Its value is chiefly instrumental: it brings about better results for the individual in question. Under a system of equal justice or with a fairness floor, some would-be litigants would do worse than under a market system. This is clearest under a system of equal justice: those individuals who would be able to afford private lawyers under a laissez-faire system of distribution may get a worse service, for their ability to purchase lawyers would be curtailed. But it could also be true if a fairness floor is established: many prospective litigants unable to afford lawyers under a laissez-faire distribution would end up with lawyers; and this could impose costs on other people in the system who now have to defend against their claims. Those who would have done better under the laissez-faire approach might say that this arrangement is unjust. Why should they be made worse off for the benefit of others?

Given the different value of that freedom to different people (depending on their wealth) some would find that deprivation more costly than others. Those who, under a laissez-faire system, would be able to buy the best lawyers might find themselves with fewer of the benefits and more of the burdens of legality under my proposed approach. Those who, in the civil sphere, had the finest lawyers in the land before might now have to make do with the lawyers most others use. This undoubtedly might make things go worse for them in individual cases: they may end up with worse settlements in civil cases, for example. Those who could have bought the finest criminal defence lawyers available might find themselves left with a state-supplied lawyer, who may be worse. These people might have an increased risk of wrongful conviction or more exacting punishment for any crime they commit.

This is more troubling than the lawyers' objection. The litigants are deprived of something they deserve as a matter of justice (i.e., justice in the outcome of their cases) or are imposed upon unjustly (e.g., with wrongful conviction). The lawyers, by contrast, had no entitlement to any particular systemic arrangement, and therefore did not lose anything to which they were entitled. The structure of the objection is essentially the same, though, and the same reason would-be lawyers have no grounds for complaint explains why would-be litigants cannot complain about the principles of a just legal system being instituted.

The distribution of lawyers either does or does not have an effect on outcomes of cases. If it has no effect, regulation of that market does not affect the interests of prospective litigants in anything but the most tangential sense: they lose the mere power to contract out, even though it is of scarce value. If it does affect the outcome of cases, any institutional arrangement is such that some individuals' benefit or burden will come at the expense of others. Some will do better under a laissez-faire system; others will do better under a system of equal justice.

So there are two levels of injustice. There is individual injustice, to which the objection points: the deprivation of justice in the outcome of cases and the wrongful conviction of those charged with crimes. Any institutional arrangement, as I have pointed out, will have an effect on these individual injustices, but no arrangement can eliminate them. Our question has been: what systematic or institutional arrangement can justify the incidence of these injustices? And we have been concerned with this second level of injustice: injustice in the institutional arrangement of the legal system. The objection only arises if my account of institutional justice is accepted; if it is rejected, an alternative account of the proper institutional arrangement must be offered. Whatever the just institutional arrangement, the structure of the objection will be the same: to raise the incidence of individual injustice to object to an institutional arrangement. We must now keep in mind the necessary imperfection here. If no institutional arrangement will work best for everyone, the mere fact that someone will be made worse off by an institutional change cannot mean that that change is ruled out.

The answer to this objection now becomes very similar to the answer to the lawyers' objection. No institutional arrangement can eliminate injustice at the individual level. Individual injustice is permissible only if it results from a just system: no individual can complain because of the distribution of risks that system generates. The sorts of benefits and risks to which any individual is entitled depend upon the benefits and risks a just institutional structure generates. On the principles I have proposed, those risks are the product of a system with a fairness floor and / or one of equal justice. Any attempt to characterise a departure from a market system as unfair to any individual litigant must assume that a market system is justified as an institutional matter: only then could it be said that the loss of benefits and the increased burdens individuals gain and incur are deprivations of things to which individuals are entitled. It is, in other words, an attempt to invoke the market as a justified institutional arrangement for the distribution of legal resources. Such proposals should be considered, of course; we cannot reject a market distribution out of hand. But they have to be considered at the earlier stage, when we think about what systemic arrangement is best.

Another way to put the same point is this. Any system will be objectionable to some, and some systems are more objectionable to some than others. The objection of would-be litigants here is that the market arrangement would work better for them than some other systems would. The response from other would-be litigants is that equal justice or the fairness floor would work better for them than the market system. How to break this gridlock?

A fair system, we might say, is one where no one can reasonably reject the institutional arrangement. The question then becomes whether those who are privileged by a market system can reasonably reject other arrangements in favour of a market system. They can only do this if they prioritise their own interests over those of their fellow citizens: a system of equal justice aims to ensure that none are better off than any others; any argument to adjust those risks will prioritise some interests over others. There may be arguments that certain individuals, such as those who are worst off overall, ought to receive preferential treatment. But the would-be litigant who wants to defend the market setting of prices does not make that argument—and anyone who would be better off when there is a power to contract out of the public option is likely to be better off overall than most. By contrast, those who are worse off under the market system can reasonably reject that system on the grounds it does not treat their interests equally with the interests of all others in society: they do not ask to be made better off than others; they only ask to be in the same position, with respect to justice, as their equals.

PATERNALISM

If individuals are given the option of legal expenses insurance or a cash transfer, Tamara Goriely and Alan Paterson point out, "one suspects that few would opt for the insurance policy."[19] There is a deep and important point here. As James Tobin says, "While concerned laymen who observe people with shabby housing or too little to eat instinctively want to provide them with decent housing and adequate food, economists instinctively want to provide them with more cash income."[20] Given Goriely and Paterson's empirical point (which sounds likely enough), someone, probably an economist, might object: why not make a cash transfer and let individuals decide how to spend the money?

The suggestion might be motivated by a few disparate concerns. Some motivations are economic: a cash transfer might be much cheaper to administer than in-kind transfers. A more interesting idea is the thought that the provision of an in-kind benefit is paternalistic. That concern may lurk beneath Goriely and Paterson's loaded question: "Why should the state make the decision for them?"[21] It is an important objection; in this section I develop and respond to it.[22]

I begin with an account of paternalism. Only if we know what paternalism is can we know whether my proposed principles are paternalistic.

The Nature of Paternalism

Suppose that you invite me to your house for dinner. I discover that you have a pack of cigarettes and that you occasionally smoke. I think that smoking is bad for you so I throw your cigarettes away. You could object to my having done this using the language of paternalism. But what makes my action paternalistic?

Paternalist actions are characterised by two attributes.[23] First, they interfere with the autonomous choice or action of another. Throwing away your cigarettes prevents you from smoking them; it interferes with your choice (about whether to smoke) and possible actions. Let's call that the "autonomy condition." Second, the paternalist substitutes (or attempts to substitute) her own judgement about the value of the other's choice or action. Maybe I am right that smoking is bad for you. But, you might say, it was your choice whether to smoke; I should not make that choice for you. Let's call that the "substitution condition."

Each condition is necessary but neither alone is sufficient to make an action paternalistic. If I see that a car is about to hit you and I grab you from the street, I interfere with your autonomy but (unless you are trying to commit suicide) do not attempt to substitute my choice for yours about the value of your actions. You were simply unaware of the car and I saved you from it. No one would call that paternalistic.[24] Similarly, if I come to dinner at your house, discover that you smoke, and try to convince you that it's bad for you, I am trying to substitute my judgement about the value of smoking for your judgement—or, more precisely, to update your judgement to match my own. But, so long as I do not attempt to interfere with any action of yours, my actions are not paternalistic.[25]

It is part of the concept of paternalism that it is in one way objectionable; to call some action paternalistic is to raise an objection to it. To complete our account of paternalism, we need to know what is wrong with it—for some actions that meet these two conditions may not be paternalistic.[26] Sometimes the problem is simply that the action will not make things better.[27] If I confiscate your cigarettes, perhaps you will double down on your habit to prove a point. And, you might say, why should I think I am a better judge of your interests than you are?

Although this argument has a very respectable pedigree,[28] it does not get to the heart of what is objectionable with paternalistic behaviour.[29] If you complain about my throwing your cigarettes away, it is no answer that I am right about the carcinogenic content of cigarettes. That would ring hollow because it does not matter whether I am right. Your objection was that it was not my choice to make. My confiscation infantilised you, expressing the judgement that you should not be allowed to live your own life.

The problem with paternalism is the negative judgement it expresses about an individual.[30] Typically this is the judgement that the individual is incapable of living, or cannot be trusted to live, an autonomous life. Paternalist action expresses contempt about the beneficiaries of that action. When we consider whether the creation of a just justice system is paternalistic, we should ask whether it infantilises its beneficiaries in this manner. The message conveyed by any action depends upon its context: a kiss on the cheek can convey affection or disdain. So it is vital to attend closely to the context.

If an individual would prefer "to spend money on a holiday than on suing his detractor," why, Lord Sumption asks, is "this a choice that should be denied to him?"[31] Sumption's objection seems to be the anti-paternalist's. It supposes, first, that there is some action of an individual that is being interfered with (or pre-empted). There is a sum of money for the state to spend; the question is whether it is to be spent on a specific good, such as legal services, or paid to individuals in cash transfers. If the state decides to spend the money on legal services, the objection must suppose, this interferes with some presumptive choice individuals might have with respect to the money: hence the autonomy condition seems to be met.

Spending the money on legal services, the objection must go on, displaces a choice an individual would make (say, to spend the money on a holiday). That substitutes the state's judgement of the value of those options for the individual's: the individual might want a holiday more than legal services, but the state thinks the individual is wrong to do so. Hence the substitution condition is also met. And Sumption's (perhaps rhetorical) question—like Goriely and Paterson's[32]—suggests that the provision of legal services might be thought objectionable in its expression of contempt. Why, he asks, should we deny people this choice?

The Response

A state's conformity with my proposed principles would not require paternalism because neither condition of paternalistic action is met. There is, in part for that reason, no expression of contempt to anyone in the creation of a just justice system.

There are better and worse distributions of legal resources. We have good reason to try to secure those distributions. The objection claims that this would be paternalistic if people would, given the option, prefer some other goods in place of legal resources. To make this claim, the objector must make two assumptions. First, she assumes a "natural" distribution of legal resources, such as a market distribution, with the question then being whether to supplement that distribution through (say) a legal aid regime. Second, that citizens are entitled to a certain amount of welfarist expenditure, the question being whether to pay citizens directly or spend the money on an in-kind benefit.

Both assumptions are flawed. No particular arrangement is natural; a legal system is a human construct. The second assumption, which develops the first, imagines that citizens are entitled to expenditure (in general): that assumption enables the objection to conceptualise legal aid expenditure as an interference with individuals (rather than the conferral of a benefit). But it is wrong to imagine that citizens have this abstract entitlement.

To see this, and why a decision to give an in-kind benefit is not paternalistic (despite the fact that the recipient would prefer to have something else from us), consider Scanlon's well-known example: "The strength of a stranger's claim on us for aid in the fulfilment of some interest depends upon what that interest is and need not be proportional to the importance he attaches to it. The fact that someone would be willing to forego a decent diet in order to build a monument to his god does not mean that his claim on others for aid in his project has the same strength as a claim for aid in obtaining enough to eat (even assuming that the sacrifices required of others would be the same)."[33] The stranger has no general claim on us for resources. His claim is for a specific good, food. It would be paternalistic if we instructed the stranger how to eat the food, or gave gratuitous dietary advice; but it is not paternalistic to provide only food as that is all the stranger has a claim for.

One way to explain why Scanlon's example does not involve paternalism is that there is no interference with any choice of the stranger. The autonomy condition is not met. The example I gave to illustrate interference was my throwing your cigarettes away: destroying something which belongs to another to prevent them from making a choice about how to use it seems paternalistic. This logic does not apply to Scanlon's example and nor does it apply to the case of legal services. Just as we do not interfere with a choice of the stranger by giving her food, the state does not interfere with any choice of an individual by giving her legal services. Individuals are not entitled to abstract resources; they are entitled to a range of goods, one of which is security from injustice, and the distribution of legal resources is a means to ensure justice in that sphere.

Something like that is the correct analysis. But it needs a little care. It is not the mere fact that no asset of another is destroyed or interfered with. If you ask me to loan you a small sum of money until you get your paycheck, and I refuse because I know that you will spend some of it on cigarettes, that also seems paternalistic.[34] My reason not to give you the money is premised on my estimation of how you would choose to spend it. So long as that choice is properly yours, the autonomy condition seems to be met.[35]

When will our decision to bestow a gift (as in Scanlon's example) or structure a state distributional mechanism (as in the example of legal services) fail to be caught by this kind of paternalism? A quite technical distinction is useful here: that between a reason being cancelled and being overridden.[36] In Scanlon's example, there is only a reason to donate to the stranger if the donation alleviates the stranger's hunger; there is no reason (or no reason sufficient to justify a transfer of wealth) to give the stranger money for a monument to his god. My reasons to give you money are, by contrast, not dependent upon your prospective choices for how to spend that money. I have good reasons to lend you money because you are my friend and you asked me for it; the loan will (jokes about lending money to friends aside) support and enrich our friendship. Those reasons remain, even if you are going to spend the gift on cigarettes. If I decide not to give you the money, that is because I think that my reason to give you money is outweighed by your reasons not to spend money on cigarettes.

This distinction clarifies why one example is paternalistic and the other is not. Talk of paternalism is intelligible when some prospective choice of the donee's is taken to give the donor a reason not to give the money. If, by contrast, the donee's prospective choice cancels a reason the donor thought she had, the situation is different.

We can now return to our own example. It might be paternalistic for the state to spend money on legal services and yet refuse to give direct cash transfers, but only if individuals have a claim against the state for welfare in general and the state is deciding in what ways to improve their welfare; or if the reason why the state does not give money to individuals is that it disapproves of the choices they would make with it. If either of these things were true, a decision of an individual, about how to spend "their" money, would be taken from them. Yet neither condition holds. The arguments I have given for specific distributions of legal resources and justice only apply to those distributions; they do not apply to transfers of money in general. Citizens do not have a general claim to be made better off, but a specific claim about the kind of legal system there ought to be. And the state's refusal to give money to individuals to spend on holidays expresses no disapproval of that option. Holidays may be great ways to spend one's time and money, but that does not mean the state has any obligation to support them. Refusing to give money that would be spent on a holiday is simply a recognition that the state has no obligation to allocate resources to individuals to spend in this way.

Citizens have claims against the state that a just justice system be set up; they do not have a claim to the monetary equivalent of setting up that system. No question of paternalism arises for no choice of an individual is being usurped.

The second condition that qualifies some action as paternalist is the substitution (or attempted substitution) of the paternalist's judgement about the value of the other's choice or action. This condition also depends on it being an open question as to whether the recipient is entitled to choose what happens in some particular situation, and the paternalist substitutes a decision for the recipient's. But it is not an open question: her only claim is that a just justice system be provided, not that wealth be transferred.

There are two deeper reasons why the substitution condition is not met. To see the first, consider again the example of the cigarettes. It was paternalistic to throw them away. It might also be paternalistic for me to not to make some gift on the basis that I disapprove of the way you are going to spend or use it. But it is not paternalistic for me to refuse to buy you cigarettes. Your smoking habit might be a legitimate life-goal of yours; perhaps I am not justified in intervening to stop your making these mistakes. (By contrast, your decision to murder people is not a legitimate goal and I am perfectly entitled to intervene to thwart that plan.) All this, though, does not mean that you can enlist me to help you make these mistakes. My refusal to help you is not paternalistic because there is no substitution of your decision for mine. The basis of my decision is not a desire to prevent your wrongdoing but a concern with my own moral status: I don't want to help you make mistakes. That is a self-regarding, not other-regarding, decision.

A similar argument can be made in our context. A just justice system is justified in part by the need to ensure that the state (and, through it, all its citizens) is not complicit in injustice. Any schematic arrangement that is unjust will lead to such complicity: the state would establish and enforce a system that is, by hypothesis, unjust; and that cannot but make it complicit in injustice. So the state's decision to expend resources on a just justice system can be justified by self-regarding considerations.

Consider what would happen if the state made transfers to each citizen (instead of creating a just justice system). Some other system for the distribution of legal resources would have to be set up. This, perhaps, would be a market in legal resources. A consequence would be, as I traced in more detail in Chapter 3, that various kinds of injustice would result. Those who could access legal resources may be able to commit injustices with greater impunity than others; they would be better able to plate their wrongs in gold. Individuals' chances of winning and losing court cases would be affected by their earlier decisions (on whether to purchase legal insurance) rather than the merits of their case: those who spent their resources on a holiday could find themselves sued by another or accused of crimes; they could be unable to defend themselves against the accusations, raising the risk of wrongful judgements and convictions. And the state would be complicit in these injustices. It would be their perpetrator: the wrongful judgments and convictions would be wrought in state courts.

The creation of a legal system brings with it the risk of incorrect court judgments. Part of the motivation for a just distribution of legal resources, and of the benefits and burdens of legality, is the concern that this risk be minimised and distributed as fairly as possible. The paternalist's objection would have us increase the risks and share them less equitably lest the state substitute its judgement for that of the citizens. Yet the state's concern is not with the citizens' judgement but with its own complicity. The decision to provide legal resources is not, therefore, paternalist. Any request that a different scheme of legal resources be established—even if twinned with cash transfers to spend on holidays—requires state complicity in the increased injustice. That request is unjustifiable.

To understand the second reason why the substitution condition is not met, think of the design of a legal system as solving a particular kind of collective action problem. It is in the collective interest to set up a just justice system. But it is in each individual's interest, narrowly conceived, to avoid the burdens of such a system: to avoid paying for it, for example. If the decision about which arrangement to create was left to the market, such that each individual was granted the choice what contribution to make, many might try to free-ride on the public good others had created. Perhaps some would spend money transfers on holidays instead of the funding of a legal system: they could enjoy the benefits of the legal system without shouldering its burdens. And if enough people went on holiday, rather than paying into the system, it would be impossible to create a just justice system.

This is to repeat points I made in more detail in Chapter 3. But their importance is somewhat distinct here. Once we see a particular design, such as mine, as an attempt to surmount this collective action problem, the charge of paternalism falls away.[37] Central control is necessary not to displace an individual's preferences but as the only mechanism by which individuals' preferences can be satisfied.

This shows why it is wrong to think of a just justice system as displacing individuals' preferences: no one would prefer a world without a justice system but there is no way to implement a just justice system without centralised control. It also demonstrates why there is no contempt conveyed through the creation of that legal system: the decision to create it is not an attempt to supplement individuals' choices but to create a framework within which individuals are able to choose what they want. The importance of creating a system for everyone is an important context when understanding the message conveyed by the system. An action is more likely to be objectionably paternalistic if it singles out an individual or class of individuals.

If, for example, a decision was taken out of the hands of only those on welfare, that might indicate that those on welfare are thought especially incapable of leading autonomous lives. By contrast, if the decision is taken for everyone in society, there is no singling out.

LIBERTY FROM GOVERNMENT

The Concern

Although often traced to Magna Carta, the tradition of subjecting rulers to law is, even in England, much older. At his coronation in 1100, Henry I of England issued a charter promising to abolish "evil" customs and to restore "the law of Edward the Confessor," last of the Anglo-Saxon kings. At their coronations and before taking up their crowns, virtually all medieval kings prior to Henry swore to rule by right and justice and to maintain good laws, repudiating the bad. John of Salisbury, the leading political theorist of the twelfth century, distinguished the tyrant and the just prince on the basis that "the latter is obedient to law."[38] It was in this long-established tradition that King John was persuaded to seal his charter at Runnymede, in 1215.[39]

To understand the requirements placed on modern states, we should distinguish between illegality and invalidity. An action is illegal if the law prohibits it; it is invalid if it fails to satisfy preconditions for some legal effect. It is illegal for people to murder: the act of killing is prohibited. It is not illegal for a judge to pass a sentence of death in a country without the death penalty: it is invalid; the judge is simply unable to pass such a sentence. An action can be invalid but not illegal; it can also be illegal but not invalid. Part of the reason to have a legal system is to prevent government illegality and to regulate validity.

Governments must act in conformity with the law: their acts should not be illegal. The fact that some wrong was committed by an agent of the state does not justify the wrong; the victim is entitled to bring the wrongdoer into court to claim compensation. Governments are also only able to act within their legal powers. When they transgress those limits, their actions are invalid. The precise limits vary from country to country. The US Constitution proscribes cruel and unusual punishment. States are simply not able to pass laws mandating cruel and unusual punishment; any attempt to do so should be struck down. In the United Kingdom, by contrast, Parliament can legislate for whatever punishments it likes. But, unlike under a tyrannical regime, for any punishment to be meted out, it must be justified by the law. Otherwise it would be illegal.

In order for these requirements to be met it is not enough that there be laws. There must also be a just administration of the laws. This is how we should understand James Madison's proposed "political maxim, that the legislative, executive, and judiciary departments ought to be separate and distinct." He explained: "The accumulation of all powers, legislative, executive, and judiciary, in the same hands, whether of one, a few, or many, and whether hereditary, self-appointed, or elective, may justly be pronounced the very definition of tyranny."[40] If the legislature or executive were able to control the application of laws to them, they would not need to obey them. Tyranny, in John of Salisbury's terms, would be possible. Madison's prediction was that the best way to prevent this tyranny is to have a separation of powers.

Any country governed by the rule of law has judges independent of the state, judges who can hold the political arm to account for any breach of the law and declare when actions are invalid. The separation of powers helps to ensure that judges are independent of the executive and legislative branches of the state.[41] If the legislature or executive controlled the judicial branch, they would be able to control the application of the laws. If the judges are in the Parliament's pocket, those judges are (the worry goes) less likely to police the politicians' actions with any rigour. In 2004, for example, the number of Supreme Court judges in Venezuela was increased from 20 to 32. The change enabled then-president Hugo Chavez to pack the court with allies. People worried that this would undermine the judges' independence from the president. These worries were borne out: the court became increasingly assertive; in 2017 it temporarily assumed the functions of an intransigent National Assembly, then Venezuela's legislative body, which was dominated by members of the opposition. The court backed down—but only when President Nicholas Maduro asked it to do so.

Why, though, is it good for the state to be subject to the laws? There are two concerns here. A central function of law, a function I have stressed in previous chapters, is to ensure that we are not exploited by other members of our community. Another important function, one I have not had much to say about (because the considerations are largely the same), is to ensure that we are not exploited by the state. A just administration of the laws is important partly to ensure that government illegality does not take place. There is another value at stake here, too. If the government could control the administration of laws, individuals would never have a certain kind of freedom, the liberty one has when one's actions do not depend upon the will of another. A slave might have a benevolent master: she might be well-treated but unfree. Just so, individuals' liberty from the dictates of the government is secure only if there are laws and if the government is not able to control their application.[42] A certain kind of freedom exists only if no one has "the capacity to interfere in [another's] affairs on an arbitrary basis."[43] This idea is principally concerned not with the things done to the person or institution but with the possibility of interference. It does not say that freedom requires no interference ever; there may be interference, but it cannot be arbitrary.

The distribution of two types of legal professionals affects the application of laws: judges and lawyers. Earlier chapters have been concerned with their distribution. If a just distribution of legal resources is achieved, that will go some way to ensure that there is no injustice in the relations between citizen and state. Where there is gross inequality of legal resources— inequality, that is, between government and citizen—then there is a risk of wrongful conviction and exploitation. Under a just justice system, each individual will have a fair level of resources. Fairness here is partly comparative: in a criminal case, whether the accused's lawyer is good enough depends in part upon how good the government's lawyer is; in a public law claim, the same point applies. Equality in the benefits and burdens of legality is also important. The burdens of legality will include unlawful administrative decisions. It is not possible, therefore, for the state to exploit certain individuals under a scheme of equal justice. Further, governments should always aim to improve the quality of their decision making, to reduce the number of illegal actions, and so on.

As the example of Venezuelan judges illustrates, however, it is not enough to have a particular distribution of legal resources. It is also important how that distribution is administered. If the government controls the distribution of legal resources, they are able (indirectly) to control the application of the laws. This would mean that they could violate the law and go beyond their powers with impunity. They could, for example, select judges who favoured the government's stance on certain issues, or choose the best lawyers for themselves (and the worst for their opponents). Would not the kind of regulation required to ensure my proposed distributions of legal resources require that legal powers be subject to political control? And would that not mean that, even if people were, in fact, treated as the principles of justice I have proposed require, the domain of liberty the legal system is supposed to provide—a domain of independence from governmental control—would be reduced?

It is in light of this concern that we can understand some of the historical claims made about legal distributions. In the 1950s, for example, one judge worried that the United States was becoming a police state: a democratic order could not long survive, he said, if a "citizen in legal conflict with the state could get no counsel except as was vouchsafed him by the state."[44] This might sound hysterical. But this was soon after Nazi Germany and, as Kenneth Willig points out, "The Nazis wanted a unified legal administration which could carry out orders efficiently and obediently. The Bar was the loose link in the chain. Consequently, the regime accelerated its process of treating lawyers as civil servants."[45] This is a serious concern. It deserves a thorough response.

The concern can be better understood when we recall the negative argument for markets, canvassed in Chapter 3. The negative argument claims that markets do not necessarily lead to a distributively just arrangement. But, it says, any other method for the distribution of resources—such as an attempt to institute equality of legal resources—will lead to a worse outcome than a market arrangement. One reason is that individuals would no longer be independent of government control, increasing the risk of capture. As debates there showed, we must be alive to two sites of power, public and private, that can endanger individual liberty. The urgency of protection from each site will vary according to context: my own concern with private power may derive in part from a sense that this poses the greatest threat to liberty today. This analogy also shows that the concern is often not normative but a matter of procedures, of discovering the best method to achieve an agreed-upon outcome.

For these reasons, there is a limit to the amount that a philosophical book can say on these questions; so much depends on empirical details, which will vary from time to time, country to country. There are, though, some general points concerning how just justice can be achieved without granting too much power to government.

The Reply

The distribution of judges already purports to adhere to principles of equal justice. Although there are, as I have said, pressures undermining the egalitarian ethos, those pressures are indirect: it remains true that you cannot pay more for one judge or another. This makes the judiciary a good place to start when thinking about whether a pattern of distribution of legal professionals will interfere with individual liberty. Three procedural mechanisms are used to ensure that, despite the egalitarian distribution, the executive or legislature cannot control the application of laws.

First is the separation of powers. Most countries distinguish, in principle and in practice, the judicial organs of the state from the legislative and executive. The theory is that their separation will insulate the judiciary from political control, furthering the goal of equal justice. It is, however, contingent whether the separation is required—or whether it will achieve its end. It is not always required. Judicial powers in the United Kingdom, for example, were, for a long time, exercised by a branch of the legislature, the House of Lords.[46] It was only in 2009 that the United Kingdom acquired a Supreme Court, and few would argue that its decisions have improved since. By contrast, there are numerous examples of countries that distinguish the judicial and political branches of government, yet where the former is not independent of the latter.

Second, the terms of appointment and tenure are often insulated from political control. The example of Venezuela illustrated the risks of state control of judicial appointments. For years, the United Kingdom was an exception here, too. The Lord Chancellor, a government minister, used to ask around and decide who the best candidates were. In 2005, an independent panel, the Judicial Appointments Commission, was created. The theory behind the change was, in part, that it would ensure that judicial appointments were not within the patronage of government ministers.

Finally, the judiciary regulates itself. A danger would arise if the government were able to select the judges to hear their disputes: not all judges are equally likely to decide in certain ways. The judiciary itself is, for this reason, usually in charge of the distribution of judges. They decide, for example, which of their brethren will sit on which cases.

These measures are usually sufficient to ensure that there is no interference with individual liberty even though there is a particular pattern of distribution for judges. They are widely thought so secure that concerns over the distribution of judges only arise when, as in the case of Venezuela, there is a political change which encroaches upon any of the three features. If there is a concern with the equal justice ideal, it arises at the level of the distribution of lawyers, not judges.

Our challenge concerns means, not ends. Our aim is to find a way of achieving equal justice without compromising political freedom. The discussion to this point suggests one crucial condition. Lawyers must be independent of, and able to act independently of, the state. No centralised political body should have unregulated control of the distribution of lawyers. If someone is charged with a crime, it would threaten liberty if the state, which brings the prosecution, were able to determine which lawyer the individual was allocated. The same goes for those situations where someone wants to accuse the government of illegality. The question is whether equal justice can be achieved consistently with this limit.

Whether a distributional system will interfere with individual freedom will depend on the proposed system. We should here distinguish between the design of the system and the precepts lawyers working within that system should follow.[47] System design is a difficult topic partly because so many have presumed that a market distribution must be used for lawyers. This has stifled discussion of practical ways to regulate these competing demands. We can, however, look to methods of regulating the distribution of judicial resources for analogies. In that context, judges' powers to change the law are limited. Rules are promulgated by legislators; they are applied by judges. Something like that model could be applied to the distribution of lawyers. A system could be created, in other words, where guidelines are issued by the central government but those guidelines are applied by lawyers.[48] The lawyers would regulate whether the guidelines were enforced; they would not set the guidelines.

Another principle we can import from the regulation of judicial powers is the separation of powers. That principle has been influential in ensuring that the equal distribution of judges does not undermine liberty. A similar principle, modified to fit the context, might be endorsed when distributing lawyers. It might be permissible for the government to have some control over the distribution of lawyers so long as that control is not localised to too few individuals or institutions. There is a world of a difference between a system that permits one government minister to issue guidelines and one where those guidelines are issued by the entire legislative body.

The second general consideration is the precepts lawyers working within the system follow. These can also be used to entrench the freedoms a distributional system might protect. Unlike their American counterparts, English barristers have ethical guidelines that include the "cab rank rule." This says that a lawyer must work for any client who requests her services, provided the work fits the lawyer's practice and expertise.[49] Something like this rule could be built into any alternative distributional mechanism. It would act as a further bulwark against any governmental interference with a particular case.

CONCLUSION

The first and main part of this book is now complete. I began with a characterisation of the problem legal systems face and proposed a principle, equal justice, that we should use to assess solutions. After criticising one institutional arrangement—the establishment of a market in legal resources—I proposed structures that can be used to secure equal justice. Each individual ought to have access to a basic level of legal resources; and, subject to the wrinkles considered in the previous chapter, the legal system should strive to achieve equal justice through the provision of equal resources. In this chapter, I rejected a number of the most plausible objections to these principles.

These are, however, not the only considerations relevant to assessment of a legal system. In Chapters 7, 8, and 9 I consider a number of further questions. Should claims of justice be dealt with in public courts? Would anything be lost if claims were resolved through an online dispute resolution process? What powers should judges have, when they decide cases? And who should pay for whatever procedures we do establish? These are some of the questions we must now approach. In public discussions, such questions are often considered in isolation. I aim to show, though, that the answers depend on the claims of the last few chapters. There is, for this reason, a continuity between the first half of the book and the second.

7

THE SITES OF JUSTICE

SITES

This chapter and the next are about where and how we should resolve claims of justice. These questions are often thought to be separate to the questions of earlier chapters, about the arrangement of legal resources. My central claim in these chapters is that this is a mistake: we cannot think sensibly about the proper arrangement of legal institutions until we have a theory about the proper distribution of the benefits and burdens of legality. The questions of these chapters are, for that reason, separate from but continuous with those of the earlier chapters.

In one way or another, a legal system needs to resolve individuals' claims of justice. Where should they do it? To answer that question, and to assess any particular legal system's arrangements, we need to know (at the very least) the various kinds of possible fora and which claims should be heard where. I address questions like these in this chapter. But they are not the only questions to ask about the design of sites of justice. Other issues depend upon a forum's powers. If, for example, a forum has the power to make laws, this should impact on its structure. There is, however, a broader preliminary question here, of whether legal fora should have this power. I defer consideration of that question, and the consequent institutional arrangements required, to the next chapter.

I begin by setting out the two topics that have concerned scholars: the fragmentation of types of legal forum and the physical location of those fora. The resolution of these topics depends on the proper arrangement of legal resources. And that, I argue, depends on the answers to the general questions of earlier chapters, of who should be allocated legal resources: the legal system should be structured to improve compliance with the general principles of justice concerning the distribution of legal resources (whatever they might be).

The next question is whether this account leaves anything out. Are there other important consequences that the arrangement of legal resources should promote? Or values that might be promoted and preserved by some arrangements but not others? I suggest that there are, and that they limit the extent to which we might permissibly privatise the judicial apparatus.

AN OVERVIEW OF THE TERRAIN

Fora

People have long worried about the complexity of legal fora, and the inequality this can engender. The *London Lickpenny,* an early fifteenth-century poem, tells the story of a Kentish man who goes to London to bring a legal claim. Our hero goes to Westminster Hall and appears before the Court of King's Bench, the Court of Common Pleas, the Chancery Court, and one final court, perhaps the Court of Exchequer. At each stage, he notes, "For lacke of money, I may not spede": for lack of money, he could not succeed.[1]

To understand the complications such complexity engenders, we should first distinguish between the range of fora and their functions. Most contemporary societies distinguish criminal and civil courts: criminal courts adjudicate on guilt and innocence, meting out state-sanctioned punishments; civil courts deal with private obligations and are, for the most part, unconcerned with punishment. This broad distinction splits into kaleidoscopic shards when we look more closely: for example, not only do most countries have an eclectic array of courts—criminal, commercial, construction, patents, planning, small claims, and so on—some also have tribunals and administrative agencies to decide on disputes. Arbitration—loosely, a privatised court system—is widespread, and a movement promoting "mediation" as an alternative to traditional methods of dispute resolution has recently risen to prominence.

Dividing fora according to the subject matter, as with courts specialising in construction disputes or intellectual property, is rarely a matter of concern. Other distinctions are less obviously benign. Consider that some courts, such as small claims courts, are specifically designed for claims of low value. These have different procedural requirements from the major courts, partly to save costs and partly to encourage litigants to represent themselves. Although the modern history of these courts begins in the 1960s,[2] the idea that a distinctive procedure should be available for claims of low value is ancient.[3] We must ask whether this is justifiable: I turn to that question later.

Judges take an oath to do justice according to law. They do not promise to reduce conflicts, to manage disputes, or to improve the economy. This suggests that we can distinguish fora according to their function: whether it is to do justice, or to do something else. Some institutions aim to do justice, to bring individuals' holdings into line with their underlying legal entitlements and obligations. A judge in court would be failing to live up to her professional oath if she approached things in any other way. Religious courts—for example, those adjudicating on marriage contracts between followers of a particular faith—and arbitration panels are no different, in this respect. Arbitration panels are, roughly speaking, private courts: subject to some complications, the point is to find out who owes whom what.

Compare, though, a justice system with one designed to maximise happiness (or to make money). A contrast can be drawn in this respect between courts and customer dispute resolution systems. People working in companies' complaints departments take no oath to do justice. When faced with an irate customer, their role is often to satisfy the customer (within limits). If the customer is unreasonably irate, doing justice might mean sending them away empty-handed; that may not be good business.

A second counter-example to the justice-tracking paradigm is the dispute-resolving paradigm. The most prominent example of the latter is mediation. This, the British government says, "is when an impartial person helps both sides work out an agreement."[4] It has become customary, even required under certain circumstances, in the United Kingdom.[5] Its purpose is to get prospective litigants to negotiate prior to going to court in the hope that they can settle their dispute. As Hazel Genn writes, "The 'spirit' of mediation is precisely to shift away from a focus on legal entitlement to a problem-solving frame of reference. It is about different interests and seeking to achieve a settlement that maximises the opportunities for both sides to achieve their interests."[6] In a passage that brings out the contrast between justice-tracking and dispute-resolving paradigms, Genn continues: "Mediation is about searching for a solution to a problem. There is no reference to the hypothesised outcome at trial. The mediator's role is to assist the parties in reaching a settlement of their dispute. The mediator does not make a judgement about the quality of the settlement. Success in mediation is a settlement that the parties can live with. The outcome of mediation is not about *just* settlement, it is *just about settlement*."[7]

This book is about questions of justice, not dispute resolution. But we should note one risk that dispute resolution fora face. They do not include the procedural safeguards of courts. For that reason Owen Fiss once warned that the dispute resolution paradigm is "at odds with a conception of justice that seeks to make the wealth of the parties irrelevant."[8] Of course, even if the justice system ought (as I have argued) to make wealth irrelevant in that sense, it does not mean that it will. Defenders of the dispute resolution model might say that things will be better if that model is endorsed wholesale. If so, it would then be no more than a regrettable necessity, "a capitulation to the conditions of mass society and should be neither encouraged nor praised."[9] But whether we need capitulate in this manner depends in part upon what the prospects of a just justice system are—and we cannot know that until we have worked out what such a system would look like. That is, of course, the point of this book.

Where Is the Forum?

The second feature we should consider is the locations of sites of justice. (For reasons that will become clear, we cannot necessarily say the *physical* locations.) Ritual and circumstance have long been important to adjudication, as a scene described by Homer in the seventh century B.C. demonstrates.[10] Hephaestus makes a shield for Achilles. It portrays two cities. One is at war, circled by "a divided army/gleaming in battle-gear."[11] In the assembly of the other,

> the people massed, streaming into the marketplace
> where a quarrel had broken out and two men struggled

over the blood-price for a kinsman just murdered.
One declaimed in public, vowing payment in full—
the other spurned him, he would not take a thing—
so both men pressed for a judge to cut the knot.
The crowd cheered on both, they took both sides,
but heralds held them back as the city elders sat
on polished stone benches, forming the sacred circle,
grasping in hand the staffs of clear-voiced heralds,
and each leapt to his feet to plead the case in turn.[12]

Two features of this scene are worth bringing out. We are accustomed
to think of legal proceedings being heard in public buildings constructed
or adapted to hear legal claims. A striking feature of Homer's depiction is
that adjudication takes place in "the place of assembly," a public space
without a building.[13] The sites of justice are a contingent fact. Athens had
structures dedicated to legal proceedings by the late fifth century B.C.,
though Athenians probably characterised courts more by their procedures
and props than the buildings that housed those things.[14] The United States
has held courts in taverns and schools; in England, few county courts are
located in buildings meant solely for justice.[15]

As financial constraints are tightened, the urge to close purpose-built
courts will increase: there will always be some office building where a court
can sit, and that might save some money. More radically, it will be asked
whether adjudication should gather individuals together at all: disputes
could be resolved online, with parties linked only by the internet.[16]

The theatre of adjudication is important in Homer's scene: the adjudication takes place in a public space, with all welcome to view the proceedings. This is an early example of a long tradition of legal fora being open
to people other than the litigants. In one speech of Demosthenes, he says
that he speaks for the "gentlemen of the jury" as well as "that circle of
hearers outside the barrier."[17] This commitment to openness is sometimes
elevated to the level of principle. The 1676 Fundamental Laws of West New
Jersey, for example, commanded "that in all publick courts of justice for
tryals of causes . . . any person or persons, inhabitants of the said Province
may freely come into, and attend the said courts, and hear and be present,
at all and any such tryals as shall be there had or passed, that justice may
not be done in a corner nor in any covert manner."[18] Contemporary courts
are usually open to the public; modern courts often try to increase access

by, for example, streaming their hearings online or, in the case of the US Supreme Court, providing recordings of oral argument.

Publicity is common to most depictions of justice (or injustice) being done. But it is not immutable, in life or in literature. In Kafka's *The Trial,* Josef K never even discovers the charge against him; contemporary trials of suspected terrorists sometimes take place in secret, with the accused not allowed to see the case against them. Whether a forum is public or private, in this sense, is scalar, not binary: a forum might be more or less open to litigants or the public at large.[19] And the crucial question is how to assess different arrangements.

SITES AND PRINCIPLES OF JUSTICE

An arrangement of legal fora is valuable chiefly in virtue of the consequences of arranging things one way or another. In principle, any good or bad consequence of a particular arrangement counts in favour or against it. There are two consequences of particular note when it comes to assessing the arrangement of legal fora.

The most salient are those that contribute to a legal system's compliance with more general principles of justice governing the distribution of legal resources. I have characterised the particular problem of justice a legal system faces and made proposals about the best way to resolve that problem.[20] It is not important here whether you agree with those principles. Instead, whatever the best principles of justice for a system are, a fragmented justice system might help secure them; it could also undermine them. The normal justification for one arrangement or another—be it fragmented fora, moving the site of justice, or deciding who runs a forum—is that it will lead to better compliance with more general principles of justice. Equally, the normal reason to object to a particular systemic arrangement is that it will lead to lower overall compliance.

In the next section I suggest a second set of consequences of particular importance: the contribution particular arrangements make to the public's acceptance (or rejection) of the burdens of the legal system. Legal systems, as a public good, must be structured in such a way to reveal their value. The preconditions for a legal system's success—such as widespread acceptance of its authority and costs—may otherwise disintegrate. This captures part, though perhaps not all, of the truth in the important idea that justice must be done and be seen to be done.

Virtues

One size does not fit all. If dispute resolution systems never varied their format based on the type of claim, they would fail to respond to the distinctive concerns different disputes raise. I will here suggest three virtues of fragmentation, arising out of that simple point. First, fragmentation can be used to promote adjudicative quality (i.e., that the fora are more likely to resolve a token dispute according to the underlying reasons of justice).[21] Consider healthcare. Those who believe that everyone should have access to the same level of health resources do not think that all health problems should be dealt with in the same way. People with cancer should see oncologists; people with heart troubles should see cardiologists; and so on.

There is nothing innately objectionable, therefore, in a legal system having a construction court as well as a patents court; it is probably a good thing. This fragmentation attempts to channel specialists into one forum or another and to ensure that the procedures are streamlined to the contextual concerns. Specialisation can improve the truth-tracking qualities of a court: it can ensure that courts get it right more often. This can lead to more justice overall.

A similar point can be made about the places where justice is done. Jeremy Bentham, for example, argued that "where there is no publicity there is no justice. Publicity is the very soul of justice. It is the keenest spur to exertion and the surest of all guards against improbity. It keeps the judge himself while trying under trial."[22] Publicity is claimed to discipline the court. It might also discipline participants, such as witnesses.[23] For any proposed arrangement, one question is its effects on the outcomes of cases. The effects are contingent: publicity does not always march in sync with legality.

The second virtue of fragmentation is efficiency. Suppose we know that a particular case was decided justly. That does not tell us very much about how good the legal system is. We would also want to know how often justice is done in cases that come before courts: perhaps that case was an aberration. Even this is not enough. Suppose that every case that comes

before the courts is decided justly: we still need to know how many possible cases there are. A legal system that deals with five cases per year is not
much good, even if it deals with every one of them expertly, if there are 5
million claims it has not had time to get to. A legal system is inefficient, we
can say, if it is not doing as much justice as it could given the resources
that are available.[24]

These examples show that we should distinguish two questions. One
question is, for a particular case, whether justice is done. The first virtue of
some systemic arrangement is its contribution to the likelihood of justice
being done in a particular case. A second question is, for a particular legal
system, whether justice is done efficiently. A second virtue of fragmentation is that some systemic arrangements are more efficient than others.

Fragmentation of legal fora can lead to greater efficiency—and, therefore, to more perfect compliance with the more general principles of justice. If a legal system only had a gold-plated service, this might do very well
for the rich, but it is not much use to those with claims of lower value: if it
were very expensive to bring a claim, it would be instrumentally irrational
for many people with good claims to bring those claims. The creation of a
small claims court can make it economically worthwhile to bring a claim
that would otherwise have gone unlitigated—and it can do so without requiring the sort of expense that the gold-plated service requires. Taking
some money from the gold-plated service to support the small claims court
might make for a more efficient justice system.

Similar things can said about movements to replace physical sites of justice, such as courts, with online courts. Online systems might be easier and
cheaper to navigate, allowing more individuals to bring their claims.
(Whether they are more efficient depends in part upon the procedures used
by the online court.) And the same thing can be said about permitting individuals to contract out of the public system, by means of (say) arbitration. Contracting out might lead to more disputes being resolved according
to their merits than might a proscription on contracting out.

These are possible virtues of fragmentation revealed through the value
of efficiency. Fragmentation can enable more individuals to bring claims
by creating a more efficient dispute-resolution system. There is nothing objectionable about this. However, when perennial concerns over the costs of
justice are combined with mistakes about value, talk of efficiency can have

profoundly inegalitarian consequences. Let me outline the issue here at greater length.

In 1648, John Cooke complained that "a man must spend above 10.l to recover 5.l" in court.[25] The principal reason costs can be worrisome is, as Roland Wilson put it, that they "render it more prudent to submit to injustice than to sue or defend."[26] This concern grounds persistent and important efforts to lower the costs of litigation.

However, we cannot infer the importance of a claim from the mere fact of its pecuniary value. A cynic, Lord Darlington says, is "a man who knows the price of everything and the value of nothing."[27] The cynic's mistake in the legal context is that claims with lower pecuniary value do not matter less simply because the sums in dispute are lower. Suppose that there is a breach of contract case worth $1 million and an employment tribunal dispute worth $5,000. If financial price were the determinant of value, the first claim would be two hundred times the value of the second. But what if the plaintiff in the first case is a rich investment banker who was denied a bonus and the plaintiff in the second case is a black secretary dismissed on the grounds of her race? We might justifiably allocate more resources to the resolution of her case than his. Partly this is because $5,000 matters more to the secretary than the banker: for her, it might make the difference between homelessness and temporary security; for him, it might determine whether he holidays upstate or in the Hamptons. There are also stronger societal reasons to ensure assurance in her case than his: elimination of racial discrimination is more important than perfect performance of contractual rights.

When scholars talk of efficiency, they sometimes shift from the reasonable claim (that a more efficient dispute resolution system is a good thing) to the unreasonable one (that this means the amount we spend on legal disputes should depend on the financial amount at stake.) That is easy to do given concerns like Cooke's. But, as I will argue at greater length in Chapter 9, this rests on a mistaken understanding of how the costs of justice should be understood. So long as we guard against this Wildean fallacy, efficiency is a good thing—and can be achieved by fragmenting legal fora.

The third virtue of fragmentation concerns bargaining positions. Enforcement procedures cast a shadow.[28] Even when individuals are not before courts, their private settlements can be affected by the fact that, if their dispute cannot be resolved, the parties are ultimately able to take their claim to a court: that is the idea of bargaining in the law's shadow. If there is no plausible enforcement procedure at the end of a bargaining process, the person who is better able to walk away will have a stronger negotiating position. If, for example, a disgruntled employee is functionally incapable of bringing a legal claim against her erstwhile employer, any argument she has that she was unlawfully dismissed will likely fall on deaf ears: an unscrupulous employer would have no interest in settling her claim, and could not be forced to engage with the argument, because the employee could not get into court. This illustrates a third dimension of importance: by leaving open paths to coercive adjudication and enforcement, a functioning justice system promotes justice in private settlements.

A legal system's success depends, this shows, not only on what happens in individual court cases but also on how wide the shadow cast by enforcement procedures is. The wider the shadow, the more likely it is that private settlements will conform with the underlying justice of individual disputes. This is part of the reason why a fair or equal distribution of legal resources is valuable: that distribution ensures a wide shadow. Insofar as fragmentation makes the legal system more accessible, providing more avenues for individuals to bring their claims, it can ensure not only greater efficiency but (by the same token) greater conformity with justice in settlements out of court. If there is a small claims court or an employment tribunal, an individual's threat to bring a legal dispute will be taken more seriously.

Vices

Most of the bad things about fragmentation of fora concern the consequences of one arrangement or another. In particular, they concern the impact of the arrangement on conformity with the general principles of justice. In that respect we can say that the vices of fragmentation are chiefly the opposite of its virtues: the virtues are increased compliance with the principles of justice; the vices are reduced compliance.

Consider the first virtue of fragmentation, adjudicative quality. Fragmentation can also mean the creation of fora that differ in quality, with none able to learn from the others. The second virtue of fragmentation was efficiency; inefficiency is a sign of a bad distributive arrangement. For example, some institutions have particularly high barriers to access: consider the consumer with a small claim on their mobile phone contract who is asked to litigate in a foreign state. Further, a dizzying array of dispute resolution fora can make it difficult for individuals to navigate the legal system. The hapless litigant of the *London Lickpenny* was able to go to four different courts because they were all in the same location; if there were four courts scattered through London, each with filing fees, getting to the right court in the first place would be important, and fragmentation can make that hard. The consequence is that some systematic arrangements will be such that not enough people with claims of justice are able to access the appropriate forum.

Certain forms of fragmentation can give rise to particular risks that deserve special note. The use of private companies to manage dispute resolution, as for example in arbitration, gives rise to twin concerns of marketisation and private power capture. Private entities might distribute their resources according to a market; that is, I have argued, an inappropriate distributional mechanism for legal resources. Or private entities might be subject to capture and control by larger entities, ones that often use the justice system. Practically important as these vices are, it is important to see that there is nothing distinctive about them: they are objectionable because they decrease conformity with the general principles of justice.

There are two additional vices that can arise from fragmentation of fora, which go beyond want of the virtues outlined above. These vices are both problems of an inegalitarian structure. First is the risk that fragmentation will lead to inconsistent decisions across the board. If there are too many and disparate fora, like cases might be funnelled into different branches of the legal system; distinct branches might approach the same case in a different way. Like cases will not be treated alike.

Second, some systemic arrangements can make it easier for two-tier justice systems to emerge. Fora can be made accessible to those with fewer means in one of two ways: subsidies (such as legal aid) can be provided to enable people to access high quality fora; or new, cheaper fora can be created (such as small claims or online courts). The risk of the second solution is that the fora will be cheaper precisely because their quality is lower. Online courts might be cheaper and thus, in principle, capable of processing more claims; however, they often rely upon written presentation of claims, which can be off-putting or impossible for those without lawyers to draft. And the kind of litigants likely to have low-value claims are those disproportionately unable to write their own claims or hire others to do it for them.

This shows a tension inherent in attempts to make legal fora accessible: a reform might be simultaneously good (opening sites of justice to individuals of fewer means) and bad (creating inequality in the provision of the instruments of justice, because the new sites are worse). This risk is exacerbated by the language of proportionality. Tribunals created for claims of lower pecuniary value are very often treated as if the claims have less urgent moral value. Procedures are simplified to make those tribunals cheaper (and, so, more "proportionate" to the sums in dispute). There is some evidence that tribunals, a type of forum created in the United Kingdom to increase the access poorer individuals have to legal resources, lead to a worse quality of justice. One report found that there was worse decision making and high error rates that were not challenged (because individuals were confused by the system or lacked the knowledge to advance their claims).[29] In that way, those with claims of lower value can end up getting a different quality of justice.

Permitting individuals to contract out of state-provided legal services—permitting, for example, individuals to arbitrate their disputes (and then have those awards enforced in public courts)—can undermine the more general principles of justice in at least two ways. First, if the private option is (for whatever reason) superior to the public option, the resultant arrangement will not be egalitarian. Second, the permission to contract out reduces the incentives those able to contract out have to support and invest in the public option. This reduces the quality of the justice system provided to those unable to contract out and, thereby, exacerbates the inequality inherent in the creation of rival public and private options.

THE PRINCIPLE OF PUBLICITY

In this section I propose four arguments for an irreducible core of "publicity" to legal institutions.[30] These constrain the pursuit of increased conformity with the legal principles enumerated in earlier chapters: the irreducible core must be met even at the expense of those principles. There are a range of practical implications of this argument: states must not permit the advent of online dispute resolution to obliterate access to information about processes and outcomes; and they must ensure that any contracting out of the instruments of justice (for example, through arbitration clauses) does not draw a veil of secrecy over those processes.

Before making these arguments I consider the language of "privatisation," an apparent antonym of "publicity."

Privatisation and Open Justice

It is customary, in contemporary debates about justice, to talk of "privatisation" of the justice system. We know that utilities, like water and electricity, can be privatised. More recent debates have asked the extent to which governments can contract out of core state activities. The George W. Bush administration's use of Blackwater to provide "security services" in Iraq—some of those in Abu Ghraib were private contractors—forced us to ask what, if anything, is wrong with a government hiring mercenaries to enact its wars.[31] The national legal system has not been spared this gaze. Can, morally, the provision of prison services be privatised? Should the legal system itself be privatised?[32]

This is an unhelpful lexicon with which to think about the justice system. "Privatisation" is a chameleon word, changing shape depending on the context in which it is used.[33] Most of the virtues and vices of privatisation can be understood in the terms already described: as more or less complete conformity with the principles of justice. There are, though, two further considerations that are sometimes discussed in this language. The first is the publicity of the doing of justice; that is the topic of this section. The second is the ability of individuals bound by the legal system to identify with that legal system. That is a topic of the next chapter.

Our question can be described as a concern with "open justice." The instruments of justice can be more or less open to the public. In this section, I argue that the justice system must be minimally open to the public if it is to sustain itself as a justice system. This limits the extent to which dispute resolution should be done in private. And that, in turn, makes general demands on the sites of justice: there must remain public instances of justice being done; it must be possible to find out the facts about how justice is done. If this is not possible, the preconditions of a successful justice system will be corroded; ultimately, they may dissolve.

Four Arguments for Publicity

ASSURANCE

John Rawls's theory of justice is developed in "ideal" conditions: "everyone is presumed to act justly and to do his part in upholding just institutions."[34] Even in these conditions, Rawls claims, people "lack full confidence in one another. They may suspect that some are not doing their part, and so they may be tempted not to do theirs. The general awareness of these temptations may eventually cause the scheme to break down."[35] To prevent this, he suggests that "a public system of penalties" is required: this means that everyone is sure that everyone else is playing by the rules. This gives us, in Rawls's terms, "assurance" that "the common agreement is being carried out."[36]

He does not develop this argument in any detail. Although he refers only to criminal law, that is not enough to convince everyone in society to obey the rules: it leaves out the entirety of private law (such as employers' treatment of their employees) and public law. If some are able to break the law with impunity, respect for the law as a whole degrades: in those countries where excuses can be bought, the law becomes a system people have to manage rather than a source of authoritative norms.

To ensure that the collective scheme does not break down there must be some minimal level of compliance with the gamut of legal rules. Compliance alone, though, will not be enough. There must also be, as Rawls implies, a "general awareness" of compliance: even if everyone is obeying the law, if decisions of courts are entirely in secret, it is hard to be sure that others are playing their part.

This is an argument for publicity: only if justice is seen to be done does everyone have assurance; only if there is assurance can the burdensome collective scheme of legality be maintained. This argument does not require that every decision on matters of justice be open to the public. It does require, though, that there is sufficient publicity that any rational person has no strong reason to doubt that all groups are doing their bit. If certain groups—such as wealthy corporations—are able to agree private "sweet-heart" deals with the government on the payment of their taxes, that undermines assurance. If other groups—such as powerful individuals—are able to resolve all disputes with their employees in private arbitration, that undermines assurance. There must be some core of publicity to the sites of justice.

TREATMENT

Only certain structures of authority are compatible with the requirement that authority be exercised over individuals in a manner that treats them with respect. Disagreements about justice are an ineliminable feature of political community. Part of the function of a justice system is to resolve those disagreements. There are winners and losers of that process. It matters, if the losers are to be treated with respect, that the reasons for the ultimate outcomes are intelligible to them.

There are a few features to this point. Legal disputes often involve both arguments of principle, about what norms ought to govern interactions, and arguments about how general principles apply to individual cases. Any process that purports to resolve those disagreements, as all legal procedures do, ought to be public to the individuals concerned: it would fail to take individuals' views about justice seriously if authoritative resolutions contrary to the individuals' views were not explained to those individuals.[37]

This justifies an openness of process to the individual litigants. But it would be too blinkered to think that dispute resolution between individual litigants is of no concern to others in society. As Thomas Christiano writes, "Each citizen has fundamental interests in being able to see that he is being treated as an equal in a society where there is significant disagreement about justice and wherein each citizen can acknowledge fallibility in their capacities for thinking about their interests and about justice."[38] It is not enough that justice is done in individual cases. It is also important that everyone is able to see that justice is done. Even if two parties' cases are dealt with in the same way, they each have an interest in knowing that the other did not receive preferential treatment. The reason this matters is partly assurance. But it also matters because any other system will fail to satisfy the interest all have in seeing that they are treated as an equal.

This point can be made in a more broad way. Not everyone will be wronged; of those who are wronged, not all will end up in court. For these groups, it matters that there is a just structure to the legal system: that has been the topic of the last few chapters. But it also matters that they see that the legal system is just, that it is protective of their interests. Publicity is important for this reason. It also puts limits on the extent of permissible fragmentation in the legal system. Fragmentation can lead to confusion, undermining the message that all are treated equally.

Public Culture

A third reason for publicity, one that relates to the argument about assurance, is shown by the trial of Orestes for the murder of his mother. Athena opens the trial with an address to those who are gathered:

> Call for order, herald, marshal our good people.
> Lift the Etruscan battle-trumpet,
> strain it to full pitch with human breath,
> crash out a stabbing blast along the ranks.[39]

After the trumpet sounds, she goes on:

> And while this court of judgement fills my city,
> silence will be best. So that you can learn
> my everlasting laws.[40]

This is a public trial, open for all to see; Athena insists upon it, calling for the city to observe. The educative function is said by her to instruct the people in the law. Whatever plausibility that might have had in Athenian days, it has an air of unreality today. How many people find out about their legal obligations by watching judicial proceedings?

But perhaps Athena's point was not the instruction on individual laws. The problem of the *Oresteia* is how to break the cycle of feud violence: Agamemnon's murder of Iphigenia begat Clytemnestra's murder of Agamemnon; this leads Orestes to murder Clytemnestra and the furies pursue him for yet further violence in retribution. The trial of Orestes is an attempt to adjudicate on his murder. It is also an attempt to institute a new order: legality in place of vengeance. This might be achieved through an appeal to reason, but reason alone might not be enough for everyone. Symbolism can inculcate the sense that the system is a good one and compliance required. The symbols of justice are a public statement of the value of the legal system; given how few people end up in courts, these symbols are some of the only ways in which citizens interact with the system.

The importance of this point can also be seen through the kind of burdens people must bear to support a legal system. Legal systems require people to do things they might not want to do—and there can be sanctions for noncompliance. There are also obligations to fund the system, discharged principally through taxation; I will examine those in Chapters 9 and 10. In these ways legal systems require people to do all sorts of things that may not be in their immediate self-interest. A central practical question any system of authority—a family, a gang, a state—faces is how to get people to comply with these obligations.

One approach is brute force. Spectacular public executions can be understood in part as an attempt to ensure people comply with at least some of their legal obligations. Gangs can enact similar spectacles: in Guatemala, one gang has been known to leave body parts of the dismembered in public places, a vivid warning of the risks of noncompliance. But brute force is costly and, for a large state, impractical. Discovering whether people are complying is expensive and it is not in the collective's immediate interests to apply heavy sanctions: an executed individual cannot pay any taxes. Much better if people comply with their legal obligations because of a sense of duty.

How can that sense of duty be inculcated? Some public goods, such as schools or hospitals, are widely used by almost everyone in society. With these goods, their benefits are quite tangible. This makes it easier to convey a sense of public duty with respect to them: although there are passionate disagreements about the level of individual obligation, few doubt that some taxes should help fund schools and hospitals. The justice system is different. Most people rarely have to go to court. Public symbols of justice are about the only contact they have with the legal system. If there was no public representation of the justice system—no courts, for example, with all legal proceedings being heard in office blocks—it would be easy to forget the ceaseless workings of that system.

This suggests a good reason to have purpose-built institutions to house courts and to make those courts open to the public at large. The buildings represent the community's dedication to having a justice system, and the kind of courts the community sets up makes a statement about their attitude to

the justice system. The statement might be about particular legal obligations. For example, a song of Bruce Springsteen tells the story of a man
talking to his son, teaching him about the town. The "flag flying over the
courthouse," he says,

> Means certain things are set in stone:
> Who we are, what we'll do and what we won't.[41]

The child is thus taught a public ethos, about the obligations of citizens,
through the image of the justice system.

The representation can also stand as a testament to the cost of living
under the rule of law. Courts are a tangible expense. When people are told
their taxes go to fund the justice system, the presence of those buildings
are a representation of the kind of things the money goes towards. It is not
so much that the obligations to fund the system can only be justified if spent,
say, on the construction of buildings. The buildings are a statement about
the collective value not only of the particular court but the system in which
that court is a part. Their construction can remind all in the community of
that value, helping to cultivate the ongoing sense of duty necessary for a
justice system to survive over time.

Openness

The Soviet Union after Stalin's rule, Hannah Arendt claimed, was not "totalitarian in the strict sense of the term."[42] As evidence, she refers to the
trial of two Soviet writers, Andrei Sinyavsky and Yuli Daniel, arrested in
1966 for publishing in foreign periodicals articles critical of the Soviet Union
and illegal at home. After a secret trial, they were sentenced to seven and
five years' hard labour, respectively. Yet fragments of their trial were reported in foreign media. For that reason, Arendt says, the writers "did not
disappear in the hole of oblivion which totalitarian rulers prepare for their
opponents."[43] Her arresting analysis: "The very fact that members of the
intellectual opposition (even though not an open one), can make themselves
heard in the courtroom and count on support outside it, do not confess to
anything but plead not guilty, demonstrates that we deal here no longer with
total domination."[44]

There is something important here though it is hard to pin down. Perhaps the idea is this: adjudication in public openly recognises the burden

of justification that states face in their legal practices. Resolving disputes through law involves an extraordinary use of force against individuals, one that brings with it terrible risks. How can these burdens be justified? One feature of that justification is self-referential: the state's open recognition of the burden it faces. Only if the state appreciates the scale of the task it faces can we be sure that it is approaching that task in the appropriate manner, and only if there is a public demonstration of that recognition can we, those ruled, be sure that the task is approached in the appropriate manner.

Publicity here relates closely to the second argument, because it relates to the manner of treatment of litigants. But the structure of the argument is a little different. The central feature of the second argument was the need to justify these processes to the individuals concerned. That is true here, too. But its central feature is the need for the state to justify itself. And it can only do this if its cumbersome apparatus of justice is open, in some sense, to inspection: so all can be sure that those caught in its tentacles are there for good reason, and that none "disappear into the hole of oblivion."

WHERE AND HOW

This chapter has been about the places where claims of justice are heard. We now turn to a related issue: how claims of justice are resolved within these sites. There is an important link here between the last points I have made and the topic of the next chapter. A concern of privatising the justice system is a concern with the identity of the person or system making the decision or taking the action in question. A legal system might be more readily justified if its institutions are those of the state, rather than if the state devolves its authority to private bodies. The central question of the next chapter is whether we need to discriminate, for the purposes of certain functions, between institutions of state. Most pertinently: should we permit judges to make law in these sites of justice? And, if we should, how should that affect the structure of the legal system?

8

JUST LAW-MAKING

INTRODUCTION

Lawmakers are able to change what people are obligated to do through a form of words. If a statute is passed saying "it is illegal to steal," the lawmakers are not trying to describe the situation before they passed the law; their statement that something is the law makes it the law. This is an extraordinary power, one that can have drastic consequences for any of the law's subjects. We should be careful whom we give the power to—and any institution with such a power should be carefully designed.

Part of the function of courts is to apply and enforce the laws made by Parliament.[1] When they do this, it is easy enough to say that they act as faithful servants of democracy. But courts are also able to create and change law. This gives rise to two questions of structural design. First, how can a legal system be structured to ensure that this power is consistent with democratic values? Second, how should the system be structured to ensure that the power is used in the best possible way? Those are the two main questions addressed in this chapter. Before turning to them, it is worth saying something about the judicial power: why judges have it and what its limits are.

JUDGES AS LAWMAKERS

The Power

Judges are sometimes portrayed as journalists. Their role, on this story, is to report the facts of disputes and their legal implications—without determining what those implications are. Judges are thus contrasted with legislators, who determine what the law actually is. Montesquieu, for example, wrote that judges are "only the mouth that pronounces the words of the law, inanimate beings who can moderate neither its force nor its rigor."[2] The judicial power to make law can be obscured by the way in which courts talk. They rarely distinguish between instances when they are making law and those when they are merely applying it; they may not even know when that line is crossed. Judges usually make law, when they make law, by asserting that the norm in question already is the law.

John Roberts, the chief justice of the US Supreme Court, seemed to embrace the contrast between journalists and legislators in his confirmation hearing. Judges, he said, should be like baseball umpires: "It's my job to call balls and strikes, and not to pitch or bat."[3] Of course, even umpires do more than report the facts. They change the facts whenever they make an incorrect call: if the umpire does not call a strike, no strike enters the record (even if the umpire made a mistake).[4] This illustrates the first aspect of the judicial power: to change the rights of litigants through a legal order. If a judge decrees that we owe another person money, we have an obligation to pay regardless of our antecedent duties; Socrates might have been innocent of corrupting the youth, but the jury's decision changed his legal status to "guilty."

Umpires do not change the rules of the game, even when they make incorrect calls. Judges are different: they can create law through their rulings and interpretations.[5] Sometimes this is through the creation of a broad set of rules: a lot of the law of contract is judge-made; the law of murder was also fashioned by the judiciary.[6] Judges also provide determinacy on questions left indeterminate by legislators. No matter how hard legislators try, legislation will always be silent on certain matters. Felix Frankfurter, a former justice of the US Supreme Court, referred to a cartoon where one senator says to another: "This new bill is too complicated to understand. We'll just have to pass it to find out what it means."[7]

Even when judges have these broader powers, they are not the same as legislators. In John Austin's Delphic phrase, a judge "legislates as properly judging, and not as properly legislating."[8] Judges only create law by adjudicating on a particular case; the law they create comes from the reasons given in the particular case. Nevertheless, one judge's decision on any of these matters binds future judges in similar cases. This is so regardless of the merit of the laws promulgated: hence Portia's warning that once something is a precedent "many an error by the same example/Will rush into the state."[9] This feature of law-making, which perpetuates error, has long been criticised. Bentham, for example, thought that following precedents was "acting without reason, to the declared exclusion of reason, and thereby in declared opposition to reason."[10] Why should we accept these powers?

The Basic Justification

Disagreements about individual cases—whether someone has breached a contract, whether another committed a crime—are inevitable. If laws are to function, there has to be some way of adjudicating on individual cases. Further, a lot of goods laws (such as those I have already mentioned: the law of contract and property, or the law of murder) were developed by judges. These two facts suggest the basic justification of the judicial power: the good consequences of allocating the power to them.

If that is the basic justification, there is a question of how the system should be designed to ensure judges can make good law. I consider that question later in this chapter. We first need to consider the democrat's objection to judicial law-making and the way in which a legal system might be arranged to ameliorate it. For there is, as former Supreme Court justice Antonin Scalia put it, an "uncomfortable relationship [between] common-law lawmaking [and] democracy."[11] Democratic election is a hallmark of political legitimacy, and judges are normally not elected: this means that they are not accountable to the population, if at all, in anything like the customary way of contemporary political procedures.

A democrat might object, therefore, that the basic justification misses the point. Legitimate law-making has two different features. Laws should, everyone agrees, be substantively just; the disagreement concerns when the law is just. But, the democrat could point out, substantive justice is insufficient for legitimacy. Suppose that a start-up in Silicon Valley decided that it could make better laws than the elected officials in the US Congress. The chief executive officer (CEO) might defend the company by saying that its laws were more just than those of Congress. She might, in other words, point to the substantive justice of its laws. And the reply might well be: "Who are you to decide that?" The objection is to the provenance of the proposed laws.[12]

Before we consider how to design the system to improve the quality of law made, we must consider the democrat's objection—and ask how the system should be designed to meet it.

DEMOCRATIC LAW

I begin with an account of the value of democracy: only if we know why democracy matters can we know whether judicial law-making is truly objectionable on democratic grounds; and, if it is, how we might ameliorate those concerns. Some judicial law-making, I argue, is necessary in a functioning democracy. Finally, I suggest two ways in which the legal system can be structured to meet the democrat's concerns.

Democratic Value

For any source of law we can ask both how good the law is and how legitimate its legislator is. Legislators' legitimacy is usually now linked with their democratic credentials. Why, though? What is the value of a democratic procedure?

Democratic procedures are sometimes valuable because they lead to better justice in the laws. Democratic legislators know that they face elections in the future. In a functioning democracy, elections provide two inducements to good legislating. First, the legislators know that they can only stay in power if they have the approval of the electorate. Second, they know that if they are removed from office they will be under the control of others; this gives them reasons to moderate their laws, in the hope that future lawmakers adopt a similar practice.

This frames the value of democracy by reference to its substantive outcomes. Democratic procedures are good, it suggests, because they tend to generate laws with good content. And there is clearly something to this. But the argument makes democracy's value a contingent matter: it all depends on whether it does lead to better laws. Not everyone agrees that democracy's value is entirely contingent in this way. Even if the Silicon Valley company was right, even if its laws were substantively just, many might baulk at the idea of outsourcing their country's legislature to the California coast. This suggests that some further value is at stake in democratic procedures.

What? Two features to democratic value are important in our context.

POLITICAL EQUALITY

An important part of the story is the problem to which "democracy" is the solution. Two features of modern societies are important: first, that very many benefits are possible only if we coordinate our activities; second, that we disagree about what ends we ought to pursue and what justice requires. These disagreements—which, as with abortion or euthanasia, sometimes concern matters of life and death—can be sincere, the underlying commitments deeply held. A central task of political institutions is to sustain a polity, ensuring that its benefits endure in the face of these disagreements. Political institutions must find some way of instituting a set of rules that we can live by, even in the face of these disagreements.

On practical grounds alone, a society must give certain people powers to resolve such disagreements: to the elders or to a monarch, for example. Any procedure that gives these powers to particular people seems to elevate that person or those persons above the rest of the community. The democrat's "Who are you to decide?" objection is felt powerfully here: a core tenet of democratic belief is that no single individual gets to decide how our disagreements are to be resolved. This means that certain demands, no matter how reasonable in content, are only acceptable if made in a certain way. The value of a democratic decision seems to be that it evades the "Who are you to decide?" objection: if a decision is made on behalf of, and justifiable to, the community as a whole, it is a reasonable resolution of disagreement about content. It is a way of securing political cooperation without raising any individual above the rest in status.

SELF-AUTHORSHIP

There is another way of understanding the "Who are you to decide?" objection. It is not the brute fact, that the person deciding is raised in political status above the others, but that their being so-raised cuts off the opportunity for an individual or group to chart their own destiny. This echoes the anti-paternalist's characteristic objection, raised in Chapter 6: the idea that there is something wrong with an individual's decision being taken for them.

That objection is clear enough when the decision is an individual's; it is less obvious how it relates to a group, such as a city or country. Democracy can be understood as a way of ensuring there is sufficient self-determination on these questions of value. If legislators are elected from the population at large, those delegated to propound the law can be understood as the population's representatives; the norms propounded can be seen as the public's norms. A democratic procedure can therefore be seen as a method of ensuring the law's subjects understand those laws as theirs.[13]

The Argument of Necessity

The important question is less whether judicial law-making is democratic than whether it is consistent with the values of political equality and individual self-authorship. I will argue that it can be so, but that these values make important claims on the structure of the legal system. First, though, I want to suggest that some measure of judicial law-making is necessary if a democracy is to function. To the extent that there is this necessary relation, judges are the servants of democracy, acquiring democratic value from their support of democratic institutions.

I distinguished two features of judicial law-making: first, judges' ability to rule on the case before them; second, their power to, by so ruling, change the rules that apply to others in society. The argument of necessity is the claim that a system of law would not work if judges were not given the first power. There must be some delegation to individuals (like judges) or groups (like juries) to rule on individual cases; without it, a system of law would not work.

The necessity arises out of two perennial features of legislation: uncertainty about the content created and disagreement about the application

of that content to particular facts. Even if everyone agrees that it is illegal
to corrupt the youth of Athens, we might have legitimate and deep disagreements over whether what Socrates did met that definition.

There is then a question of how to respond to these facts. Bentham
thought that judges should ask Parliament to rule on any points of uncertainty.[14] But this is utterly unworldly. Legislation can be incredibly complex, requiring very many interpretive rulings; given that the courts have
not the time to hear all of them, it is unrealistic to suggest that Parliament
could. The options are to give up the practice of government by legislation
or to delegate power to some individuals to administer the laws. If the
second option is the only way to preserve a system of democratic legislation, the judicial role in ruling on individual cases can be reframed: not as
a threat to democracy, but as a necessary part of a democratic legal order.

If this argument is accepted, the question is then how far it carries. Can
it justify permitting judges to create laws through these rulings? It is doubtful
that this is a necessary part of a working legal order: numerous systems
disclaim any such power, and they seem to function perfectly well. But there
are serious risks in not granting this power. Where the law is indeterminate, if the individual ruling does not generate a precedent, a judge in a
future case can decide in a different way. Once there has been an individual
ruling, the doctrine of precedent means that future judges are bound by the
first ruling. Their power to decide in the individual case is minimised and
the prospect that like cases will be treated alike is advanced.

The grant of the second power to judges can, therefore, be understood
as a constraint on their first power: the permission to rule on individual
cases raises the risk of arbitrary and unequal distinctions in rulings; the
power to make law is granted to minimise the risk of that arbitrariness.
This also explains the curious feature of judicial law-making, that the judge
"legislates as properly judging, and not as properly legislating."[15] The
second judicial power only arises through the exercise of their first; and the
first power is required in a democracy.

Legitimate Lawmakers

This goes a long way to justifying the judicial power to make laws. A just
justice system must still be structured to ensure that the law-making power

is, where possible, consistent with the democratic values outlined above. Two important features of institutional design have received insufficient attention.

Rights of Access

Legislatures can be more or less democratic. The mere fact that everyone in society has a vote does not tell us everything we need to know. In the United States, a series of Supreme Court decisions has removed most restrictions on the amount corporations and non-profit groups can spend on federal elections, and how much individuals can donate to political action committees.[16] In the election campaign of November 2016, 0.5 per cent of Americans made donations larger than $200; that 0.5 per cent accounted for nearly 70 per cent of the money spent in the campaign.[17] Facts like these make people worried that the legislature does not serve each vote equally: the voice of certain members of the community is much louder than others. If a legislature becomes too corrupt, it is no longer possible to regard it as speaking for a community. That is so even if it has some formal features— for example, one person, one vote—that appear democratic.

Similar points can be made about judicial law-making. Judicial decisions arise out of individual litigants' arguments. The kind of arguments made in courts can influence the laws that are made. This input is one reason why the law in different countries can diverge. Different communities place different weight on the same reasons. When it comes to balancing rights to free expression against rights to privacy, for example, Europeans tend to favour the latter interest more than Americans. An important consequence is that if only certain interests are represented in legal arguments, only certain laws will be made. This might make the content of laws less just. For example, if only rich and powerful companies litigate about contractual disputes, concerns about inequality of bargaining power might be ignored.[18] But the concern is not only with the content of the law. Just as differential voice in the legislative process is a sign that the ultimate law may be less democratic, differential voice in the legal process can deprive the law judges make of democratic value.

This shows an important way in which the topic of this chapter relates to the topics of earlier chapters. To know what kind of voice citizens are entitled to have, we need more general principles: principles, that is, to say what would make access to courts just. It is not enough that access be formally equal. The fact those people could access a court if they were to pay enough money does not make access to courts just if many cannot afford the filing fees. My suggested principles were egalitarian: it matters that legal systems equalise the justice benefits and burdens of legality, and this is likely to mean a reasonable equality of legal resources. Even if my arguments there were unsuccessful, the demands of democratic law are likely to converge on similar requirements. Citizens must see judge-made law as "*their* laws."[19] Inequality in access to courts means inequality in the ability to make arguments about law. And inequality in that ability makes it harder to see the law as theirs.

Judicial Appointments

It is sometimes said to be important that judges represent the community they judge. This is sometimes a claim about the quality of laws made by judges: a judiciary with no women, for example, might fail to recognise the interests of women. But the claim also seems related to the concern that judicial law-making is undemocratic; a representative judiciary might be thought to evade those concerns.

Notions of representation must be treated with quite some care. When "representation" is thought of as a reflection—with judges having the same characteristics of the population—the idea becomes hard to make sense of as a normative ideal. G. Harrold Carswell, one of Richard Nixon's proposed appointees to the US Supreme Court, was said by George McGovern "to be distinguished largely by two qualities: racism and mediocrity." Senator Roman Hruska of Nebraska replied, in Carswell's defence, that the mediocre "are entitled to a little representation."[20] Hruska's claim is absurd because mediocrity is not a characteristic that should be represented by the judiciary.

Which characteristics, if any, should be represented? That is not an easy question to answer. One reason mediocrity might be ruled out is that no one self-identifies as mediocre. By contrast, when there are calls for increased representation of certain groups, the groups' status tends to be an important feature of their identities. For example, collectives can and do self-identify, and are identified, as women. This, though, merely pushes the question back a stage: why should this kind of self-identification matter?

Even if these questions could be answered, the very idea of a representative judiciary is not easy to make sense of. Many judicial decisions are taken by one individual; very rarely, decisions are taken by larger panels, but almost never more than a handful of judges. What would it be for a one-judge panel—or even a three-, nine-, or twelve-judge panel—to represent the community? I am not sure. Perhaps it could be done if there were very few identities that matter. But on any view there are many important characteristics. To name only the most obvious, these include race, class, gender, and sex. Given this, even if diversity and representation on the bench were possible in theory, how could it be achieved in practice?

It may be that proposals to reform the racial, sex, or gender composition of the judiciary can be explained by two more obvious notions: that our judges should be good judges and that all in society should have an equal opportunity to become good judges. A good judge would take into account a litigant's individual circumstances and characteristics, when relevant: they would ensure greater conformity overall with the principles of justice developed in earlier chapters. Further, insofar as the desire for a representative judiciary is motivated by the idea that a representative panel demonstrates equality of opportunity, the desire for a representative panel is really only a desire to ensure that a fair system exists in society for the distribution of jobs. If it is a problem that a judicial panel is composed entirely of white males, the root of the problem is, on this account, the societal structure that allows white males to get ahead.

If so, we should focus more closely on methods of judicial appointments. Niko Kolodny notes the intuition that "legislators must be directly elected with short, fixed terms" while "certain judges . . . may be appointed by elected officials for longer or indefinite terms."[21] The reason, he suggests, that we might be happier with life appointments for judges is that they do not "make laws": they merely "apply or execute the laws."[22] Once this is seen to be a mistaken characterisation of their roles, the question arises whether we ought to think of judicial appointments more along the lines of legislative appointments. Should judges be appointed by election?

There are two considerations here. One is whether an appointment procedure and the conditions of tenure (e.g., life terms versus fixed terms) will lead to good judges being appointed and good decisions being made once they are appointed. Some systems will be better than others at selecting judges best able to do justice; some conditions of tenure will make judges more likely to do justice in individual cases. A second consideration is whether a particular appointment procedure lends the judiciary greater legitimacy. If legitimacy is a function of something other than the justice of decisions, these two considerations are irreducible.

Often, when thinking about judicial appointments, people tend to focus on the first consideration. It is certainly important. Yet many methods of judicial appointment would be unintelligible if that was all that was at stake. For example, some jurisdictions hold elections for judicial office. This method is impossible to defend if the first consideration were all that mattered: elections are a bad way of selecting judges, leading to injustice and partiality. Yet the desire to elect judges is intelligible. It reflects an attempt to democratise a method of judicial law-creation.

Similar points can be made about appointments to the US Supreme Court. Justices to the Supreme Court are nominated by the president and appointed after the "advice and consent of the Senate."[23] For the last hundred years or so, the Senate has held public hearings, some of which are quite widely watched, to test the nominees. It is hard to regard this process as a method of finding out who the best judges are: usually, neither the president nor the Senate has any particular legal expertise, so their judgement on which judges are best is unlikely to be perfect. Yet their involvement is perfectly intelligible: it is a way of trying to ensure that the judges who are appointed are seen as a representative of the community. The nominee has to answer to that community, represented by the legislature, about how they will go about their law-making role.[24]

This second consideration means that certain procedures can be ruled out. Judges cannot be thought to speak for the community if they are appointed by the litigants themselves. Judges stand, in this way, in contrast to arbitrators, who are selected by the litigants. The different method of appointment is one reason why we deny arbitrators law-making powers. (It might be tempting to think that party nomination would lead to bias, but that need not be true: litigants in arbitration, at least, seem to think their appointments immune from this risk.) It is unlikely, though, that there is one particular appointment mechanism guaranteed to ensure that the judges speak for the community. Different communities, with different cultures and traditions, can approach the question of judicial appointments in different ways. Any reform to judicial appointments, though, must bear in mind the importance of the procedure in ensuring that the judge does speak in this way; otherwise objections to judges' law-making powers will be readily available.

LAWMAKERS AND LAW-MAKING

Law-Making and Case Selection

It is justifiable to give judges a power to make laws. This creates a new problem. Judges only make law through reasoning on the disputes that come before them. The law that is made will, therefore, depend in part on the disputes they hear.[25] How should the legal system be structured to ensure that the right kind of cases come to court?

This question dovetails with those considered in earlier chapters. To this point, I have assumed a quite formal notion of what it is for justice to be done in an individual case. Roughly, we have been concerned with ensuring that each litigant gets what they are legally entitled to. This is obviously not enough for a complete picture of what matters about a legal system. Some laws are better than others. One thing legislators should try to do is to replace bad laws with good ones. Judges should do the same.[26]

It might seem as if, for judges to do this, they need to hear a lot of cases. If so, there is a serious worry with contemporary legal systems. There has been a dramatic decrease in the number of cases going to trial. Sociologists refer, following Marc Galanter, to the "vanishing civil trial." In the United States, federal civil trials fell from 12,529 in 1985 to 4,569 in 2002.[27] In the United Kingdom, as Hazel Genn writes, "civil disputes are now not coming near the courts."[28] Sometimes people worry about this because they think it will reduce the amount of law being made. But that is not the right way to think about it. The raw number of cases being litigated is less important (when we are concerned with law-making) than the fact that the right law—and the right amount of law—is being made.

Two considerations are worth emphasising. First, and rather obviously, only those cases that come to court can make law in court. So we need to ensure that the right kind of cases are channelled into courts, not that some raw number of cases is adjudicated. This means that the system should be designed to ensure that a sufficient range of cases will be heard. Something has gone wrong if the only cases being heard by courts are some particular group (be they contractual claims, public law claims, or any other): it is implausible that there is only one area of law worth updating.

Second, perhaps less obviously, a diverse range of litigants can improve the quality of law-making.[29] The way in which cases are argued will affect the kind of considerations judges take into account in deciding those cases. In a society where the only contractual claims that are litigated are those of large companies, concerns surrounding contractual exchange (such as worries about exploitation) will receive far less attention than a society where all claims concern labour relations. The system should ensure that the cases in court feature a diverse range of interests and individuals.

With these two considerations in mind, what systemic arrangements would best promote good judicial law-making?

Selection Methods

A just justice system would improve immeasurably upon a market system, which suffers both from the influence of market principles on adjudication and a tendency unduly to narrow the selection of cases. To see this, we must first notice that the cases that end up in court are filtered by two factors. First, only certain cases are in principle permitted into the public courts. Second, given the procedures of those courts, only certain cases end up going to adjudication. Both factors require attention in the design of a system, but the greatest downsides of contemporary systems would be ameliorated if the fairness floor was built and equal justice held.

Courts should be open to those who might bring cases raising points of law. That is trivial in theory, but not so in practice. The United States provides a useful case study in how to go wrong. Over 300 million people in the United States have cell phones; 99.9 per cent of subscribers to the major networks have arbitration clauses in their contracts.[30] Many of these arbitration clauses bar citizens from litigating their claims in public courts. The law created by those arbitration clauses is, for that reason, very difficult to establish. You cannot always discover your rights simply by reading a document: your rights are the legal effects of a contract's words, not the meaning of the words themselves; and the content of a contract can sometimes go beyond the explicit meaning of words, as where contracts have so-called implied terms. The exclusion of citizens from public courts means that their rights are very hard to establish.[31]

What of the second factor? Of the cases that are permitted into public courts, which ones end up going to adjudication? We have long left the initial selection of cases to the market: those willing and able to litigate do so.

Legal aid interventions have provided a partial interference with this market. But control of litigation has always remained with the litigants: lawyers look wistfully upon interesting disputes that settle on the court steps. Might the market work just fine? Although not impossible, it would be surprising. To see why, I need to say something more about the nature of the benefit the creation of law brings.

Some benefits, like the light on a reader's nightstand, are enjoyed only by a particular person; other benefits, like a lighthouse, are (or can be) enjoyed by anyone.[32] Goods that can be enjoyed by everyone (in the purest case, goods where one person's enjoyment is neither rivalrous with nor excludes the use of others) are known as "public goods." Goods that are or can only be enjoyed by a particular person are, by contrast, private. Law is non-rivalrous and non-excludable. The resolution of a dispute in a public forum is, therefore, a hybrid good: part private (resolving the dispute between the parties) and part public (creating law applicable to everyone in society).[33]

Law created through courts is a public good. And all economists agree that a free market underproduces public goods. This is intuitive. Law-making is costly and, as David Luban puts it, "Why would litigants who engage the services of a rent-a-judge want to pay extra for a reasoned opinion enunciating a rule that benefits only future litigants?"[34] Given this, we should treat the market production of legal knowledge with some suspicion.[35] We should also put some pressure on the idea that the market here is "free." There are numerous barriers to entry into public courts from court fees, scant legal aid, fragmented fora and costs orders. All this gives another reason to doubt the wisdom of a market distribution of legal resources, and to feel confident that compliance with the principles I have enumerated will help to promote the creation of just law.

Beyond this, it would be dangerous to formulate precise reforms. The proper structure of a legal system will depend upon many contextual factors: it is impossible to generalise across all legal systems about how best to ensure the right cases come to court. Any prospective reform should be easier to assess now we have the proper range of considerations on the table. Consider a common proposal: that we channel cases from private arbitration into public courts. That, it should now be clear, is no panacea. Parties have legitimate reasons to want to go through arbitration. More importantly, the law created in courts is inevitably moulded by the concerns of the litigants:

if those litigants are rich enough to contract out, their concerns are also likely to be distinct to their community. English contract lawyers sometimes point out that English contract law is chosen by commercial parties world-wide, as if this were a sign of the quality of the law. It may be—for commercial parties worldwide. But the law must serve everyone, and a law sculpted only by commercial parties will not attend to everyone's interests. Courts must not become sites where law is only made in expensive commercial cases. This entails some public investment, paying for citizens to access courts even when those citizens cannot afford to litigate themselves.

CONCLUSION

This chapter is my final positive proposal about the structure of a just justice system. I set the scene in Chapter 1. I proposed principles to assess distributions of both legal resources and the benefits and burdens of legality in Chapters 2 through 5, as well as objections to those principles in Chapter 6. Finally, in the previous chapter and this one I have considered some structural questions about the way claims of justice should be heard and adjudicated.

All this might sound attractive. It might also sound expensive. How should we pay for it? That is an important question to answer if my proposals are to be endorsed. I turn to it in the next chapter.

9

THE EXPENSE OF JUSTICE

WHO PAYS?

At the Twenty-Fifth Anniversary Dinner of the Legal Aid Society in New York, Vice President Teddy Roosevelt gave a short set of remarks.[1] "I am not sure," he said, "that there could be a change in the law which would make it the duty of the State to try to carry the burden that your society has carried."[2] That was in 1901. Just seven years later, then governor-general of the Philippines William H. Taft, wrote that "it is sufficiently in the interest of the public at large to promote equality between litigants, to take upon the government much more than has already been done, the burden of private litigation."[3]

These remarks reflect a long history of debate about who should bear the considerable costs of dispute resolution.[4] Controversy over who should pay for "the expense of justice," as Adam Smith aptly termed it, has been with us since at least the ancient Greeks.[5] Yet there has been almost no consideration of what principles should determine its distribution.[6] This has hampered the debate and led to some indefensible policy proposals.

In this chapter I claim that the two principles most often used to justify imposing the expense of justice on litigants more naturally lead to a system of public funding. I also argue that attempts to make litigants pay are often attempts to introduce a market mechanism for the distribution of legal resources, a principle I have already rejected. These claims might seem to have quite radical implications. I suggest, however, that a system of fees is justifiable. Fees may be imposed not as a means to fund the justice system;

instead, they may be imposed to help secure compliance with the principles of justice set out in earlier chapters. Although there are some radical
implications to these points, therefore, their conclusions are not as startling
as might first seem.

COSTS AND DISTRIBUTION

The costs of running a justice system can be vast. The 2019 budget for the
US Department of Justice was $28 billion; the same budget for the United
Kingdom was £6 billion.[7]

A legal system has two principal expenses. The first is its fixed costs. Any
justice system worthy of the name requires court buildings and most will
include prisons; these can be very expensive. The US Supreme Court
Building, which opened in 1935, cost nearly $10 million to build.[8] The full
cost of capital expenditure is far higher: the United Kingdom, for example,
spent £600 million in 2018.

Second are labour costs. Some people who work in the justice system,
such as judges, jurors, or court reporters, receive salaries from the state;
those salaries must be funded in some way. In a system with a legal aid regime, the state also pays the wages of some lawyers. Customarily, however,
lawyers are funded by private litigants. When their prices are set by an
open market, they can be very expensive.[9] The final labour expense is for
experts and witnesses: these people, particularly expert witnesses, are often
paid and are sometimes paid substantial sums.

These costs must be paid; some distributional arrangements are fairer
than others. To know which we should favour, we need principles to determine what the just distribution of costs would be. Such principles might be
negative or positive. Negative principles say that certain people ought not
to bear the costs of justice; positive principles say who ought to bear them.
Almost every jurisdiction in the world, for example, has a rule of "costs
shifting."[10] The party who wins a legal dispute is usually entitled to "shift"
her costs—both court fees and labour costs—onto the losing side. The negative principle here is that a victorious litigant ought not to have to fund
the justice system; the positive principle is that a losing litigant should. These
proposals are separable: we might say that neither litigant bears special responsibility for the cost of the system. The most important question is

what positive principles we should endorse. These dictate who should bear the burdens of funding the system.

I will argue that the costs of the legal system should be funded by taxpayers as a whole. I also say that we should not ask litigants, as a group, to pay more to fund the justice system. That does not mean, though, that we should not ask litigants to pay more than others: a system of fees is permissible. The point is simply that the reason to ask them to pay more is not a matter of cost recovery.

Although I will explain this argument in more detail below, it is worth stressing that this system of fees is not, strictly speaking, related to the question of this chapter. It is no part of the case for the fee that the user pays the costs of the system. It is, on my view, no part of the justification for imposing the fees that the activity in question (e.g. litigating) is costly; fees might be imposed even if legal resources were not costly. The justification of the fee, instead, is that the system of fees helps to allocate legal resources (rather than the expense of legal resources) to appropriate individuals. For example, a decree of the Synod of Westminster in 1175 said that "in actions between clerks for the recovery of money, the party who should be the loser should be condemned to pay the costs."[11] This is, on its face, a principle to determine who bears the costs of litigation. However, the reason given for the measure is that it will "put a check on litigation."[12] The justification of the fee is deterrence of vexatious claims, not a belief that the loser should pay the actual costs of litigation.

As this description of my proposed fee regime shows, it is important to distinguish the principles for the distribution of legal resources ("resources principles") from principles for the distribution of the costs of those legal resources ("costs principles"). The question then arises how these principles interrelate.

One possible view is that costs principles must be resolved prior to resources principles. The intuition here is that it is impossible to say what justice in the distribution of legal resources requires until we know how much money we have to fund those legal resources—and that we cannot know how much money we will have until we know who is going to pay. If this is the right way to think of things, that is bad news (for me). I have developed my own principles for the distribution of legal resources on the explicit assumption that the question of cost could be deferred until later. Happily (for me) this is the wrong way to think of things.

For this to be the right analysis, the amount of money that we could demand from each other (to fund the system) could not depend upon the broader demands of justice—such as the right distribution of legal resources. This is for reasons of logical sequencing: if we have to resolve costs principles before resources principles, costs principles cannot depend upon a view about resources principles. But this seems an implausible position. The need to find costs principles comes from the fact that certain distributions of resources are called for as a matter of justice. If those distributions were merely ideals—in the way it might be ideal if everyone had access to cheap, high-quality champagne—there would be no urgency to fund projects that might realise the ideal. Given this, we need resources principles before we think about who ought to pay to bring about those distributions.

A slightly different position claims that costs principles and resources principles must be worked out at the same time. This view depends on the justice of each set of principles interrelating. The intuition here is that we cannot say what a just distribution of legal resources is without having some view about how that distribution ought to be funded.

This view is sometimes plausible. Suppose that we want to know how to distribute champagne and plovers' eggs. A reasonable principle for the distribution of these goods is a market measure. Those willing and able to pay for these things should get them; those unwilling or unable should not. The principle of resource distribution, the market, is at one and the same time a principle to determine who is to fund that distribution. When this feature is present, one cannot propose a resources principle without proposing a costs principle; and one cannot propose a costs principle without proposing a resource principle.

To this extent, I have already considered and rejected one costs principle: a market distribution of legal resources. I have, therefore, rejected a user-pays model of the justice system. This is important to stress as, otherwise, a market distribution could acquire illicit support, a resources principle masquerading as a costs principle alone. As this example demonstrates, we should always be suspicious of attempts to develop distinctive principles over who pays for certain features of the welfare state: they are often disguised assaults on the distributive foundations of the system.

The proper approach is to consider resources principles first, as I have in earlier chapters, before turning to the question of how the just distribution of resources should be funded. Approached in this way, costs principles can be general or local. The most general principle holds that expenses should be distributed according to principles of justice in taxation. On this view, there is no question of distribution local to the justice system: the costs of justice should be picked up by those who ought to fund the other costs of running a state, whoever they might be. I call this the "simple view" because it has the fewest costs principles for questions of justice: the same principles govern the expenses of legal services as, say, healthcare. Local principles build on the idea that there are special considerations that bear on the distribution of costs in the context of the justice system. This view is more complex because it multiplies the principles we need to consider: there might be different considerations in healthcare and defence than, say, justice.

I examine both the general and local approach. These positions come to the same conclusion: that costs should be borne by the population at large; in other words, that the costs principles are simply principles of just taxation.

THE SIMPLE VIEW

Justice in Taxation

There are things—things like justice, healthcare, and security—that should not be distributed through a laissez-faire market. We need to quantify the costs of ensuring the just distribution of these goods and to work out how to raise the requisite revenue. The simple view holds that we should establish all the things required as a matter of justice and then think about how to raise the revenue to meet those demands. It is wrong, in other words, to think about how to raise money for defence or for the legal system; we should think instead about how to raise money for all the things that ought to be privately funded. The project of working out how to do this, and what methods of raising revenue ought to be permitted, is the project of justice in taxation—and lawyers have no special expertise in that.

John Locke proposed a principle of justice in taxation to meet this problem: "every one who enjoys his share of the Protection, should pay out of his Estate his proportion for the maintenance of it."[13] That principle may be acceptable so far as it goes, but a lot of disagreement remains concerning the nature of each individual's "proportion." This, though, is not our concern: it is a question for the philosophy of taxation. The important point about the simple view is that it subsumes the question of the expense of justice within this more general question, concerning justice in taxation.

A counterintuitive consequence of the simple view is that there is no reason why the costs of litigation should be paid by the litigants. The task of this section is to motivate the simple view through analogies with the funding of other goods and to resist the idea that there are counterintuitive consequences to the view. Although there are no funding reasons to localise litigation costs to the litigants, it is sensible to establish a system of fees that shapes prospective litigants' choices. A system with just costs principles would not, for this reason, be dramatically different from the present system.

Analogies

Our question—who should pay for the justice system?—is a species of a wider genus. In the context of, for example, national defence, policing, and healthcare, the same questions arise: how much defence, policing, or healthcare should there be? How should that defence, policing, or healthcare be distributed? And how should these arrangements be paid for? There are few links between the first two questions and the last. The two principles sometimes raised in the legal context, the responsibility and benefit principles (discussed later), are rarely, if ever, raised outside the justice context.[14]

Debates over the proper levels and distribution of defence or policing are quite familiar. Should the United Kingdom renew Trident, its nuclear deterrent? Should troubled communities get more police "on the beat"? Whatever the right answers to those questions, those answers do not also determine who ought to pay for the collective schemes.[15] No one argues that those in vulnerable parts of the country should pay more by way of taxes than those in more secure areas; or that victims of crimes the police investigate should pay a super-tax to cover the cost of the service they receive. The burden of taxation should be spread throughout the country according to principles of just taxation (whatever they might be).

The Role of Fees

All that I have said thus far indicates that there is no reason to make individual litigants pay the costs of their suit, howsoever calculated. This might sound not only deeply revisionary but also unworkable. It is neither. That is because individual litigants can justifiably be—and often are—required to pay fees.

Legal resources are scarce. They must be rationed. Any system of rationing should aim to support the best principles for the distribution of legal resources, of justice, and of injustice. The current system rations according to a market. I have already argued that this is a bad principle. If there were no filing fee, another system of rationing would have to be found. We should try to design it to ensure that the best outcomes are met. We should implement whatever fee regime would lead to more perfect compliance with the best principles of justice about the distribution of legal resources. The question is then whether some particular fee arrangement might achieve a just distribution of legal resources, justice, and injustice.

Distributive arrangements can go wrong if access to them is free. It is a contingent question whether imposing a charge for the use of some good makes things go better. Although we tend to assume that people will consume less of a good as its price goes up, charging for goods can lead to increased consumption. In one famous example, a day-care centre introduced fines for parents who picked their children up late; late pickups increased.[16] Even so, as a general rule, the more you charge for a good, the less people will consume.[17] If some good were to become free at the point of use, consumption would be likely to increase.

In the context of the law, this means that there is a risk of bad cases—"vexatious litigation"—being brought to court. Sometimes, even though there is no good reason to bring a claim to court, the litigant pursues it anyway. A fee has the potential to deter such litigants, ensuring that there is some downside to litigation: people will not engage in litigation without giving it some thought. This explains the 1175 decree of the Synod of Westminster: a costs regime was instituted to "put a check on litigation."[18] This is an example of a fee regime in service of a distributive principle.[19]

There are two important consequences of this analysis. First, absent some further argument justifying the measure, there is no reason to set the litigant's fees at the cost of providing any particular legal resource. Certainly there is no reason for a government to pursue a policy of full cost recovery. Although it is less palatable, perhaps, litigants can be asked to pay more than the cost of providing the legal resource in question. Setting fees at a level above cost will often be wrong because it will disrupt the just distribution of legal resources. But if charging individuals more than cost will better secure compliance with principles of distributive justice, there is a good reason to do so.[20]

Second, there is a serious danger inherent in a flat fee for all users. Given that there is no equality of material resources and that individuals have varied levels of risk-aversion, a fixed fee regime will be highly imperfect. As Frank Michelman writes, "Modest, flat fees make no dependable contribution to dissuading the affluent from theoretical or extortionate litigation; but they can make it absolutely impossible for the indigent to litigate in good faith."[21] A flat fee is a blunt instrument for deterring vexatious litigants. Wealthy individuals with bad cases will not be deterred; poor individuals with good cases might be. We have some anecdotal evidence that this is so: some rich individuals are notorious for their abuse of the courts.[22]

It is not always easy to establish the rationale for legal fees imposed. There are good grounds, though, to think that most countries do not impose fees in order to recover costs; instead they approach things as I have said they should: imposing fees to ensure that legal resources are distributed to those who ought to get them. This can be seen from two features of most systems.

First, court fees are not hypothecated to the justice system. Money from court fees can justifiably be spent on schools and hospitals. If the fees were imposed to fund the system they ought rationally to be spent on the system. The United Kingdom has passed legislation holding that any profits made from court fees "must be used to finance an efficient and effective system of courts and tribunals."[23] This hypothecation was probably included to sweeten the bitter pill—the above-cost fees were met with fierce resistance. But it is notable chiefly because it is so different from most approaches: I know of no other attempt in other legal systems to hypothecate fees in this way.

Second, rarely do countries attempt to set fees with reference to the costs of claims. The level of court fees tends to be plucked out of thin air. Nevertheless, it is clear that the guiding principle is not the cost of the justice system. Again, this can be illustrated by contrast with the United Kingdom. The *Treasury, Fees and Charges Guide* (1992) said that "the purpose of charging for services is to ensure that resources are efficiently allocated. Charges should normally be set to recover the full cost of the service."[24] It is the only country in the world to adopt such a policy. Whatever most countries' policies with respect to fees are, they do not involve the recovery of costs of the justice system. The most plausible conclusion is that these countries aim to use fees to secure a just distribution of legal resources.[25]

In this section I have claimed that there are no principles local to the justice system that should determine who pays for the justice system. However, people do sometimes propose special principles to justify the distribution of expenses for certain activities. In the next two sections I consider two such principles; both, I claim, lead to the same conclusion: that legal expenses should be funded out of general taxation.

THE RESPONSIBILITY PRINCIPLE

The Basic Idea

Consider again the analogy with the costs of healthcare. We might (and governments do) impose a tax on smokers to deter the activity. This would be, as with my own proposed system of legal fees, a method of securing a better outcome: say, reduced demands on the healthcare system. But the tax might be justified in another way. Where socialised healthcare is provided, smokers create costs—their healthcare, and the healthcare of second-hand smokers—which the public as a whole would otherwise be forced to pay. Smokers, we might say, are responsible for the costs they create through their own voluntary activity, and a tax might be imposed to localise that cost to them.

A similar argument can be made in the legal context. Someone might argue, that is, that individuals responsible for the creation of legal costs ought to bear the burden of those costs. The Roman jurist Ulpian, for example, wrote that "he who . . . has without cause summoned the other party to court will be obliged to pay the other party's traveling expenses."[26] The limitation of this principle to those claims brought "without cause" suggests that the individual should be responsible for the travelling expenses because they (irresponsibly) imposed them on the other party.

The principle is difficult to parse in part because the word "responsi-bility" is used in so many different ways.[27] In this section I will argue that although there is some intuitive attraction to the principle, it is much more complicated than it might first appear. When these complications are drawn out, it seems that the only counsel the principle might give is: distribute costs to the population at large. But that, of course, is not a rival principle to the one I have already proposed: it claims that the expense of justice should be borne according to principles of just taxation.

Assessing the Principle

In ordinary morality we can acquire obligations, for example to repair damage we do, even though we do not consent to those obligations. This is the moral in some shop's norm: "You break it, you bought it." Something like the shop's norm is the basis of the responsibility principle: if your actions generate the costs of running the legal system, you ought to pay those costs.

If I break a vase in a shop, there is a relatively clear line of responsibility from my action to the cost of replacing the vase. Things are different in the legal context. An individual litigant does not determine the cost of the court building or the salary of judges, nor do they determine the procedures that govern their case: insofar as their decision to litigate imposes costs, they do not determine the size of those costs. Further, we have to resolve our disputes through the legal apparatus; self-help is not just discouraged but often illegal. The appropriate analogy is something like this. Imagine that the state nationalises the car industry and provides only Rolls Royce cars. It could have provided much cheaper alternatives, but a select few are quite partial to the Rolls Royce brand. When someone—carelessly, suppose—damages one of the Rolls Royce cars is it reasonable to demand that they pay the market cost of repairs? Responsibility for the cost is attributable, at least in part, to those few who wanted the Rolls Royce system and im-posed it on the others; their responsibility should not drop out of the pic-ture. Just so in the legal context, it is a collective decision of a polity to have a particular legal system with particular cost implications. All of those in the polity are partially responsible for those costs. For this reason, the responsibility principle points towards a system of general taxation to fund the bulk of the costs.

But surely, you might say, the individual's responsibility does not drop out entirely? Surely they are *a bit* more responsible for these costs than everyone else? Any notion of responsibility is extremely defuse. Think again of my action, smashing of the shop's vase. Two features seem important: my voluntary action (for example, tipping the vase with a careless arm) and my fault (in my carelessness). Neither feature is normally present in the legal context.

Consider the criminal law. Those charged with crimes are hauled into court by the state; we cannot simply opt out of the criminal law. It does not make much sense to say that these individuals are responsible for the cost of the court proceedings.[28] Those who are ultimately convicted of crimes are responsible for the court proceedings in this loose sense: if they had not committed the crime and defended themselves from conviction, those costs would not have arisen. But this is a looser sense of responsibility than is present in the shop. Committing the crime does not incur any costs automatically. It is more like entering the shop in the first place; defending oneself (the act that incurs the costs) is more like breaking the vase. Yet the criminal's blame is in committing the original act; the careless shopper's blame is in the cost-creating act.

Similar points can be made about civil claims. Defendants have no choice whether to be called into court: someone else calls them to answer a claim. Plaintiffs, provided they are acting in good faith, are not in a materially different position: they believe that they have been wronged and that they are entitled to reparation, so while they could simply submit to perceived injustice, their decision to litigate is not voluntary in the way the careless shopper's act is. More important still, litigants are not blameworthy for going to trial. The act of litigating can be a public good in its generation of assurance and new laws. Further, most legal disputes arise not because individuals pursue hopeless cases in bad faith. It is often unclear who is responsible for what, and confusion may arise in part because the law on some matter is unclear. Sometimes a litigant might have a good case given the law that applied at the time the facts arose, only for a court to change the law in their case.

The shop's norm also talks of "buying." This gives rise to further problems, ones that make it extremely difficult to say what responsibility each litigant has for which cost. The only expense the shopper is called on to carry is the value of the vase. It is easy enough to determine the quantum of that: it has a market value. The shopkeeper cannot ask the shopper to pay for their employees' labour or the shop's heating costs. In the legal context the analogical claim must say that the individual should only pay for those costs they actually create. But what are those? When an individual's case is heard in court, there can be many different costs: of the judge, the jury, the lawyers, the fixed costs of the court room, incidental costs (e.g., heating the court room, security at its entrance), and so on. If some individual is thought to have wrongfully prolonged a case, which of these costs are they responsible for? The judge's salary would have been paid anyway; the courtroom was already there; the heating would not have been turned off. The most plausible cost for which the litigant is responsible is the lawyers' time, but principles of cost recovery rarely concern only those costs.

A concrete example might illustrate these points. In *Coventry v. Lawrence,* the defendant's motor-racing track generated noise.[29] The plaintiff objected to this. Sometimes the noise generated by an activity is so invasive as to give rise to a tort, known as nuisance; prior to the case, the law usually granted an injunction to prevent nuisance. The dispute concerned whether the defendant's activities amounted to an actionable nuisance—and, if so, whether an injunction could be issued. Some of the questions were factual: how much noise was generated? On how many days? Other questions were legal: did it matter that the defendants had planning permission for their racetrack? Under what circumstances would an injunction be granted? These issues were heard in numerous courts, ultimately coming before the Supreme Court. They decided that there was a nuisance and granted an injunction. The successful plaintiff had spent over £1,000,000 on legal fees en route to their ultimate victory. With respect to those costs—forget the court costs for now—who was responsible?

Part of the reason why the costs were so high is that the labour market for lawyers is privatised. This meant that the plaintiff's lawyers were able to charge high fees. Less obviously, but no less important, the plaintiff's fees were paid for by a "no win, no fee" arrangement. These arrangements depend upon an "uplift" to cover the risk of the lawyer losing: the idea is that, if the lawyer takes enough of these cases, the uplift in the cases they win will cancel out the work they end up doing for free in the cases they lose. Neither the plaintiff nor the defendant were responsible for either the privatised market nor the "no win, no fee" arrangement. If anyone is responsible for those arrangements, it is the population as a whole.

Might we say that the plaintiff is responsible for the costs? They chose to litigate, after all. But, as I pointed out, the sense in which they are responsible for that choice is attenuated: their civil rights were being infringed by another and they pursued the mandated method to resolve that dispute. When, as in England, these costs are put onto the losing defendant, "no win, no fee" arrangements privatise the costs of a more open justice system: they shift the costs of enabling individuals to bring claims from the public at large to an individual wrongdoer. Is that because those costs are the defendant's responsibility? The defendant had no real choice, either: they could have closed their business, of course, but that is not something many would do unless forced. And their argument that their actions were legal was far from risible: although they lost in the Supreme Court, they won in the Court of Appeal. It is only if you have a very strict notion of responsibility—whereby an individual, acting in good faith and for good reasons, can be responsible for the costs they generate—that you can plausibly think these costs are the responsibility of the defendant.

Conclusion

The responsibility principle faces enormous difficulties if it is to justify imposing costs on one litigant or another. If the responsibility principle has any purchase, it seems to reach the same conclusion as the simple view: that the costs should be borne by taxpayers as a whole, distributed according to principles of justice in taxation.

In the next section I consider the second possible principle. My conclusion is precisely the same as here: if there is anything to the principle, it counsels us to distribute the costs to the public as a whole.

THE BENEFIT PRINCIPLE

Paying for Benefits

It is sometimes said that those who are "able" to pay more should do so. This is not a particularly persuasive argument. "Ability to pay" may be a necessary condition for someone to be called on to pay for some project but it is not sufficient. I might as well argue: I would like to take a surfing holiday in luxurious surroundings; therefore, those who are able to subsidise my desire to do so should be made to contribute. That argument has found disappointingly limited support amongst those I have canvassed.[30]

There is more promise to Adam Smith's claim, that "the subjects of every state ought to contribute towards the support of the government, as nearly as possible, in proportion to their respective abilities; that is, in proportion to the revenue that they respectively enjoy under the protection of the state."[31] At first glance, Smith seems to be making the same argument: people should contribute "in proportion to their respective abilities." Yet Smith means something quite different: he says that people should contribute "in proportion to the revenue which they enjoy under the protection of the state." This limit is incompatible with the "ability" principle: if a subject has revenue overseas, they are able to pay using that revenue. Smith seems to believe, though, that it would be unjustifiable for a government to assess the subject's contribution with reference to those funds.

Why should contributions to state costs be assessed relative to funds protected by the state? Immanuel Kant suggests an argument: "The wealthy have acquired an obligation to the commonwealth, since they owe their existence to an act of submitting to its protection and care, which they need in order to live; on this obligation the state now bases its right to contribute what is theirs to maintaining their fellow citizens."[32] Kant's key claim, with Smith, is that taxpayers benefit from the system of cooperation and that this explains why they can be called upon to fund the system. Hence, the reason why Smith is concerned with payments only in proportion to the "protection" offered is to ensure that beneficiaries of the state pay only in proportion to the benefit received.

The question then becomes: Why should the beneficiaries of a cooperative scheme be called upon to pay? Two quite distinct reasons could be given. First is the idea of "internalising" costs. A great deal of economic theory approaches problems in this way: various activities have "externalities" which, for the market to function efficiently, must be internalised by the actor. A factory, for example, might pollute the river, reducing the quality of water downstream. That is a "negative externality," a cost of the factory's operation that should be borne by those running the factory. It does not matter, on this rationale, whether the factory owner benefits. It is simply a condition on the permissibility (or efficiency) of their operation that they pay for the costs of production. The argument is no different from the one I have already proposed: that fees can be justifiably imposed only when those fees lead to greater compliance with the best principles of justice.

Second are duties of "fair play." This is an old idea. Jeremy Bentham, for example, thought it "incontrovertible" that "the burthen of an establishment ought to lie on those by whom the benefit is reaped."[33] H. L. A. Hart's discussion is the usual launchpad for the modern debate. He introduced the idea in the following terms: "when a number of persons conduct any joint enterprise according to rules and thus restrict their liberty, those who have submitted to these restrictions when required have a right to a similar submission from those who have benefited by their submission."[34]

Not every benefit individuals receive engages the principle. For example, the fact of benefiting does not seem normatively salient when it is possible to exclude individuals from enjoying the benefit of cooperative actions—and the benefit is bestowed anyway. As an English judge once put it, "One cleans another's shoes; what can the other do but put them on? . . . The benefit of the service could not be rejected without refusing the property itself."[35] The cleaner did not have to clean the shoes and the beneficiary did not ask them to. So the owner of the shoes does not have to pay the cleaner for the benefit received.

Some goods are different. Consider national defence. It is a "pure public good." The benefit of living in a secure state, free from foreign invasion, is enjoyed by everyone who lives in that state: if I am protected from foreign attack, my neighbour will be, too. Two features are notable: first, one individual's enjoyment of the benefits of national defence does not reduce the amount of national defence available to others; second, it is not possible to parcel the benefits up into individual packets or to exclude certain individuals.[36] A secure state benefits all who live in it. That is one reason why we all ought to pay for this security.

Where, on this spectrum, does law lie?

Fair Play and Law

We should distinguish between two types of benefit the justice system brings. First are the public benefits of living under a legal system governed by the rule of law. These include: a public statement of values and rules with which to guide actions and plan lives; increased responsiveness of distributions to reasons of justice; increased security because of that responsiveness to reasons; and the value of power-creating institutions like those of contract and private property. Second is the "private" benefit of having some dispute resolved within that system, such as the court order that keeps the trespassers off your land or that forces your employer to pay your wages.[37] This suggests two classes of beneficiary: the public as a whole and individual litigants. That the benefit has this dual character is why I termed law a "hybrid" good.

The provision of a just justice system is, for this reason, more like national defence than the cleaning of another's shoes. The principle of fair play seems to apply to both categories of beneficiary: the public cannot be excluded from the first benefit and the litigants choose to take the second benefit by litigating. This suggests an argument for a system of public funding—as I have proposed—but with contributions from individual litigants. For example, Costa e Silva has argued that "given that the user of Justice is a beneficiary of the provision of a service, it is reasonable to require from him the payment of a certain amount for the service provided."[38]

Things are slightly more complex than this. Many of the public benefits of a legal system are like those of a system of national defence: they cannot be split into discrete sections and allocated to individuals; if there is increased security in my neighbourhood, that is better for me and my neighbours. It is often useful to refer to the value of a justice system as being shared by all the public. So long as this is used to argue that the public should pay according to principles of justice in taxation, there is no conflict with the simple view. If, by contrast, it is said that all should pay equal amounts because they share in the benefits equally, that requires rather more care.

To see the complexity, consider the value of a public statement of values and rules with which to guide actions and plan lives. This is certainly part-public; it is hard, if not impossible, to prevent particular individuals from benefiting from this. Yet the actual value to individuals varies depending on the content of the law. The more difficult it is to understand, for example, the more its benefits will be enjoyed only by those with sophisticated legal advice. Although the benefit is public, the benefit is not always equally shared. Similar remarks could be made about any of the other goods. An institution of contract and private property benefits some more than others.

The benefit principle suggests that those who enjoy more of the benefits of a legal system should pay more for its upkeep. Usually this will mean that those with more assets should pay more—which is also the likely conclusion of any argument about justice in taxation.

The beneficiaries of a legal suit are, intuitively, the two parties to that suit. This intuition is sometimes the basis of policy reform, privatising the costs of the legal system to the litigants. The United Kingdom, for example, has sought to shift the cost of litigation from the public at large onto individual litigants. The rationale for this was often said to be that those who benefit from the justice system should pay for its upkeep. But there is something spurious about the privacy of these benefits—hence why I have talked of "private" benefits. This means that the benefit principle makes few demands of individual litigants.

First, private litigation partly constitutes the public benefits. A justice system only functions because individuals bring legal claims to public courts. The litigation serves as a reminder to the unscrupulous that the state can step in to coerce performance of their duties. If no claims were brought in court, this would either be because no wrongs were being committed (an unlikely hypothesis) or because the repair of injustice is impossible. If the repair of injustice is impossible in some particular legal system, the system offers scant security.

Not only do individual litigants in this way ensure that the rule of law is maintained, their claims also help to constitute the law itself.[39] Judges can change the law. Unlike legislators, they cannot change the law when they feel like it; they must wait for a relevant case to come before them. Law is made in judges' decisions: that is the system of precedent. So there is an element of artificiality to unpicking the benefits of a legal system and attributing them to some particular group.

The second reason is that beneficiaries in the second class, individual litigants, have—almost by definition—received less of the public benefits of living under a legal system than others. In his "Protest against Law Taxes," Jeremy Bentham objected to a civil law tax. His comments apply with equal force to court fees: "The persons on whom the whole of the burthen is cast, are precisely those who have the least enjoyment of the benefit: the security that other people enjoy for nothing, without interruption, and every moment of their lives, they who are so unfortunate as to be obliged to go to law for it, are forced to purchase at an expense of time and trouble, in addition to what pecuniary expense may be naturally unavoidable. Meantime, which is of most value?—which most worth paying for?—a possession thus cruelly disturbed, or the same possession free from all disturbance?"[40] Bentham's point is this. Victims of injustice have not received the fullest extent of the public benefit that justice systems promise: part of the point of the legal system is to protect individuals against injustice.

What benefit do individuals gain from going to court? In most cases they ideally get rectification to the position they would have been in had there been no injustice in the first place. Litigants, through the proper operation of the justice system, receive rectification in private for their failure to receive the public benefit all others have got.

These two points mean that the attempt to drive a wedge between the public and private benefits of the justice system is a fool's errand. It also means that attempts to shift the costs of the justice system from the public purse to private citizens are not justifiable: the fair play argument, which is the principal argument in policy debates, points towards a system of public funding.

CONCLUSION

Running a just justice system is expensive. Funding has to be found. Presented in this way, the puzzle might seem like one for legal philosophers: who should pay for their system? The puzzle is more general than that; it can only be answered with a broader theory of justice in taxation. To propose such a theory is well beyond the scope of this book.

My own argument—that the public as a whole should pay for legal resources in a just justice system—seems like it implies that all legal services should be free at the point of use. Not so. To control access to the system— to ration the scarce legal resources—it is justifiable to charge fees. Those fees should not be set by reference to the cost of those resources. I have proposed a number of outcomes in earlier chapters, outcomes we should tailor fees to achieve. Others will disagree. The point of this chapter is to say that whatever the best outcomes are—whatever the best principles of justice to guide the structure of a legal system—we ought to set fees so as to ensure that those outcomes are reached.

10

JUST INJUSTICE

The common problem, yours, mine, every one's
Is—not to fancy what were fair in life
Provided it could be,—but, finding first
What may be, then find how to make it fair
Up to our means: A very different thing!

—Robert Browning, "Bishop Blougram's Apology"

IDEALS

"Reason," Immanuel Kant writes, "will not command the impossible."[1] Due to claims like these, many attribute to Kant the maxim that "ought implies can."[2] In contemporary scholarship, this principle leads some people to reject a certain kind of abstract philosophical reflection upon moral demands or political structures. As James Griffin writes, "Moral norms must be tailored to fit the human moral torso. . . . There are no moral norms outside the boundary set by our capacities. . . . Moral norms regulate human action; a norm that ignores the limited nature of human agents is not an 'ideal' norm, but no norm at all."[3] Equally, someone can argue, a political principle that counsels the impossible is no norm at all.

This suggests another objection to my discussion in this book. If it is impossible or infeasible to comply with my proposed principles, what was the point of proposing them in the first place? If a just justice system is an impossible ideal, perhaps there is no point in trying to say what such a system would look like in the first place. That, I argue in this chapter, is a mistake. The model I have proposed is far from infeasible. And, even when it is not immediately possible to comply with all the principles, a model of just justice is vital for practical reflection in our imperfect world. The ideal serves as a guide, helping us to choose amongst possible options. As John Rawls wrote, "By showing how the social world may realize the features of a realistic Utopia, political philosophy provides a long-term goal of political endeavor, and in working toward it gives meaning to what we can do today."[4] Without an ideal of just justice, law reform will lack "an objective, an aim, by reference to which its queries can be answered."[5]

Objections to idealism, I suggest later, are often a covert disagreement with proposed principles or a resistance to the costs of compliance with those principles. Even so, there are some societies where it is economically or politically infeasible to achieve compliance: in these societies, the objection of idealism has some purchase, and my own proposals should be considered in light of that. I close with a consideration of how to apply my principles to those situations so as to reduce injustice in society. There are two questions to consider: first, what to do where there is injustice in taxation or political intransigence, such that justice in the distribution of legal resources is not possible; second, what injustice in the distribution of legal resources means for principles of taxation.

REALISM AND FEASIBILITY

Realism about Justice

The impetus to formulate principles of a just justice system is the imperfection of our world. A degree of realism is, for that reason, baked into my approach. There are three constraints worth noting.

I began this book with a summary of the problems in a world without law. Many of those problems would not arise in a society of angels. If no rights were infringed, the urgency of a system of justice to repair rights violations would fall away. If no distributions were ever disrupted, there would be no need for a system to correct distributive injustices. The project of formulating principles of just justice only makes sense in a world that is imperfect from the point of view of justice. The enterprise assumes that there is, and will continue to be, injustice in the world.

That concession to reality is a minor one. No theorists of justice assume that we are in a world of angels. Very many theories, however, go on to assume that all humans in society act in good faith, intending to uphold principles of justice. Rawls's theory of justice is built on the assumption that "everyone . . . act[s] justly and [does] his part in upholding just institutions."[6] Rawls suggests that, when this is so, there is no need for principles of just justice as a part of ideal theory; he does not engage with the questions of this book. This is a mistake. Even if everyone acts justly, distributions can be upset; even if everyone *intends* to act justly, there can be disagreements about what justice requires. Principles of just justice are necessary even in Rawls's ideal world.

My own assumptions are distinct from those of Rawls. I made no assumptions about citizens' support for legal institutions, though I did propose principles that may command their assent: my aim was to establish a system that will ensure fairness even in the event that some people are perennially committing injustice, and despite the fact those people have no desire to repair their wrongs voluntarily. A fair distribution of legal resources is required, for example, in part to protect against the oppression that could occur if there was an unjust distribution.[7]

The third assumption built into my own system is that it is impossible to build a perfect justice system, where everyone with a good claim to justice gets justice. The next best thing to that might be for everyone who would value time with a lawyer or a judge getting that time. That, too, is impossible. We need to accept, as David Luban has written, that "our technology of justice is *necessarily* imperfect, that costs and confusions of adjudication are as ineliminable a part of the normative world as friction is of the physical world."[8] Principles of just justice are necessary only given that ours is, and will always be, an imperfect world.

Feasibility

In what sense are my own principles infeasible or impossible? To bring some order, we should distinguish four ways in which a particular proposal might be infeasible. A proposal might, first, be logically impossible, like a plan to build an education system in which all children are above average.

Next are practical constraints furnished by contingent but unchanging facts about humans. Many humans, for example, are selfish. That fact is taken for granted in the formulation of Rawls's principles of justice. He argued that distributive inequality (of wealth or authority) was consistent with justice to the extent that it benefited the "the least advantaged members of society."[9] This assumes that members of society are willing to work to benefit the worst off only if they are able to enjoy some of the fruits of their labour: no distributive inequality would arise if people were not selfish, for they could work just as hard and give all their income to the worst off. Jerry Cohen long argued that Rawls's concession to selfishness was one a theory of justice should not make.[10] He refused, in other words, to build contingent facts about human motivations into his theory.

Third are political constraints, those furnished by facts about institutions. In the United States, for example, certain reforms to the legal system are possible only by the passage of legislation through Congress. Given how those institutions are composed—given, for example, how elections to the Senate and the House are run—there are very powerful arguments that many theoretically feasible principles are politically infeasible. This may not reflect anything about the preferences of those in these communities; it reflects how those preferences are refracted through these political bodies.[11]

Finally, there are economic constraints. In a pre-industrial economy, or a country where most people live beneath the poverty line, many political proposals are unaffordable. The United States has enough money to institute a basic legal aid regime; Somalia may not. Even if everyone in society wanted a basic legal aid regime, even if Somalia's parliament could pass such a measure, it would fall still-born from the legislative process.

Which of these objections, if any, might the realist raise against my principles? The first objection is obviously irrelevant: nothing I have proposed is logically impossible. The second objection can also be set to one side. I made no assumptions contrary to basic facts about humans. To the contrary, unedifying assumptions about human dispositions were central to my account; principles were designed to protect against those facts. Many of the motivations for proposing the equal distribution of the justice benefits and burdens of legality, for example, derive from a belief that humans will, if given the chance, prefer their own interests to those of others.

All this said, the implementation of an egalitarian regime would conflict with human selfishness. Lawyers would prefer to make their market salaries; individuals would rather have the finest lawyer money can buy rather than the one an egalitarian system allocates to them. But these facts are consistent with every regulation of a market in any industry: employers might rather there were no minimum wage laws; doctors might prefer to sell their services on the market than under a system of socialised medicine; and litigants might wish that they could pay extra for a certain judge. Such facts about humans cannot be ignored when it comes to the design of the system. They must always be taken into account in regulatory structures. But they do not show that any proposed principle is mistaken.

The third and fourth feasibility constraints have more salience. In many, perhaps most, countries the political institutions are such that it may be impossible in the near-distant future to comply with all the principles I have proposed. That is for a range of reasons. As a general matter, the justice system tends to receive less attention than other features of state expenditure and many people in society are quite happy with that. Perhaps this is because legal services are only contingently necessary and many assume that they will never end up in a court room.

There are also contingent reasons, applicable to different societies, why my principles might be politically infeasible. The United States is a good example. Many of my proposals would not favour the interests of larger corporations: those groups enjoy more benefits and fewer burdens of legality than others in society; they stand to lose both those privileges if my principles were enacted. The US Supreme Court's decision in *Citizens United v. Federal Election Commission* removed restrictions on the amount corporations can spend on federal elections.[12] Were any quixotic candidate to place reform of the justice system at the centre of their platform, those corporations could exercise a loud voice through attack ads. It is an empirical question how persuasive that voice will be, but it is plausible that a louder voice will, on average, persuade more people. All this indicates that the charge of political infeasibility might well stick; I will consider the implications of this in the next subsection.

The fourth feasibility constraint, economic constraints, has salience in some societies but not all. Of course, in any country compliance with my principles will come at a cost: it will, in other words, entail that other valuable goods will not be realised. Prioritising justice, I have argued, is justifiable. For now, it is enough to note that justice has a central concern in most conceptions of a good society; this gives some grounds for thinking that the loss of other goods (in favour of justice) is a price worth paying.

Responses to Infeasibility

In theory and in practice, the appropriate response to political gridlock should sometimes be a flat refusal to accept the status quo. If we know that a certain arrangement is best as a matter of justice and that our political structures make its realisation impossible, the thing to change should be our political structures. And charges of infeasibility should be treated with some caution. Entrenched interests can accuse unpalatable theories—such as the idea that the benefits and burdens of legality be equally shared—of infeasibility or impracticality as a way of stifling reform. To call a proposed reform infeasible is facially a factual claim about present circumstances. Yet the assessment may be driven by, for example, the fact that the proposal would harm the assessor's interests. (Think of a financier's rejection of a wealth tax as politically infeasible.) And that assessment is, properly understood, one about the different weights of individuals' interests: the assessor might simply be placing their interests above others' and masking that normative ranking beneath talk of impossibility. Factual claims of impracticality can, this shows, be used to cloak the absence of normative argument.

It would, however, be too glib to ignore political practicality. A political party that ignored existing political institutions would have scant impact on society; it would not move closer to realising the ideals of justice. Politics must often attend to feasibility constraints of the here and now. The fact that feasibility is important to election cycles, though, should not be used to dismiss or sideline more ambitious reforms. Partly this is because we can misjudge the limits of the possible. Numerous campaigns that began as utopian ended as inevitable: in the last century these have included women's suffrage, civil rights and marriage equality. My proposal is that a just justice system be added to the roster of realisable utopias. Further, any systemic feasibility limit imposed on the pursuit of justice suggests the need to reform the system.

If there is not enough money to realise a just justice system, there is little that can be done immediately. But we should be cautious before accepting claims of economic infeasibility.[13] First, claims of economic infeasibility can be used as an excuse by those unwilling to incur the (affordable) costs of realising justice. This excuse can be occluded by the fact that normative judgements are often concealed beneath apparently factual claims. Consider, for example, the debate on single-payer healthcare. Some claim that the costs of that regime are not worth paying, a normative judgement. This conclusion is sometimes expressed in apparently factual terms, as a claim about the infeasibility of the system: that the costs could not be paid. A related concern is that our judgements about factual matters can be influenced by our normative judgements. Many who claim that single-payer healthcare is unaffordable are not themselves competent to assess the economic data on which their assessments depend. Their conclusions about economics will be affected by whom they listen to. And whom they listen to may be influenced by normative considerations. (The same charge can be made against those on the other side of the debate: those pre-committed to single-payer healthcare may be led to read and listen to those who support that conclusion.)

A second reason to be cautious about accepting charges of economic infeasibility is that the charge may put the cart before the horse. There is often said to be a link between economic prosperity and just justice systems (although the point is more often made using the language of the "rule of law"). Daron Acemoglu and James Robinson, for example, offer an account of why certain nations were politically and economically successful. One of the vital preconditions, they claim, is the rule of law.[14] If economists like these are correct, societies with just justice systems are more likely to develop the kind of economic resources that enable them to maintain such systems.

THE PRIORITIES OF JUSTICE

Two Kinds of Priority

If there remains political or economic infeasibility, the practical question is how to order priorities between the principles of a just justice system. We should distinguish two kinds of reason to prioritise one cause over another. First is normative priority.[15] An activist might think it more important that there be universal healthcare than that there be easy access to national parks. They might, for that reason, spend their time lobbying for universal healthcare.

Second is practical priority. Even if they think healthcare more important than national parks, an activist might spend their time lobbying for easy access to national parks because they believe that a sufficient number of legislators favour the measure; maybe universal healthcare is Panglossian. Practical reasons to favour one proposal or another will be highly contingent on facts about particular societies: political possibilities will differ from country to country, time to time. And philosophical inquiry has essentially nothing to say about this. We should concentrate, then, on normative reasons for prioritisation.

So the question is: what normative priority, if any, do some proposed principles have over the others?

The Priority of Principles

I proposed that equal justice should be the lodestar of reforms and that this should be achieved through a fairness floor and access to equal resources. Ensuring equal justice is the central concern here; the institutional reforms are instrumentally valuable, justified as attempts to realise equal justice. For the most part, then, realising equal justice would thereby also realise whatever value is latent in the institutional arrangements I set out in Chapters 4 and 5.

When it comes to prioritising the institutional reforms, it would be better to secure an equal distribution of legal resources than a fairness floor. That is for the simple reason that equality of legal resources would also realise the value of the fairness floor; an equal distribution is likely also to be a fair one. The basic explanation for this is that the value of lawyers is often comparative. This has the important, if counterintuitive, implication that an absolute reduction in the quality of lawyers might improve the quality of lawyering and increase the amount of justice being done. This may need a little explanation.

The proscription of private contracting for lawyers might lead to many people quitting the legal industry. This might drain some of the best resources from the legal system, when "best" is understood apart from any context. However, it may not lower—"level down"—the quality of legal resources available to litigants. Lawyers' value to litigants is comparative, dependent in part upon the absolute ability of other lawyers. In that sense, then, the quality of an individual lawyer to an individual litigant may not be reduced by an excellent lawyer quitting the legal industry. From this it follows that some lawyers quitting might lead to more benefits and fewer burdens of legality. Something like this was my argument for why the proscription of contracting out may not have the pernicious effects some anticipate.[16] In short, once equality of legal resources is achieved, the quality of legal service might be improved; it is hard to argue that this, combined with each individual being treated in the same way by the legal system, is unfair.

The Priority of Interests

Many societies endorse a qualified fairness floor.[17] They recognise, in other words, an entitlement to a basic level of legal resources only for certain types of claims. In the United States, for example, there is a constitutional right to a legal aid lawyer in criminal cases.[18] However, the Supreme Court has said, "an indigent litigant has a right to appointed counsel only when, if he loses, he may be deprived of his physical liberty."[19] This means that there is no constitutional right to a legal aid lawyer in civil cases. The implicit determination is that it is worse to lose your physical liberty than to lose "merely" civil rights.

Regardless of whether the particular assessment the United States makes is true—in *Lassiter v. Department of Social Services*, Abby Gail Lassiter stood to lose her parental rights over her three-year-old son, something many parents would regard as worse than temporary incarceration[20]—their approach only makes sense if some notion of ranking is invoked. The implicit determination must be that some injustices are worse than others.[21] This determination will look ad hoc absent the identification of a principle to say why (for example) the risk of a two-year jail sentence is so weighty that a right to counsel should be provided, whereas the risk of losing one's livelihood in a civil case is not. An ordering of this form is particularly important where a fairness floor or an equal distribution of legal resources cannot be achieved: it tells us which interests we should prioritise in political movements.

As well as distinctions between the criminal and civil spheres, we also need to draw further distinctions within the civil sphere. Just as some public health regimes distinguish elective from non-elective surgery—funds from general taxation can be used to pay for the latter but not the former—when money is scarce, budgeters should direct legal aid resources to the most important claims. If a negligent driver crashes into my car, breaking the passenger door and paralysing the passenger, two claims arise: my claim to have my car repaired and the passenger's claim for the medical expenses, pain and suffering, and so on. If a legal aid system had to choose to support only one of us, everyone should agree that (absent further facts) the passenger's claim should be prioritised. A legal aid scheme has to draw numerous distinctions of this form between classes of individuals. Given the distinct interests in play, perhaps it is more important to have legal aid lawyers for cases where the litigant stands to lose their children than it is to have lawyers where they stand to lose their job; or perhaps, given the structural power disadvantages, it is more important to have legal aid in employment disputes than in defamation claims. If we want to make any claims of this form, we need to be able to explain in virtue of what one claim is more important than another. We need, again, some kind of principle to structure and weight possible claims.

One line it seems possible to draw concerns access to valuable legal institutions. Many people, for example, would benefit from the provision of a tax lawyer to order their affairs: it is doubtful that many people pay the minimum tax they could were they advised as well as (for example) Apple or Amazon. Yet few will be tempted by the thought that the government should supply these lawyers; it just does not seem unfair to let individuals order their own tax affairs. This is best explained by the distinction between justice and welfare benefits. The tax system in a society is ultimately a matter of welfare and, so, subject to the best principles concerning the distribution of welfare in society. There is no egalitarian stringency in that domain. If there are objections to these inequalities, they are objections to the more general inequalities in society, ones that might counsel more general political reform, rather than inequalities that can be salved by the provision of legal resources.

This distinction, between justice and welfare, may not explain everything. Consider that some arguments about the distribution of legal resources do not depend upon there being an injustice or even a dispute. Suppose that two people want to get divorced. There is no acrimony and both agree on the terms of settlement. They do not become divorced simply by agreeing to certain terms. People must be able to access the requisite legal procedures. If they cannot do this, it is unfair: the state claims the sole right to terminate the marriage but has set up conditions of access these people cannot meet; they are forced to remain in a legal arrangement neither wants simply because they lack the money to escape from it. Justice John Harlan made this exact argument: "given the basic position of the marriage relationship in this society's hierarchy of values and the concomitant State monopolization of the means for legally dissolving this relationship, due process does prohibit a State from denying, solely because of inability to pay, access to its courts to individuals who seek judicial dissolution of their marriages."[22]

One explanation might be that there would be an injustice in this second case if there were no provision of legal resources. But the more general point is that the sharp lines a practical regime will have to draw may not match up to the philosophical theory. The universe is not carved into perfect joints by moral principles. Yet the fact that philosophy cannot solve all the problems does not mean that it cannot solve any of them. It can, in particular, clarify the kind of questions we should ask when thinking about these issues. It can also, as I will show, clarify the considerations we should take into account in this context.

Suppose that two individuals have plausible claims that they have been wronged and each wants help preparing their case. A lawyer has only one hour of free time and has to decide to whom it should go; the only way to help, they conclude, is to spend the entire hour on one of the individuals. What, ethically, should they take into account?[23] There would be a wide range of contingent questions. Who might benefit more from the advice? Does the lawyer know one area of law better than another, such that they can do more to help? Contingencies apart, two features seem salient to any case. First, the interests at stake; second, the extent of the injury to those interests occasioned by an individual wrong.

Legal rights protect a range of different interests. Our physical integrity is important. The legal system, therefore, recognises rights to physical integrity (not to be murdered, raped or battered, and so on). Our livelihood is also important. This interest serves to justify a variety of further rights, including rights to property (e.g., to exclude others from our homes) and to contractual outcomes (e.g., to be paid our wages). The violation of any of these rights is an injustice and can justify a claim that the law recognises. But some rights violations are worse than others. It is generally worse for an individual's physical integrity to be interfered with—for someone to be assaulted, for example—than it is for her to have some property stolen. These violations are usually worse because the interest affected is more important. Wrongful imprisonment is a grave injustice because it interferes with the most important interests we have as humans; wrongful execution is worse, depriving us of the ability to have any interests at all. This shows one important consideration when assessing the justice or injustice of certain states of affairs. If we could choose between a world where there is one physical assault and no breaches of contract or a world where there is one breach of contract and no physical assaults, we should choose the latter world.

The second thing that matters, when ranking claims, is the amount of loss suffered by the victim of injustice. The greater the loss, the more reason there is to provide legal resources to the victim. When it comes to creating a system, the implication of this is that more legal resources should be channelled to those claims where there is an increased risk of greater loss. Two people might work in the same factory and injure their hands in the same way. That description of the injury is incomplete. It leaves out the different options these people might lose as a result of the injury. It matters what these people would have done—or could otherwise have done—with their hands intact. If one of the workers was a pianist, any aspirations of a professional music career might be ended; if the other was an aspirant long-distance runner, her future might be unaffected by the injury. When thinking about the extent of loss, we must not have too blinkered a view of what counts as loss: in particular, it is important not to consider only financial interests.

When we think about the design of the legal system, there is never only one person we can help. There are very many injustices and very many possible beneficiaries of the legal system. When thinking about system design we need to consider all of them.

Imagine a very simple scenario. There are one thousand people seeking compensation for breach of contract and one individual seeking compensation for physical assault. Scarcity is such that we can either create a court that deals in breach of contract claims or a court that deals in physical assault claims. (This, of course, is an unreal assumption. But bear with me: it is helpful to simplify things like this because it will throw some light on the actual problems we face.) Which should we prioritise? If faced with one assault and one breach of contract, the question of priority usually looks easy. But there must be some amount of injustice lower-level in scale than physical assault which, conjunctively, is as bad as one physical assault. How should we weigh these different claims on the scales of justice? There is no easy answer to that—and it is not a topic philosophers have examined in much depth.[24] It seems implausible to say that we should never aggregate claims against each other: again, there must be some number of lower-level injustices that can outweigh one worse injustice.

The issue is complicated yet further by the other possible things money can go towards in the legal system. I have concentrated largely upon the repair of injustice, but the legal system also has a value in its creation and distribution of benefits. Instead of providing lawyers to argue claims in courts, money could be spent on advice bureaus: these could advise individuals before an injustice occurs. A housing association might be prevented from exploiting its tenants—evicting them unlawfully, say—if the tenants have good legal advice. Access to legal services can also generate more small-scale goods: tax-efficient planning, improved contractual rights, and so on. In principle, these things might also be traded off against the value of lawyers (for the reparation of injustice).

A final complication is temporal. Injustices have occurred in the past and will occur in the future. The structure of the legal system that we set up will affect which claims are channelled into it and how well they are resolved—and we might predict that the character of wrongdoing in society might change over time. This means that we have, in designing a legal system, to decide whether to prioritise existing claims of justice or future possible claims. Should we think of all future claims for justice as equally weighted with extant claims? If so, we might trade off the repair of one injustice today in exchange for two repairs of injustice tomorrow.

Doing More with Less

Even if there are financial feasibility constraints, those constraints entail no particular amount or arrangement of legal resources. Some of my principles depended upon the fact that certain distributions will affect the amount of legal resources to go around. It is worth stressing this point because it raises the prospect of supply-side reforms. Even if we do not have enough money for a just justice system, we should endorse those structures that lead to the most perfect compliance with the principles of justice. Certain structures, for example, might generate more or fewer legal resources, leading to more or less compliance with just justice principles. To illustrate what I have in mind, I will say something more about judges.

The state decides how many judicial positions there are and how to fill them. There is substantial variation in the number of judges appointed to apex courts worldwide. At the lower end of the scale, for example, the High Court of Australia has 7 judges and the Supreme Court of the United States has 9. Germany's Federal Court of Justice, by contrast, has 127. An increase in the number of judges might increase costs to the state, but not necessarily: it might bring in more court fees and more taxes (because of the possible increase in the number of cases being heard). The first question is the number of judges—and there can be increases without greater expense.

Who is willing to become a judge depends on push and pull factors. Quite how attractive the job is depends partly upon factors such as judicial pensions, the nature of the work, and so on. Another important factor affecting whether enough people—and enough of the best people—want to be judges is the character of private practice. The English judiciary is undermined, ironically, by its own quality. The quality of the English judiciary has made England a very popular place to litigate. This has dramatically increased the cost of private sector lawyers; a substantial number of the highest paid are, inevitably, some of the best lawyers, the sort of lawyers we should want to become judges. That has deterred many from applying to become judges: it entails a substantial pay cut. (There are other factors, too, deterring applicants today.) If we were to institute a fixed fee regime, this might decrease how attractive private practice is. It is possible that this would discourage some individuals from becoming lawyers. However, it would also increase lawyers' incentives to become judges.

INJUSTICE IN THE LEGAL SYSTEM

In earlier chapters I argued that we cannot think about certain questions— such as the proper structure of the court system—without an appreciation of principles of just justice. What if the legal system does not conform to those principles? What implications does this have for downstream questions? In this section I consider the implications for obligations to fund the legal system.

Justice in Taxation

The Gotha Program proposed "free instruction" in school. Karl Marx criticised the proposal on the grounds that it, combined with an unequal distribution of access to education, would entail "defraying the cost of education of the upper classes from the general tax receipts."[25] A similar problem applies to justice. With a suggestive question, Marx highlighted the problem: "The administration of . . . civil justice is concerned almost exclusively with conflicts over property and hence affects almost exclusively the possessing classes. Are they to carry on their litigation at the expense of the national coffers?"[26] The previous chapter considered how a just justice system should be funded. When the justice system operates to the benefit of few, funding it out of general taxation can compound the initial injustice. How should funding considerations be approached where the justice system is itself unjust?

This question seems novel, but it raises no new problems. My claim in the last chapter was that the justice system should be funded according to principles of justice in taxation. That claim holds regardless of the underlying justice of the legal system. Any plausible theory of justice in taxation will say that the principles applicable should be sensitive to the nature of the system the taxes are to fund. On the benefit principle, for example, tax burdens should be parcelled out according to the benefits individuals in fact receive: if the system only benefits the few, those few should pay.

It follows that we do not need new principles to determine who should pay for an unjust justice system: once we have buck-passed that question to the broader issue of justice in taxation, those principles will address the salient issues. There is, however, one issue local to our domain: the responsibilities of lawyers in an unjust system.

Lawyers' Obligations

In 1295, the Archbishop of Canterbury said that "advocates and proctors, and other officers in the Ecclesiastical Court, in the cause of paupers, should render their services gratis."[27] And in 1648, John Cooke proposed twelve propositions for social reform. His twelfth was "that Lawyers would give every Tenth Fee to the poore."[28]

To single out lawyers in this way presupposes that they, as a group, bear a special responsibility—beyond, that is, their basic responsibility as citizens—to ensure that the justice system is properly resourced (such that there is compliance with the best principles of justice).[29] Very many policy discussions suppose that this is the case. Reginald Heber Smith, a key figure in early twentieth-century debates in the United States, wrote that "Legal Aid is an essential part of the administration of justice in a democracy; and the primary responsibility for the establishment and maintenance of an adequate number of legal aid officers and committees in all parts of the nation is one of the cardinal obligations of the legal profession."[30]

Why think that lawyers do bear a special responsibility? One argument is that "there exists a moral obligation on the part of the profession, in return for the monopoly in the practice of law that it enjoys, to render gratuitous legal assistance to those members of the community who cannot afford to pay for such assistance, provided that no undue burden is thereby cast upon any individual members of the profession."[31] It is difficult to tease out the precise argument. It seems to be something like the fair play argument applied to lawyers: lawyers receive a particular benefit from the scheme so they should contribute to its upkeep. Without the legal system, lawyers would not be able to pursue their careers. In that sense, they owe their entire livelihoods to the system. However, most legal systems permit non-lawyers to appear in court and argue their own cases; the rules on legal appearances have been considerably loosened in recent years. And very many people depend upon lawyers. Anyone who uses contracts or wills to structure their affairs probably depends upon them. There is no deep distinction between lawyers and others in society: we all have a duty to ensure the justice system goes well; lawyers are not special in that respect.

This discussion assumes that there is a just justice system. Lawyers would, in that system, not earn the wages they earn on the free market, just as doctors in the United Kingdom are less well paid than their counterparts in the United States. When that condition does not hold, things are different.

Lawyers, like all workers, are only morally entitled to the income they would earn from a just labour relation. Were there just conditions in the legal system, lawyers would not earn market salaries. This means that they have no claim of justice to their earnings above the amount they would earn in a just justice system; any extra is surplus to which they have no strong moral entitlement. It is, therefore, justifiable for the state to call on lawyers to surrender their salary above the amount they would earn in a just justice system.

Political philosophers disagree about moral demands on individuals in circumstances of injustice. The most generous view (to individuals) is that individuals must do their share, the amount they would have to do were everyone to do what is required by justice, but no more.[32] This may limit the obligations that can be placed on lawyers. However, it does not justify lawyers' salaries. Were everyone to do what is required by justice, many lawyers would earn much less than they currently do. Doing the amount required by justice means doing what a just justice system entails. And that entails giving up the possible income of a market system.[33]

If lawyers have no entitlement to their surplus income, what are their consequent responsibilities? Their special responsibility is sometimes said to be, as in the 1295 instruction, a requirement to engage in pro bono work, to do work for which they are not paid. The proposal makes little sense. City solicitors are trained in transactions, not asylum and immigration; instead of donating an hour of their time, they would do more good if they paid an hour's wages to a legal charity. Many lawyers are paid generously; were they to contribute the equivalent of an hour's fees, this could help fund more specialised work by other lawyers. If lawyers should contribute more to the legal system, therefore, it should normally be more money, not more time. Perhaps Cooke recognised that: he proposed a donation of money.

But there is an important preliminary question. If lawyers have a special responsibility, is it owed to the population at large or to the legal system? If their obligation is to give up, the money should go to the population at large; if it is to give back (to the legal institutions), the money (and any extra tax revenue) should be hypothecated to further compliance with principles of just justice. The form of their obligation depends on the resolution of broader and under-examined puzzle about the nature of benefit-based obligations. These are obligations individuals acquire through their benefiting.[34] My view, which I have not the space to defend, is that there are stronger reasons to give benefits derived from injustice to the amelioration of the underlying injustice than there are to put it towards justice more generally. If so, extra taxation (or professional obligations) levied on lawyers should be put towards the justice system. If I am wrong, the revenue should go to the public fisc.

CONCLUSION

We have not given enough thought to the legal system and its structure. This neglect has impoverished many practical and policy debates. It has allowed very unjust structures to persist in plain sight; the flaws of those systems have often been missed. And it has allowed a number of good features of modern legal systems to be eroded without any real appreciation of the harm those changes wrought.

The prospects of progress are bleak unless we think more clearly about the nature of the questions we face. I spent some time clarifying the topic. We should, I said, think about two levels of goods: the benefits and burdens of legality; and legal resources. I spent more time making various proposals about those goods: defending the principle of equal justice, rejecting the market as a means of distributing legal resources, and developing two systemic principles (the fairness floor and equality of legal resources). Even if readers reject every one of these proposals, I hope that they find their disagreements clarified and opposing arguments sharpened by the framework I have set up.

If what I say has even a grain of truth to it, there are profound implications for the structure of most modern legal systems. No longer should we tolerate a system that permits individuals' chances of justice or risks of injustice to depend on their class, race or wealth. This may, as I have sought to explain, entail substantial changes to the structure of our legal systems: from a legal system structured around market relations to one based upon a quite different system of distribution. Those reforms will be hard won, if they come at all. But it is only with a clearer picture of our ideals that we can begin to bend reality towards them.

NOTES

ACKNOWLEDGMENTS

INDEX

NOTES

Introduction

1. Plato, *Crito* (circa 360 B.C.), in *Euthyphro. Apology. Crito. Phaedo. Phaedrus,* ed. Harold North Fowler, Loeb Classical Library (Harvard University Press, 1914), 50B.

2. This is why the laws say that Socrates was wronged, if at all, "not by . . . the laws, but by men": Plato, *Crito,* 54c. Socrates bears quite a lot of responsibility for his own demise. He was intransigent and impractical: his conduct at trial virtually compelled the jury (having found him guilty) to sentence him to death: Adriaan Lanni, *Law and Justice in the Courts of Classical Athens* (Cambridge University Press, 2006), 30–40.

3. One complication is Socrates's claim that there is a "law which provides that the decisions reached by the courts shall be valid": Plato, *Crito,* 50c. That is not a natural way for a modern lawyer to think of these things. One suggestion that Socrates thought there was a distinction between laws and court orders is in Plato, *Apology* (circa 360 B.C.), trans. Harold North Fowler, Loeb Classical Library (Harvard University Press, 1914), 29C–30C (where Socrates suggests that he might disobey a jury's decision).

4. This is the response of a participant in a working group: Roderick A Macdonald, "Access to Justice and Law Reform," *Windsor Yearbook on Access to Justice* 10 (1990): 287, 292.

5. Thomas Nagel, "Justice and Nature," in *Concealment and Exposure* (Oxford University Press, 2002), 113.

6. A trend in moral philosophy, to emphasise individual choices irrespective of background factors that condition those choices, can thus be seen to have contributed to the neglect of the questions of this book. For remarks to this effect, see Allen Wood, "Humanity as an End in Itself," in *On What Matters,* ed. Samuel Scheffler (Oxford University Press, 2011), 2:66–82.

7. My claims here are similar to Michael Walzer's account of "dominant" goods. A good is dominant "if the individuals who have it, because they have it,

can command a wide range of other goods": Michael Walzer, *Spheres of Justice* (Basic Books, 1983), 10. The structure of my claim is slightly different, particularly given the stress I give to the constitutive importance of just justice. I have, for that reason, not presented things in overtly Walzerian terms.

8. On justice across generations, see generally John Rawls, *A Theory of Justice,* rev. ed. (Belknap Press of Harvard University Press, 1999), Sections 11, 14; first published 1971; John Rawls, *Justice as Fairness: A Restatement,* ed. Erin I. Kelly (Belknap Press of Harvard University Press. 2001), 14.1.

9. Beyond the various passages considered in the following pages, see also Hobbes's discussion of whether "a Lawfull Kings command may be disobeyed": Thomas Hobbes, *Behemoth, or The Long Parliament,* The Clarendon Edition of the Works of Thomas Hobbes, vol. 10, ed. Paul Seaward (Oxford University Press, 2009), 173–74; first published 1682 (discussing a command to a son to execute his father). As that passage shows, Hobbes's principal concern was with obedience to *the law.* He does say that there is a right to a "publique hearing": Thomas Hobbes, *Leviathan, The English and Latin Texts (i),* The Clarendon Edition of the Works of Thomas Hobbes, vol. 4, ed. Noel Malcolm (Oxford University Press, 2012), 484; first published 1668. And his view about the proper structure of legal procedures depends in part on his views about law: he says, for example, that "The Judge is to take notice, that his Sentence ought to be according to the reason of his Sovereign": Hobbes, *Leviathan,* 424.

10. Though see John Locke, *Two Treatises of Government,* ed. Peter Laslett (Cambridge University Press, 1988), Sections 20 and 142; first published 1689.

11. Immanuel Kant, *The Metaphysics of Morals,* ed. Lara Denis; trans. Mary Gregor; 2nd ed. (Cambridge University Press, 2017); first published 1797.

12. Rawls, *A Theory of Justice,* 308–12. He does make some rather programmatic remarks about the rule of law: Rawls, *A Theory of Justice,* 206–13.

13. Though see Robert Nozick, *Anarchy, State and Utopia* (Basic Books, 1974), chap. 5, which contains numerous thoughts.

14. For example, H. L. A. Hart, *The Concept of Law,* ed. Joseph Raz and Penelope Bulloch, 2nd ed. (Clarendon Press, 1994); Ronald Dworkin, *Law's Empire* (Belknap Press of Harvard University Press, 1986).

15. H. L. A. Hart, *Punishment and Responsibility: Essays in the Philosophy of Law* (Oxford University Press, 1968); Ronald Dworkin, *A Matter of Principle* (Harvard University Press, 1985).

16. Though see Ronald Dworkin, "Principle, Policy, Procedure," in *A Matter of Principle.*

17. Aristotle, *The Nicomachean Ethics,* ed. Leslie Brown; trans. Sir David Ross, rev. ed. (1925; Oxford University Press, 2009), 1131^{a}10, 1131^{b}25.

18. See, however, John Gardner, "What Is Tort Law For? Part 2. The Place of Distributive Justice," in *Philosophical Foundations of the Law of Torts,* ed. John Oberdiek (Oxford University Press, 2014).

19. "Mr. Roosevelt Praises the Legal Aid Society," *New York Times,* March 24, 1901, 3 (address to the Twenty-Fifth Anniversary Dinner of the Legal Aid Society). William Brennan, former associate justice of the US Supreme Court, was so impressed by Abbott's turn of phrase that, almost sixty years later, he saw fit to lift it (without attribution) for a speech of his own: Justice William Brennan, "The

Community's Responsibility for Legal Aid," *Legal Aid Briefcase* 15 (1956): 75 (an address to the Fourth Annual Meeting of the Monmouth, New Jersey, County Legal Aid Society). Brennan also borrowed, without attribution, from Reginald Heber Smith, "Introduction" in *Emery Brownell, Legal Aid in the United States: A Study of the Availability of Lawyers' Services for Persons Unable to Pay Fees* (Lawyers Cooperative Publishing, 1951).

20. Reginald Heber Smith, *Justice and the Poor* (Charles Scribner, 1919), 5.

21. Smith, *Justice and the Poor,* 12. See, too, his dark warning that "Marxian Communism" was teaching people that "law is a class weapon used by the rich to oppress the poor through the simple device of making justice too expensive": Smith, "Introduction," in *Justice and the Poor,* xiii.

22. Deborah L Rhode, *Access to Justice* (Oxford University Press, 2004), 3. The very idea of unmet legal needs is a little difficult to grasp, but an intuitive sense—of a need to access legal resources to vindicate a claim of justice—is enough for now.

23. February 16, 1951. See Harrison Tweed, "A Great Judge Retires," *American Bar Association Journal* 37 (July 1951): 504.

24. For example, Rose Elizabeth Bird, "Thou Shalt Not Ration Justice," *Human Rights* 13 (1985): 24.

25. Aristotle, *The Nicomachean Ethics,* 1131^{a}15.

1. The Problems of Justice

1. Dred Scott v. Sandford, 60 U.S. (19 How.), 393, 403 (1857). The *Dred Scott* case was the central concern of Abraham Lincoln in his "House Divided" speech.

2. *Codex Theodosianus* 1.16.7 ("Aeque aures iudicantis pauperrimis ac divitibus reserentur").

3. The precise effect of the law is a matter of scholarly dispute. For discussion, see John Dillon, *The Justice of Constantine: Law, Communication, and Control* (University of Michigan Press, 2012), 139–46. It is certainly true that attempts were made to regulate judicial fees: see *Codex Iustinianus* (456 A.D.?), 1.3.25.3; *Novels of Justinian* 17.3.

4. 11 Henry VII, 1495, c.12 ('An acte to admytt such psons as are poore to sue in formâ paupis'). Seventy years earlier, James I of Scotland provided that "if there be any poor creature [person] that for want of skill or means cannot or may not follow his cause" (i.e., argue his own case), "a lawful [i.e., person skilled in the law] and wise advocate" would be provided for him: Parliament at Perth, 12th March 1424, Cap 24 (special thanks to Mary Wellesley for the translation from Older Scots). James's statute, which may have its origins in the French provisions of the early fifteenth century, seems concerned with fairness; Henry's statute, by contrast, is openly egalitarian.

5. Lassiter v. Department of Social Services, 452 U.S. 18 (1981), 27.

6. William Shakespeare, *The First Part of the Contention of the Two Famous Houses of York and Lancaster* (1590), in *The Oxford Shakespeare: The Complete Works,* ed. Stanley Wells and others, 2nd ed. (Oxford University Press 2005),

4.2.78. We should assess the informal settlements of the farmers of Shasta County in this light: it does not matter that they do not use lawyers, so long as their resolutions are more just than the alternative. The farmers seem to have something approaching a legal system, albeit an informal one: Robert C. Ellickson, *Order without Law: How Neighbors Settle Disputes* (Harvard University Press, 1991).

7. See, for example, the speeches of Cicero: "Chronological List of Cicero's Known Appearances as an Advocate," in Jonathan Powell and Jeremy Paterson, eds., *Cicero the Advocate* (Oxford University Press, 2004), 417–22.

8. Thomas Hobbes, *Leviathan: The English and Latin Texts (i)*, The Clarendon Edition of the Works of Thomas Hobbes, vol. 4, ed. Noel Malcolm (Oxford University Press, 2012), 193; first published 1668. Noel Malcolm calls this "a theoretical absolute which may be approached but never reached": *Aspects of Hobbes* (Oxford University Press, 2002), 452.

9. For a succinct analysis, see Thomas Hobbes, *De Cive: The English Version,* The Clarendon Edition of the Works of Thomas Hobbes, vol. 2, ed. Howard Warrender (Oxford University Press, 2012), 129–30; first published 1642. For a similar account, see David Hume, *A Treatise of Human Nature,* ed. David Fate Norton and Mary J. Norton (Oxford University Press, 2008), 3.2.7; first published 1740. Hume, though, does not distinguish justice and welfare benefits: the benefits are the "sweets of society and mutual assistance."

10. David Hume, "Of the Origin of Government" in *Essays, Moral, Political, and Literary,* ed. Eugene F. Miller, 2nd ed. (Liberty Fund, 1987), 37; first published 1742.

11. James Madison, *Federalist 51,* in Alexander Hamilton, James Madison, and John Jay, *The Federalist Papers,* ed. Lawrence Goldman (Oxford University Press, 2008), 259; first published 1788. See, too, Jean Bodin's claim, that "kings were never for other thing established than for the administration of justice": Jean Bodin, *The Six Bookes of a Commonweale,* ed. Kenneth Douglas McRae; trans. Richard Knolles (Harvard University Press, 1962), 500, F–G; first published 1576.

12. An apparent counterexample is Hobbes, *Leviathan,* 196: "Where there is no common Power, there is no Law: where no Law, no Injustice." But Hobbes would not disagree with the thrust of this claim. His concept of "justice" applies only in civil society, but he adds that "they that have Soveraigne power, may commit Iniquity; but not Injustice . . . in the proper signification." As he explains (in a passage substituted in the Latin version): "I have not denied that the sovereign can act iniquitously [or: "inequitably"]. For that which is done against the law of nature is called 'iniquitous', and that which is done against the civil law is called 'unjust.' For justice and injustice did not exist before the commonwealth was set up": Hobbes, *Leviathan,* 270 and n. 21. Part of the justification of the state is, in Hobbes's language, to protect from *iniquity.*

13. Adam Smith, *An Inquiry into the Nature and Causes of the Wealth of Nations,* The Glasgow Edition of the Works and Correspondence of Adam Smith, vol. 2, ed. William B. Todd (Oxford University Press, 1976) 689; first published 1776.

14. Smith, *The Wealth of Nations,* 708.

15. Smith, *The Wealth of Nations,* 708–9.

16. Hobbes, *De Cive,* 74–75 (VI. 9).

17. Hume, *A Treatise of Human Nature,* 3.2.2. It is a contingent question which things are scarce. At one point Hume talks of air as bountiful: David Hume, *An Enquiry Concerning the Principles of Morals,* in *The Clarendon Edition of the Works of David Hume,* ed. Tom L Beauchamp (Oxford University Press, 1998), 3.1.4; first published 1740. But if there are stowaways on the space rocket, there might not be enough oxygen for everyone to return to earth. If some are to survive, one must die: Hergé, *On a Marché Sur la Lune* (Casterman, 1954).

18. Jeremy Bentham, "Preface to *A Fragment on Government,*" in *A Comment on the Commentaries and A Fragment on Government,* The Collected Works of Jeremy Bentham, ed. J. H. Burns and H. L. A. Hart (Oxford University Press, 1977), 393 (emphasis removed); first published 1776.

19. This statement requires some care. Rawls's difference principle, for example, allows inequalities that favour those with certain talents; those talents are, for Rawls, "arbitrary from a moral point of view": John Rawls, *A Theory of Justice,* rev ed. (Belknap Press of Harvard University Press, 1999), 14, 63; first published 1971. The mere interrelation between arbitrary facts and outcomes does not, therefore, necessarily render those outcomes unjust: the outcomes are unjust unless justified in some other way (e.g., by the difference principle). I have tried to capture these complications with the reference to a "determinative" role.

20. Practical debates usually concern not the abstract claim—that there is injustice when an allocation is made on the basis of the wrong kind of facts—but what the right kind of facts are. For example, Bernard Williams claimed that "the proper ground of distribution of medical care is ill health": Bernard Williams, "The Idea of Equality," in *Problems of the Self* (Cambridge University Press 1973), 240. Those who disagree with him claim that Williams is wrong to think ill health is the only relevant fact in that context; they do not doubt that there is injustice when irrelevant facts control distributions.

21. Aristotle, *The Nicomachean Ethics,* ed. Leslie Brown; trans. Sir David Ross, rev. ed. (1925; Oxford University Press, 2009), book V, chap. 2, 1131^a.

22. See Aristotle, *The Nicomachean Ethics,* 1132^{a}30, on "arithmetical" equality.

23. James W. Nickel, "Justice in Compensation," *William and Mary Law Review* 18 (1976): 379, 381–82. See, too, Robert Nozick, *Anarchy, State and Utopia* (Basic Books, 1974), 151.

24. I have made things easier for myself here than they are in the real world. My assumed state, like Nickel's, is one where a just distribution is disturbed. What if, though, an *unjust* distribution is disturbed? The point is considered by Jules L Coleman, *Risks and Wrongs* (Oxford University Press, 1992), 304–5, 352–53.

25. Thomas Hobbes, *The Elements of Law,* ed. J. C. A. Gaskin (Oxford University Press, 2008), II.10.8; first published 1640. For the descendants of this passage, see Hobbes, *De Cive,* 74–75, and Hobbes, *Leviathan,* 193. Hobbes's own example, which concerns whether an individual counts as a human, is more controversial than the basic point about the value of conventions. See, too, Hume's observation that humans have a "remarkable partiality in their own

favours," a partiality that is cured by legal officials: Hume, *A Treatise of Human Nature,* 3.2.7.7.

26. I mean here that laws can and should help us establish what we ought morally to do. The fact that the law is one way or another might also determine what we ought, prudentially, to do (for example, to avoid punishment).

27. See, for example, Hume, *A Treatise of Human Nature,* 3.1.7.8.

28. Here I use the term "assurance" in its non-technical sense. Free-rider cases, where an individual is able to obtain the benefits of cooperative schemes without incurring their costs, give rise to more complicated problems; and in that scholarly domain "assurance" has a more technical meaning, which I consider later. Consider things like tax evasion, where it seems as if the core of the wrong is that some individual is gaming the system, acquiring the benefits of a coopera-tive scheme without paying in. I will return to these questions in Chapter 9.

29. For example, Hume, *A Treatise of Human Nature,* 3.2.2, 3.2.5.

30. *Old Bailey Sessions Papers* 285 (July 1757): 263, 269. For this passage and other evocative examples, see John Langbein, *The Origins of Adversary Criminal Trial* (Oxford University Press, 2005), 317–18.

31. William Chatwin and John Davis, *Old Bailey Sessions Papers* 429 (June 1788): 561, 562.

32. The incidence of absolute injustices may also be an injustice if unequally distributed. I consider here, though, the pure case where the injustice is in the mere differential treatment, where the treatment (such as conviction of crime) is (comparative questions aside) warranted.

33. Bob Dylan, "The Lonesome Death of Hattie Carroll" in *The Lyrics, 1962–2012* (Simon and Schuster, 2016), 95–96.

34. William Zantzinger, the person on whom Dylan based the song, was convicted of manslaughter and assault. He received a six-month sentence—and he was permitted to bring in the tobacco crop from his farm before beginning his sentence.

35. Max Weber, "Politics as a Vocation," in *From Max Weber: Essays in Sociology,* trans. H. H. Gerth and C. Wright Mills (Routledge, 2009), 334 (emphasis removed); first published 1919.

36. Philosophers have disagreed about the case in which I did take your crops. Some think that there is such a power of private punishment.

37. *Selden Society* 30 (1914): 2–3.

38. We do not know what the court thought of Alice's claim. The particular bill from which I have quoted is one that she failed to prosecute. It appears that she withdrew the bill and put forward another with a slightly amended—less literary—complaint. Alice and Thomas settled the complaint of the second bill with the permission of the court. My thanks to Paul Brand for help piecing this together.

39. Aristotle, *Politics* (circa 350 B.C.), trans. Carnes Lord (University of Chicago Press, 2013), 1282b.

40. Williams, "The Idea of Equality," 240. There is a complication here, one that I ignore in order to try to keep the discussion intelligible, concerning the distinction between value monism and value pluralism. The monist thinks that all values are ultimately reducible, which makes it possible to propose a general

principle, like Bentham's, for the distribution of all goods. The pluralist thinks that values are not reducible in this way. Inevitably, any proposed distributive principle will be more local in its application.

41. Powell v. Alabama 287 US 45, 68–69 (1932). The facts of *Powell* are vivid and illustrative of some earlier claims of mine about the importance of law in securing freedom from private vengeance: see 51–52 of Justice Sutherland's opinion.

42. Gideon v. Wainwright 372 US 335, 344 (1964). There is widespread evidence of the importance of lawyers to outcomes. In one study, legal representation was found to increase an immigrant's chance of winning an immigration case by up to twelve times: Vera Institute of Justice, "Evaluation of the New York Immigrant Family Unity Project" (November 2017). Although the empirical literature on this is still developing, the value lawyers add to clients seems to depend, unsurprisingly, on context: D. James Greiner, Cassandra Wolos Pattanayak, and Jonathan Hennessy, "The Limits of Unbundled Legal Assistance: A Randomized Study in a Massachusetts District Court and Prospects for the Future," *Harvard Law Review* 126 (2013): 901. Some claims I will make depend on there being a certain degree of interrelation; those claims are, in that sense, a hostage to the developing literature. Others, though, are not. I will try, when developing my arguments, to make clear when my claims do depend on this interrelation.

43. To put this point another way, legal resources are both a thing to be distributed *and* a procedure to distribute the benefits and burdens of legality, but justice in the distribution of legal resources depends largely on its effects on the distribution of the benefits and burdens of legality.

44. This division aims to bring some order to our thought. But the line between procedures and outcomes can be blurred: when assessing a distributive arrangement, it is always possible to characterise the use of a procedure as an "outcome." (See, analogously, Bernard Williams, "A Critique of Utilitarianism," in *Utilitarianism: For and Against* [Cambridge University Press, 1973], 83). So long as no weight is attached to the fact that some consideration is procedural rather than outcome-based, the complication should not pose a problem.

Despite the complication, failure to distinguish the grounds of a distribution (such as "need", as in Karl Marx, *Critique of the Gotha Programme*, ed. Robert C. Tucker, 2nd ed. [W. W. Norton and Company, 1978], 531; first published 1875) from the method used to achieve the distribution (such as "queues") is an obstacle to clear thought. Compare Michael J. Sandel, *Justice: What's the Right Thing to Do?* (Farrar, Straus and Giroux, 2009), 41 ("markets and queues are not the only ways of allocating things. Some goods we distribute by merit, others by need, still others by lottery or chance").

45. For example, James Harrington's example of two friends cutting a cake, where the procedure is designed to incentivise the cake-cutter to cut the cake in half: James Harrington, *The Commonwealth of Oceana and A System of Politics*, ed. J. G. A. Pocock (Cambridge University Press, 1992), 22; first published 1656. The example demonstrates "perfect procedural justice": Rawls, *A Theory of Justice* 74. The difference between this and an "imperfect procedural justice" is a matter of degree, so it can be left to one side.

46. This is "pure procedural justice," which Rawls claimed is the appropriate perspective to take when considering the justice of the basic structure: Rawls, *A Theory of Justice,* 75.

47. This point is important to bear in mind when discussing which procedure to use in a certain context. Some, for example, ask whether a queue or a market is a better means of getting goods to those who need them: Martin L. Weitzman, "Is the Price System or Rationing More Effective in Getting a Commodity to Those Who Need It Most?" *Bell Journal of Economics* 8 (1977): 517. This is, though, merely one dimension of justice.

48. The hereditary feature is incidental to my point. The Athenian Stranger, for example, says that offices of state should be assigned to the "most obedient to the established laws": Plato, *Laws,* trans. Thomas L. Pangle (University of Chicago Press, 1980), 715c, p. 102. This is no different in form from hereditary rule: an outcome-based norm is proposed for the distribution of political power.

49. This is not to say, as I stress in Chapter 3, that the consequences of using these methods is unpredictable. These models might be understood differently by different cultures, too: in the *Iliad,* for example, a lot is understood as revealing Zeus's will. It is, under those circumstances, selection with a particular outcome in mind: allocation to the one chosen by Zeus. See Homer, *The Iliad* (circa 1260–1180 B.C.), trans. Stephen Mitchell (Weidenfeld and Nicholson, 2011), 7.170–190.

50. This is the argument of Chapter 2.

51. See Chapters 4 and 5.

2. Equal Justice

1. Thucydides, *The War of the Peloponnesians and the Athenians,* ed. and trans. Jeremy Mynott, (Cambridge University Press, 2013), ii.37.1. This passage is translated in various ways, each of which casts a subtly different light on the quote. Thomas Hobbes's translation refers to "an equality amongst all men in point of law": Thucydides, *The Peloponnesian War,* ed. David Grene; trans. Thomas Hobbes (University of Chicago Press, 1989), 109; first published 1629. Martin Hammond's translation says, "Our laws give equal rights to all in private disputes": Thucydides, *The Peloponnesian War,* trans. Martin Hammond (Oxford University Press, 2009), 92.

2. For example, the Legal Action Group has argued that "anyone with a legal problem [should have] equal access to its just conclusion so that disputes are determined by the intrinsic merits of the arguments of either party, not by inequalities of wealth or power": Legal Action Group, "The Scope of Legal Services," in *A Strategy for Justice* (Legal Action Group, 1992). The key idea here is that the "intrinsic merits of the argument" should win out: we need no reference to equality as a value for that.

3. F. A. Hayek, *The Constitution of Liberty,* ed. Ronald Hamowy (University of Chicago Press, 2011), 222; first published 1960.

4. John Rawls, *A Theory of Justice,* rev. ed. (Belknap Press of Harvard University Press, 1999), 51; first published 1971.

5. "La majestueuse égalité des lois interdit aux riches comme aux pauvres de coucher sous les ponts, de mendier dans la rue et de voler du pain": Anatole France, *Le Lys Rouge*, 14th ed. (Callmann-Lévy, 1894), 118.

6. There may be a more profound demand nascent in the precept. Consider, for example, the reference to a law that "forbids the introduction of any law that does not affect all citizens alike,—an injunction conceived in the true spirit of democracy. As every man has an equal share in the constitution generally, so this statute asserts his equal share in the laws": Demosthenes, "Against Timocrates" in *Orations* (circa 353 B.C.), trans. J. H. Vince, Loeb Classical Library (Harvard University Press, 1935), 3: line 59. Or consider John Locke's requirement that all governments "govern by promulgated established laws, not to be varied in particular cases, but to have one rule for rich and poor, for the favourite at court, and the country man at plough": John Locke, *Two Treatises of Government*, ed. Peter Laslett (Cambridge University Press, 1988), 2: section 142 (emphasis removed); first published 1689. Locke is writing about formal equality, but the egalitarian instinct, which I develop under my principle of equal justice, is clear.

7. Hayek, *The Constitution of Liberty*, 222.

8. Whitney Seymour, *Annual Report of the Standing Committee on Legal Aid Work of the American Bar Association* (1961), 7.

9. Herodotus, *The Landmark Herodotus: The Histories*, ed. Robert B. Strassler; trans. Andrea L. Purvis (Anchor Books, 2007), 3.80.6.

10. "Otanes . . . presented the proposal that the government of the Persians should be a democracy": Herodotus, *The Landmark Herodotus: The Histories*, 6.43.3.

11. For (contrasting) philological discussions of *isonomia*, see Gregory Vlastos, "Isonomia," *American Journal of Philology* 74 (1953): 337; Martin Ostwald, *Nomos and the Beginnings of Athenian Democracy* (Clarendon Press, 1969), part 2, chap. 3; Kurt Raaflaub, *The Discovery of Freedom in Ancient Greece*, trans. Renate Franciscono (University of Chicago Press, 2004), 94–96.

12. Ostwald, *Nomos and the Beginnings of Athenian Democracy*, 120.

13. Ostwald, *Nomos and the Beginnings of Athenian Democracy*, 113.

14. Euripides, *Suppliant Women, Electra, Heracles* (circa 420 B.C.), ed. and trans. David Kovacs, Loeb Classical Library (Harvard University Press, 1998), 433–34, 437. This is the only reference in the fifth century B.C. to *written* law as guaranteeing equal justice. Compare Thucydides, *The War of the Peloponnesians and the Athenians*, ii.37.1.

15. Euripides, *Suppliant Women, Electra, Heracles*, 465–66.

16. The first concern deals with equality in an individual suit: so long as right wins out in individual claims, the ideal is secured. The second concern deals with equality across the legal system: if right is prevailing more for some than others, the ideal is infringed.

17. Thucydides, *The War of the Peloponnesians and the Athenians*, II.37.1.

18. Thucydides, *History of the Peloponnesian War*, trans. Benjamin Jowett, 2nd ed. (Clarendon Press, 1900), II.37.1. See, too, Thucydides, *The History of the Peloponnesian War*, trans. Richard Crawley (Longmans, Green, 1874), II.37.1 ("If we look to the laws, they afford equal justice to all in their private differences").

19. See, for example, Griffin v. Illinois 351 US 12, 17, 19 (1956) ("In criminal trials, a State can no more discriminate on account of poverty than on account of religion, race, or color. . . . There can be no equal justice where the kind of trial a man gets depends on the amount of money he has" [Black, J.]).

20. Michael Walzer, *Spheres of Justice* (Basic Books, 1983), 85.

21. Thomas Hobbes, *Leviathan: The English and Latin Texts (i),* The Clarendon Edition of the Works of Thomas Hobbes, vol. 4, ed. Noel Malcolm (Oxford University Press, 2012), 534; first published 1668.

22. For example, David Dyzenhaus, "Normative Justifications for the Provision of Legal Aid," in *Report of the Ontario Legal Aid Review: A Blueprint for Publicly Funded Legal Services* (1997), 490–91 ("The law, through its promise of equality before it to all those subject to it, suggests that the benefits it delivers are equally open to all subjects").

23. Figures taken from Dave Fowler, "Titanic Survivors," *Titanic Facts,* https://titanicfacts. net / titanic-survivors/, accessed October 15, 2018.

24. Thomas Schelling, *Choice and Consequence* (Harvard University Press, 1985), 115–16.

25. Schelling himself does not draw out this moral; he makes few proposals for equality in our world. In Thomas Nagel's sharp phrase, Schelling "seems to think that . . . we're all in the same boat only if we're all literally in the same boat": Thomas Nagel, "Schelling: The Price of Life," in *Other Minds: Critical Essays 1969–1994* (Oxford University Press, 1995), 186.

26. This is a weaker claim than the one I attribute to Schelling's hypothetical: I have softened "shared equally" to "roughly equally." Otherwise I would be committed to the claim that a state of anarchy, namely, a state without a legal system, is better in all cases than one where the benefits and burdens of the scheme are not shared equally. And that would be implausible. The problem posed here is similar in structure to that raised by Jean-Jacques Rousseau, *Discourse on the Origin and Foundations of Inequality among Men,* ed. and trans. Victor Gourevitch (Cambridge University Press, 1997), first published 1754. See, too, Nagel and Murphy's reference to the idea that "the market will in certain respects leave *everyone* worse off than they could otherwise be": Liam Murphy and Thomas Nagel, *The Myth of Ownership* (Oxford University Press, 2002), 86 (emphasis added).

27. Herodotus, *The Landmark Herodotus: The Histories,* 3.83.

28. Hannah Arendt, *On Revolution* (Penguin Books, 2006), 20; first published 1963. For a more recent reference, see Niko Kolodny, "Rule over None II: Social Equality and the Justification of Democracy," *Philosophy and Public Affairs* 42 (2014): 287.

29. For Rawls these rights are included within the basic liberties: Rawls, *A Theory of Justice,* 53. On my own presentation, such political rights are distinct from our natural rights, such as those to be free from, in Rawls's terms, "physical assault and dismemberment." So far as is possible, I have tried to avoid specifying these rights with too much precision; my claims concern, not these liberties, but what follows from their recognition and the manner of their protection.

30. Rawls, *A Theory of Justice,* 220. See, too, Immanuel Kant, *The Metaphysics of Morals,* ed. Lara Denis; trans. Mary Gregor, 2nd ed. (Cambridge

University Press, 2017), 6:237; first published 1797; H. L. A. Hart, "Are There Any Natural Rights?" *Philosophical Review* 64 (1955): 175.

31. There is an important disagreement in the history of ideas about the basis of equal rights. Some have thought equal rights a necessary bulwark against individuals' natural inequality; others derive the concept from humans' natural equality. Thomas Hobbes, a proponent of the latter view, proposes an argument to unite these views: "If Nature therefore have made men equall, that equalitie is to be acknowledged: or if Nature have made men unequall; yet because men that think themselves equall, will not enter into conditions of Peace, but upon Equall termes, such equalitie must be admitted": Hobbes, *Leviathan,* 234.

32. Compare Hayek, *The Constitution of Liberty,* 71.

33. For this language see Rawls, *A Theory of Justice,* 179; see also 198. See, too, Hayek, *The Constitution of Liberty,* 20–21, 133.

34. Compare Tuttle v. Buck 119 NW 946 (Minnesota 1909), a case concerning rival barbers in Minnesota.

35. Kant, *The Metaphysics of Morals,* 6.271.

36. For example, James W Nickel, "Justice in Compensation," *William and Mary Law Review* 18 (1976): 379, 381–82; Arthur Ripstein, *Force and Freedom* (Harvard University Press, 2009), 303–4; John Gardner, "What Is Tort Law For? Part 1. The Place of Corrective Justice," *Law and Philosophy* 30 (2011): 1.

37. See, for example, the reference to *vanishing* rights in a book about the difficulties of *enforcing* those rights: Margaret Jane Radin, *Boilerplate: The Fine Print, Vanishing Rights, and the Rule of Law* (Princeton University Press, 2014).

38. I cannot defend that assumption here, though it is widely accepted: Ronald Dworkin, *Sovereign Virtue* (Belknap Press of Harvard University Press, 2002), 6; T. M. Scanlon, *Why Does Inequality Matter?* (Oxford University Press, 2018), chap. 2.

39. T. M. Scanlon, "The Diversity of Objections to Inequality," in *The Difficulty of Tolerance: Essays in Political Philosophy* (Cambridge University Press, 2003), 206.

40. The principle is somewhat more complicated than this: Scanlon, *Why Does Inequality Matter?,* 7, 17–19.

41. March 3, 1863: *An Act for Enrolling and Calling Out the National Forces, and for Other Purposes,* 12 Stat. 731.

42. Section 13 provides that "any person drafted . . . may pay . . . such sum, not exceeding three hundred dollars . . . for the procuration of [a] substitute" soldier. "[T]hereupon such person . . . paying the money, shall be discharged from farther liability under that draft."

43. James Tobin, "On Limiting the Domain of Inequality," *Journal of Law and Economics* 13 (1970): 263, 270.

44. The historical position is somewhat more complicated than this bald assessment suggests. Commutation clubs formed that enabled individuals to pool their risk and, thus, buy themselves out the draft notwithstanding their inability to meet the $300 fee. Thus James Geary has argued that, "through the use of private resources, community contributions, insurance societies . . . most drafted men could escape military service": James W Geary, *We Need Men: The Union Draft in the Civil War* (Northern Illinois University Press, 1991), 168.

45. Leslie M Harris, *In the Shadow of Slavery: African Americans in New York City, 1626–1863* (University of Chicago Press, 2004), 280.

46. David M. Barnes, *Draft Riots in New York City, July 1863: The Metropolitan Police: Their Services during Riot Week* (Baker and Godwin, 1863), 115. Jones's widow, Mary, was only able to identify his body by the loaf of bread he had carried.

47. *Evening Express,* July 14, 1863. See, generally, Iver Bernstein, *The New York City Draft Riots: Their Significance for American Society and Politics in the Age of the Civil War* (Oxford University Press, 1991).

48. John Rawls made a similar point about the Vietnam War–era draft: Robert J Samuelson, "Faculty Shelves Draft Resolution after Debating for Hour and Half," *Harvard Crimson,* November 1, 1967. See, too, John Rawls, *Justice as Fairness: A Restatement,* ed. Erin I. Kelly (Belknap Press of Harvard University Press, 2001), 47.

49. It only "suggests" this because the lottery might be thought objectionable for incidental reasons, such as efficiency. I will consider this kind of argument in Chapter 6.

50. My caveats are to take account of the fact that, for example, women and black Americans were not drafted.

51. Aeschylus's *Suppliants* suggests that a principal argument in favour of democracy was that decisions about war ought to be taken by all those likely to be affected: Kurt Raaflaub, "The Breakthrough of *Demokratia* in Mid-Fifth-Century Athens," in K. A. Raaflaub, J. Ober, and R. W. Wallace, *Origins of Democracy in Ancient Greece* (University of California Press, 2007), 139. This is a good argument for democratic procedures for the resolution of such decisions; it is different from the equal burden principle, though, because it is not an argument for how those burdens should be allocated.

52. Bureau of Justice Statistics, *Homicide Trends in the United States, 1980–2008* (2011), 3, https://www.bjs.gov/content/pub/pdf/htus8008.pdf.

53. This example also demonstrates a complication in the notion of a benefit of legality being shared equally. It is not enough to examine the different incidence of, for example, various wrongs on different groups; that does not tell us whether the inequality is a function of the social institution. The mere inequality in the incidence of wrongs between groups is not itself an injustice. It is doubtful, though, that grave inequality could result from anything but an institutional prejudice.

54. Adam Smith, *An Inquiry into the Nature and Causes of the Wealth of Nations,* The Glasgow Edition of the Works and Correspondence of Adam Smith, vol. 2, ed. William B. Todd (Oxford University Press, 1976), 689, 708; first published 1776.

55. For the analogous argument, see Rawls, *A Theory of Justice,* 312. Rawls argues that "the burden of injustice [of unjust laws] should be more or less evenly distributed over different groups in society, and the hardship of unjust policies should not weigh too heavily in any particular case. Therefore the duty to comply is problematic for permanent minorities that have suffered from injustice for many years."

56. See the analogous claim of Ronald Dworkin, "Principle, Policy, Procedure," in *A Matter of Principle* (Belknap Press of Harvard University Press, 1985), 85: "a decision to adopt a particular rule of evidence in criminal trials treats citizens as equals, because each citizen is antecedently equally likely to be drawn into the criminal process though innocent, and equally likely to benefit from the savings gained by choosing that rule of evidence rather than a socially more expensive rule."

57. Michelle Alexander, *The New Jim Crow: Mass Incarceration in the Age of Colorblindness* (New Press, 2010), 96–97.

58. David B. Mustard, "Racial, Ethnic, and Gender Disparities in Sentencing: Evidence from the U.S. Federal Courts," *Journal of Law and Economics* 44 (2001): 285, 304.

59. Hobbes, *Leviathan,* 534 n. 75. This is Noel Malcolm's translation of Hobbes's Latin edition of *Leviathan.* The Latin is itself a substitution for the passage on the equal administration of justice, quoted previously. It is a shame both passages were not included in a single version of *Leviathan;* they have somewhat distinct, mutually supportive, content.

60. This derives from the Robert Nozick's example of the basketballer, Wilt Chamberlain: Robert Nozick, *Anarchy, State and Utopia* (Basic Books, 1974), 160–64.

61. These questions, Rawls said, subject "any ethical theory to severe if not impossible tests": Rawls, *A Theory of Justice,* 251.

62. Nozick's central claim, that "whatever arises from a just situation by just steps is itself just," is a yawning non sequitur: Nozick, *Anarchy, State and Utopia,* 151. No defence of that claim is provided in the book. For further criticism of this formulation see G. A., "Justice, Freedom and Market Transactions," in *Self-Ownership, Freedom and Equality* (Cambridge University Press 1995), especially p. 61.

63. John Rawls, "The Basic Structure as Subject," in *Political Liberalism* (Columbia University Press 1993), 265–69. Cf. Rawls, *A Theory of Justice,* section 43.

64. Rawls, "The Basic Structure as Subject," 266.

65. Rawls, "The Basic Structure as Subject," 268.

66. Nozick did not consider justice in the rectification of injustice; he simply said that injustices should be rectified: Nozick, *Anarchy, State and Utopia,* 151. He failed, in other words, to think about the mechanics of a legal system. Rawls makes passing remarks about the legal system's import: Rawls, *A Theory of Justice,* 6 ("the legal protection of freedom of thought and liberty of conscience, competitive markets, private property in the means of production, and the monogamous family"); Rawls, *Justice as Fairness: A Restatement,* section 4.1 ("The political constitution with an independent judiciary, the legally recognized forms of property, and the structure of the economy").

67. Cicero, *On Moral Ends* (45 B.C.), ed. Julia Annas; trans. Raphael Woolf (Cambridge University Press, 2001), v. 67; p. 140. See, too, Plato, *Republic, Books 1–5* (circa 380 B.C.), trans. Christopher Emlyn-Jones and William Preddy, Loeb Classical Library (Harvard University Press, 2013), iv. 422; p. 397 (Justice

aims "to make sure that individuals neither end up with other people's belong-ings, nor are deprived of their own").

68. Scanlon, *Why Does Inequality Matter?*, 19.

69. Anthony Trollope, *The Last Chronicle of Barset* (Penguin Classics, 2002), 208; first published 1867.

70. Socrates is an early example of a philosopher taking his argument a bit too far. Even Thomas Hobbes (often thought an absolutist in these respects) permitted an exception to such obligations when an individual's life was at stake. He did say that "every subject in a Commonwealth, hath covenanted to obey the Civill Law": Hobbes, *Leviathan,* 419. But he also wrote that "if the Soveraign command a man (though justly condemned [to death],) to kill, wound, or mayme himselfe; or not to resist those that assault him; or to abstain from the use of food, ayre, medicine, or any other thing, without which he cannot live; yet hath that man the Liberty to disobey": Hobbes, *Leviathan,* 111–12. See, too, Thomas Hobbes, *De Cive: The English Version,* The Clarendon Edition of the Works of Thomas Hobbes, vol. 2, ed. Howard Warrender (Oxford University Press, 2012), 98 ("if therefore I be commanded to kill my self, I am not bound to doe it"); first published 1642. An excellent general account of Hobbes on rights to resist is given by Susanne Sreedhar, *Hobbes on Resistance: Defying the Leviathan* (Cambridge University Press, 2010).

71. Some views of authority will make things too easy for these officials. Bates says that "if [the king's] cause be wrong, our obedience to the king wipes/the crime of it out of us": William Shakespeare, *The Life of Henry the Fifth,* in *The Oxford Shakespeare: The Complete Works,* ed. Stanley Wells and others, 2nd ed. (Oxford University Press, 2005), 4.1.131–32; first published 1599. That is too optimistic a view: officials' lives can go wrong if they follow unjust orders. As a countermeasure, there are exceptions to officials' obligations to obey. Gustav Radbruch, a jurist who lived through the Nazi era, proposed a formula to resolve conflicts between what the law and justice requires: "The positive law, secured by legislation and power, takes precedence even when its content is unjust and fails to benefit the people, unless the conflict between statute and justice reaches such an intolerable degree that the statute, as 'flawed law,' must yield to justice": Gustav Radbruch, "Gesetzliches Unrecht und übergesetzliches Recht," *Südde-utsche Juristen-Zeitung* 1 (1946): 105–8. The translation is from Gustav Radbruch, "Statutory Lawlessness and Supra-Statutory Law (1946)," Bonnie Litschewski Paulson and Stanley L. Paulson, trans., *Oxford Journal of Legal Studies* 26 (2006): 1, 7. For further discussion of the general point, see David Estlund, "On Following Orders in an Unjust War," *Journal of Political Philosophy* 15 (2007): 213; Jeff McMahan, *Killing in War* (Oxford University Press, 2009), 68–69.

72. Plato, *Crito,* in *Euthyphro. Apology. Crito. Phaedo. Phaedrus,* trans. Harold North Fowler, Loeb Classical Library (Harvard University Press, 1914), 50b.

73. Hobbes stressed this point often: see Thomas Hobbes, *The Elements of Law,* ed. J. C. A. Gaskin (Oxford University Press, 2008), II.10.8; first published 1640; Hobbes, *De Cive,* 74–75; Hobbes, *Leviathan,* 193.

74. For an enjoyable account, see N. A. M. Rodger, *The Command of the Ocean: A Naval History of Britain 1649–1815* (Penguin, 2006), 720–27.

75. "Dans ce pays-ci il est bon de tuer de temps en temps un amiral pour encourager les autres," translated in Voltaire, *Candide, and Other Stories* (trans. Roger Pearson [Oxford University Press, 2006], 65; first published 1759), as "in this country it is considered a good thing to kill an admiral from time to time so as to encourage the others."

76. Rodger, *The Command of the Ocean*, 738–39.

77. Compare E. F. Carritt, *Ethical and Political Thinking* (Clarendon Press, 1947), 65.

78. See the text to note 46.

79. Compare here Thomas Christiano's argument that "in order for a state to be authoritative, it must be just either in the substance of its laws or in the process by which it makes those laws": Thomas Christiano, "The Authority of Democracy," *Journal of Political Philosophy* 12 (2004): 266, 280. My point is that even if both these conditions were met, injustice in the application of the laws could undermine a state's authority. A similar claim is made about obligations to obey unjust laws in Peter Singer, *Democracy and Disobedience* (Oxford University Press, 1974), 30 and following; compare Joseph Raz, "The Obligation to Obey the Law," in *The Authority of Law: Essays on Law and Morality* (Oxford University Press, 1979), 241–42. There is also an analogy, though a looser one, with Tom Tyler, *Why People Obey the Law,* rev. ed. (Princeton University Press, 2006); first published 1990. (The analogy is looser with Tyler because his claims are empirical, whereas mine are normative.)

80. For example, Boddie v. Connecticut 401 US 371, 375 (1971) (Harlan, J.): "the State's monopoly over techniques for binding conflict resolution could hardly be said to be acceptable" if there were not a procedural guarantee of an individual's rights. Commenting on this case, the editors of the Harvard Law Review wrote that "access to the courts for all citizens induces willingness to relinquish self-help and submit to the rule of law; and ability to litigate just claims . . . gives legitimacy to the state's coercive power." "The Supreme Court, 1970 Term," *Harvard Law Review* 85 (1971): 104, 109–10.

81. United Kingdom, *Report of the Royal Commission on Divorce and Matrimonial Causes* (1912), Cd 6478, para 82.

3. A Market in Legal Resources

1. John Messer, "The Ship William Brown," *Court and Lady's Magazine, Monthly Critic and Museum* 21 (1841): 226. The best account of the event doubts this was ever said: Brian Simpson, "The *William Brown* and the *Euxine,*" in *Cannibalism and the Common Law: A Victorian Yachting Tragedy* (University of Chicago Press, 1984), 167. Simpson is relying, not Messer's earlier statement, but on an account in the London *Times,* published on July 24, 1884. He gives no explanation for his doubt. Simpson also notes that the sacrifice of life was unnecessary: the boat was rescued at 7 A.M. the next morning.

2. United States v. Holmes 26 Fed.Cas. (1842), 360, 367.

3. The reasonably lenient sentence—the maximum sentence for the crime was three years—was partly a function of the fact Holmes had already been jailed for six months awaiting trial and also, perhaps, of the jury's recommendation that Holmes receive mercy. President John Tyler refused a pardon on procedural grounds, though a fine that was initially imposed was remitted.

4. Debra Satz, *Why Some Things Should Not Be for Sale: The Moral Limits of Markets* (Oxford University Press, 2010), 79–80.

5. F. A. Hayek, *The Road to Serfdom* (Routledge Press, 1944); Gary Becker, *The Economic Approach to Human Behavior* (University of Chicago Press, 1976), 10.

6. I discuss the concept of public goods, and their relation to law, in more detail later in this chapter. Compare, on this general point, Ronald Coase, "The Problem of Social Cost," *Journal of Law and Economics* 3 (1960): 44.

7. For example, Daniel Kahneman and Amos Tversky, "Prospect Theory: An Analysis of Decisions under Risk," *Econometrica* 47 (1979): 263 (on humans' asymmetric attitudes to benefits and burdens); Bruce Greenwald and Joseph Stiglitz, "Externalities in Economies with Imperfect Information and Incomplete Markets," *Quarterly Journal of Economics* 101 (1986): 229 (on moral hazard and adverse selection).

8. I here invoke a distinction in value theory between, as Glaucon put it in Plato's *Republic,* those goods we would want due to "a desire for [their] consequences" from those we would want "for [their] own sake": Plato, *Republic, Books 1–5* (circa 380 B.C.), trans. Christopher Emlyn-Jones and William Preddy, Loeb Classical Library (Harvard University Press, 2013), 357b–d. The first kind of value, where things have value due to the consequences they bring about, is customarily called "instrumental" value; the second kind of value, where things have value "for their own sake" is customarily called "intrinsic."

9. Adam Smith, *An Inquiry into the Nature and Causes of the Wealth of Nations, Volume 1,* The Glasgow Edition of the Works and Correspondence of Adam Smith, vol. 2, ed. William B. Todd (Oxford University Press, 1976), 412; first published 1776.

10. Smith, *The Wealth of Nations,* 157–58.

11. Smith's own views on the importance of liberty were obscured by as early as 1790s: Emma Rothschild, *Economic Sentiments: Adam Smith, Condorcet, and the Enlightenment* (Harvard University Press, 2002), 70–71. I present freedom as an instrumental benefit of the use of markets (with freedom itself, perhaps, having an intrinsic value); others may use "intrinsic" and "instrumental" in different ways, but this should not obscure the basic structure of Smith's argument.

12. Instances are collated in Michael J Sandel, *Justice: What's the Right Thing to Do?* (Farrar, Straus and Giroux, 2009).

13. A helpful discussion of these various approaches, including some claims about the importance of legal services consonant with my own, can be found in Ronald J. Daniels and Michael J. Trebilcock, "Legal Aid," in *Rethinking the Welfare State: Government by Voucher* (Routledge, 2005).

14. In Chapter 9 I distinguish two reasons why a user should bear these costs. The first is the idea that the user is in some sense *responsible* for them. The second is that the allocation of those costs to users leads to a better distribution

of legal resources. The second reason, I argue, might justify localising costs to users; the first reason cannot.

15. I discuss these reforms in more detail in Chapter 4.

16. The modern phenomenon, where individuals are encouraged to settle their disputes, has long been a topic of academic controversy: for example, Owen Fiss, "Against Settlement," *Yale Law Journal* 93 (1984): 1073. What has been less often remarked upon, and what is perhaps most important, is its inegalitarian implications.

17. "CEDR: Court of Appeal Mediation," https://www.cedr.com/solve/courtofappeal/.

18. John Rawls, *A Theory of Justice*, rev. ed. (Belknap Press of Harvard University Press, 1999), 87; first published 1971. (Unlike Rawls, I do not think that only institutions can have this property; justice is a virtue of [good] people as much as [good] institutions.)

19. Rawls, *A Theory of Justice*, 87.

20. I presume here, and in this book, that the best way to think about justice in this sphere is *holistic* rather than *individualistic*. That is, to paraphrase Samuel Scheffler, the justice of any individual's claim to legal resources and/or the benefits and burdens of legality depends, directly or indirectly, on the justice of the wider distribution of those resources, benefits, and burdens: Samuel Scheffler, "Rawls and Utilitarianism," in *Boundaries and Allegiances* (Oxford University Press, 2001), 166–68. That is because the problem we face is institutional: not what justice requires in a particular instance, but how our institutions should be arranged given that we cannot secure perfect justice in all cases. I explore this feature in more detail in Frederick Wilmot-Smith, "Just Costs," in *Principles, Procedure and Justice: Essays in Honour of Adrian Zuckerman*, ed. Rabeea Assy and Andrew Higgins (Oxford University Press, 2020).

21. This kind of argument is developed in Satz, *Why Some Things Should Not Be for Sale*, chap. 9.

22. William Shakespeare, *The Tragedy of Hamlet, Prince of Denmark*, in *The Oxford Shakespeare: The Complete Works*, ed. Stanley Wells and others, 2nd ed. (Oxford University Press, 2005), 3.3.57–60; first published 1600.

23. This point is often made. See, for example, Ronald Coase, *The Firm, the Market, and the Law* (University of Chicago Press, 1988), 7, 9; Satz, *Why Some Things Should Not Be for Sale*, 26. This point should be borne in mind if, for example, someone were to argue that the public good problem of law can be overcome by assurance contracts: David Schmidtz, "Contracts and Public Goods," *Harvard Journal of Law and Public Policy* 10 (1987): 475.

24. This argument should be acceptable even to those libertarians who regard the only unjust exchanges as those that are coerced: the legal system is the archetypal method of coercive enforcement.

25. Rawls, *A Theory of Justice*, 63; see, further, John Rawls, *Justice as Fairness: A Restatement*, ed. Erin I. Kelly (Belknap Press of Harvard University Press, 2001), section 13.2.

26. For more examples, see Thomas Hobbes, *Leviathan: The English and Latin Texts (i)*, The Clarendon Edition of the Works of Thomas Hobbes, vol. 4, ed. Noel Malcolm (Oxford University Press, 2012), 228; first published 1668.

Hobbes defines distributive justice as "the distribution of equall benefit, to men of *equall merit.*" Also see G. A. Cohen, who says that "there is injustice in distribution when inequality of goods reflects not such things as differences in *the arduousness of different people's labors, or people's different preferences and choices with respect to income and leisure,* but myriad forms of lucky and unlucky circumstances": G. A. Cohen, *Rescuing Justice and Equality* (Harvard University Press, 2008), 126. The emphasis is added in both passages to demonstrate the set of circumstances any equal outcome is to be measured against. For Hobbes, those of different merit should not be allocated equal benefit; for Cohen, there is no injustice per se in inequality between those who put in different labour.

27. The extent to which markets have had this effect is a contested matter in the literature, one I do not pretend to have resolved. See, generally, Gary Becker, *The Economics of Discrimination,* 2nd ed. (University of Chicago Press, 1971); first published 1957. Compare M. G. Coleman, "Contesting the Magic of the Market-Place: Black Employment and Business Concentration in the Urban Context," *Urban Studies* 39 (2002): 1793.

28. The difference between lotteries and markets, in this respect, is illustrated by the story of the *William Brown.* Francis Askin offered Alexander Holmes five sovereigns to spare his (Askin's) life. Holmes replied, "I don't want your money, Frank," and threw him overboard.

29. "Winning" here should be taken to include favourable settlement terms, more substantial damages awards and costs orders, and so on.

30. Lassiter v. Department of Social Services 18 US 452 (1981). By contrast, a right to counsel is recognised in criminal cases. Gideon v. Wainwright 372 US 335 (1964). Whether this is a sensible distinction to draw is one of the questions any theory of the justice system must answer.

31. William Shakespeare, *The History of King Lear: The 1610 Quarto,* in *The Oxford Shakespeare: The Complete Works,* ed. Stanley Wells and others, 2nd ed. (Oxford University Press, 2005), 4.6.161–63; first published 1610. Lear's concerns are not fanciful: a solicitor of the sixteenth century advised his client that "if ye send the [judge] a firkin of sturgeon, it will not be lost": letter from George Rolle to Lady Lisle (1534), State Papers series 3/13, folio 74. This is an objection to *Market* both as a matter of quantum (it will not lead to justice being done) and as a matter of distribution (the rich escape the justice system's burdens).

32. This argument forms the core of Alan Wertheimer, "The Equalization of Legal Resources," *Philosophy and Public Affairs* 17 (1988): 303.

33. Rawls, *A Theory of Justice,* 65. See, too, my discussion of Bentham in Chapter 1.

34. Frederick Engels, "Outlines of a Critique of Political Economy," in *Economic and Philosophic Manuscripts of 1844,* trans. Martin Milligan (Prometheus Books, 1988), 186; first published 1844.

35. The source of this line is disputed. It is customary to attribute it to Mr. (or Lord) Justice Matthew, but Lord Birkett said he had heard the same joke attributed to Lord Justice Bowen and Lord Justice Chitty: Stanley Jackson, *Laughter at Law* (Arthur Baker, 1961), 11. See, too, the earlier (very similar) line of Horne Tooke. "Law," he said, "ought to be not a luxury for the rich, but a remedy to be

easily, cheaply and speedily obtained by the poor." Some spoke up. English courts of justice are open to all without distinction, they said. "And so," Tooke replied, "is the London Tavern—to such as can afford to pay for their entertainment": Henry Kett, *The Flowers of Wit* (Lackington, Allen, and Co., 1814), 71–72.

36. Ronald Dworkin, *Justice for Hedgehogs* (Belknap Press of Harvard University Press, 2011), 356.

37. For a full discussion see Ronald Dworkin, "What Is Equality? Part 2: Equality of Resources," *Philosophy and Public Affairs* 10, no. 4 (1981): 283, part 4; Ronald Dworkin, "Equality, Luck and Hierarchy," *Philosophy and Public Affairs* 31, no. 2 (2003): 190, 191. It is interesting to wonder how this feature of Dworkin's auction, where "brute" luck is converted to "option" luck, relates to the features that made the lottery attractive. Dworkin considers lottery tickets at pages 293–94 of "Equality of Resources," but this is where individuals want to take part in gambles; that is not the situation faced, for example, by those on the *William Brown*.

38. Although it is more contentious, the same point can be made in the context of criminal cases: if some people purchase insurance (or make enough money to purchase lawyers when necessary), their risk of being falsely convicted will be reduced. This, I will argue, comes at the expense of others in society.

39. This is one way to understand the arguments of some in the Chicago School, such as George Stigler's claim that regulatory capture is such that regulation "as a rule" benefits industry: George Stigler, "The Theory of Economic Regulation," *Bell Journal of Economics* 2 (1971): 3.

40. Insofar as there is a remaining objection, it is best thought of as an objection to proposed distributions of legal resources. The objection is not to claims about the best distribution of the benefits and burdens of legality, but it raises practical concerns about the prospects of achieving that distribution. I consider concerns like these in Chapter 6.

41. I am grateful to John Gardner for prompting me to stress this point (and the nice point about buying the auction house).

42. Something similar happened when Millard Fillmore sought, in 1852, to nominate justices after the election of Franklin Pierce but before Pierce took office.

43. "Judicial Crisis Network Launches $10 Million Campaign to Preserve Justice Scalia's Legacy," *Judicial Crisis Network,* January 9, 2017, https://judicialnetwork.com/jcn-press-release/judicial-crisis-network-launches-10-million-campaign-preserve-justice-scalias-legacy-support-president-elect-trump-nominee/.

44. AT&T Mobility v. Concepcion 563 US 333 (2011); American Express Co v. Italian Colors Restaurant 570 US (2013). These cases are discussed in an excellent three-part series, *Behind the Fine Print,* by Jessica Silver-Greenberg and Robert Gebeloff: "Arbitration Everywhere, Stacking the Deck of Justice" *New York Times,* October 31, 2015; "In Arbitration, a 'Privatization of the Justice System,'" *New York Times,* November 1, 2015; "In Religious Arbitration, Scripture Is the Rule of Law," *New York Times,* November 2, 2015.

45. Carnegie v. Household International Inc. 376 F 3d 656, 661 (7th Circ. 2004).

46. Epic Systems Corp v. Lewis 584 US (2018).

47. *Epic Systems Corp v. Lewis* at 28.

48. Why, someone might ask, restrict the inquiry to *justice* consequences rather than consequences in general? Perhaps an unjust state of affairs in the justice system could be justified by concomitant gains in some other sphere. There are three reasons to restrict our focus in the bulk of the inquiry.

First, the restriction can be seen as a first step to make the question intelligible and approachable. To ask about consequences *in general* is to ask a very complicated and perhaps intractable question: quite apart from any empirical difficulties, it would require a discussion of the different goods at stake and their relative value; and it would require some method of commensuration.

Second, a global inquiry could be dangerous. There is a risk that attention would be paid to goods of comparatively limited, but quantifiable, value to the detriment of those, such as justice, which are of greater value (but which are hard to quantify). This is a consequence of the commensuration concerns of the first reason.

Finally, there are independent reasons to think that justice benefits are the salient consequences to consider when assessing the justice system.

49. More arguments are given in Daniels and Trebilcock, "Legal Aid," 75.

50. This definition comes from Paul Samuelson, "The Pure Theory of Public Expenditure," *Review of Economics and Statistics* 36 (1954): 387.

51. It does not follow from this that governments should intervene: that will depend on what the consequences of intervention would be. See, for example, Paul Samuelson, "Indeterminacy of Government Role in Public-Good Theory," in *The Collected Scientific Papers of Paul A. Samuelson,* ed. R. C. Merton (MIT Press, 1972), 3:52.

52. Adam Smith, *An Inquiry into the Nature and Causes of the Wealth of Nations,* Vol. 2, in *The Glasgow Edition of the Works and Correspondence of Adam Smith,* ed. William B. Todd (Oxford University Press, 1976), 723; first published 1776. See, too, the earlier discussion of David Hume, *A Treatise of Human Nature,* ed. David Fate Norton and Mary J. Norton (Oxford University Press, 2008) 3.2.7, pp. 344–45; first published 1740 (discussing the creation of a legal system as a means of curing co-ordination problems).

53. This is the message of George Akerlof, "The Market for 'Lemons': Quality Uncertainty and the Market Mechanism," *Quarterly Journal of Economics* 84 (1970): 488, concerning the market in cars with serious defects. The paper is not directly analogous because it concerns goods (cars) that individuals can retain. It is hard to see how Gresham's law could apply to the market in lawyers.

54. Kenneth J Arrow, "Uncertainty and the Welfare Economics of Medical Care," *American Economic Review* 53 (1963): 941, 948.

55. Arrow, "Uncertainty and the Welfare Economics of Medical Care," 951.

56. Arrow, "Uncertainty and the Welfare Economics of Medical Care," 967.

57. I am not aware of any systematic argument to this effect. However, Arrow himself recognised the analogy: Arrow, "Uncertainty and the Welfare Economics of Medical Care," 948.

58. Arrow, "Uncertainty and the Welfare Economics of Medical Care," 948. I take the language of "adventitious need" (as opposed to a "course-of-life need") from David Braybrooke, *Let Needs Diminish That Preferences May Flourish* (University of Pittsburgh Press, 1968), 90.

59. William Shakespeare, *The Comical History of the Merchant of Venice, or Otherwise Called the Jew of Venice (1596–7)*, in *The Oxford Shakespeare: The Complete Works*, ed. Stanley Wells and others, 2nd ed. (Oxford University Press, 2005), 1.3.158; first published 1597.

60. Antonio thinks the ships lost: "Sweet Bassanio, my ships have all / miscarried, my creditors grow cruel, my estate is very / low, my bond to the Jew is forfeit": Shakespeare, *The Merchant of Venice*, 3.2.313–15. But the ships eventually come in: "I read for certain that my ships / Are safely come to road": Shakespeare, *The Merchant of Venice*, 5.1.287–88.

61. There is here a more fundamental point: the fact that they fail to insure is not, from the point of view of justice, a salient fact justifying a differential outcome. This point is the argument from justice.

4. A Fairness Floor

1. For the intellectual origins of this idea, see Philippe Van Parijs and Yannick Vanderborght, *Basic Income: A Radical Proposal for a Free Society and a Sane Economy* (Harvard University Press, 2017), chap. 4.

2. John Stuart Mill, "The Subjection of Women," in *Essays on Equality, Law, and Education, Collected Works of John Stuart Mill*, ed. John M. Robson (University of Toronto Press, 1984): 21:272; first published 1825.

3. Elizabeth S. Anderson, "What Is the Point of Equality?," *Ethics* 109 (1999): 287, 315.

4. T. M. Scanlon, "The Diversity of Objections to Inequality," in *The Difficulty of Tolerance: Essays in Political Philosophy* (Cambridge University Press, 2003), 205.

5. These claims relate both to the republican ideal of freedom and the relational ideal of equality: Philip Pettit, "Republican Freedom and Contestatory Democratization," in *Democracy's Value*, ed. Ian Shapiro and Casiano Hacker-Cordon (Cambridge University Press, 1999), 165; Anderson, "What Is the Point of Equality?," 315.

6. John Locke, *Two Treatises of Government*, ed. Peter Laslett (Cambridge University Press, 1988), vol. 2, section 22; first published 1689.

7. That a legal system is the best method to ensure equal freedom is a signature claim of Immanuel Kant, *The Metaphysics of Morals*, ed. Lara Denis; trans. Mary Gregor, 2nd ed. (Cambridge University Press, 2017); first published 1797. But I am not aware of any real appreciation—in Kant's work or his recent interpreters—of the procedural dimension to the equal freedom ideal. Note, however, Arthur Ripstein, *Force and Freedom* (Harvard University Press, 2009), 24, where Ripstein points out that certain legal procedures can ensure "that no person is subject to the power or judgment of others."

8. Demosthenes, "Against Meidias," in *Speeches 20–22*, The Oratory of Classical Greece, Vol. 12, trans. Edward M. Harris (University of Texas Press, 2005), 137. See, too, Hobbes's claim that "It belongs to the sovereign to see that the common body of citizens are not oppressed by the great ones, and much more that he himself does not oppress them on the great ones' advice": Thomas

Hobbes, *Leviathan: The English and Latin Texts (i),* The Clarendon Edition of the Works of Thomas Hobbes, vol. 4, ed. Noel Malcolm (Oxford University Press, 2012), 536 n. 76 (an addition to the Latin edition); first published 1668.

9. There are, doubtless, more conditions. It is also a problem, for example, if the law's remedies for violations of rights fail to ensure adequate protection. The initial sanction in Roman law for *actio iniuriarum,* an action to protect an individual's dignity, was twenty-five asses. That was a substantial sum when initially imposed, around 450 B.C.; three centuries later, it was not. Thus Lucius Veratius was said to amuse himself, slapping the faces of people he met as he walked; a slave followed in tow, tasked with paying twenty-five asses to each victim: Gellius, *Attic Nights, Volume 3: Books 14–20,* trans. John C. Rolfe, Loeb Classical Library (Harvard University Press, 1927), 20, 1, 13; p. 411.

10. William Blackstone, *Commentaries on the Laws of England,* ed. David Lemmings, book 1, *Of the Rights of Persons* (Oxford University Press, 2016), 95; first published 1765.

11. Blackstone, *Of the Rights of Persons,* 95. For the antecedent to this passage, see Sir Edward Coke, *Institutes of the Laws of England* (London, 1642), 55–56.

12. Demosthenes, "On the Dishonest Embassy," in *Speeches 18 and 19,* The Oratory of Classical Greece, vol. 9, trans. Harvey Yunis (University of Texas Press, 2005), *The Oratory of Classical Greece* (University of Texas Press, 2005), 297.

13. Before a public official exercises a discretionary power, by way of example, they are bound to consider relevant evidence, to avoid bias, and so on. These requirements are justified instrumentally insofar as they serve to constrain the arbitrary exercise of power; the existence of those constraints can also be justified by its elimination of unjust power dynamics between officials and citizens.

14. Locke, *Two Treatises of Government,* vol. 2, section 20.

15. Compare Steel and Morris v. United Kingdom (2005), 41 EHRR 22 (ECtHR), where the European Court of Human Rights found that such inequality in a case was so grave as to amount to a denial of a right to a fair hearing.

16. The most illuminating analogy is with a national health service, where medical treatment is allocated according to need rather than wealth. For such a policy proposal, see the Bishop of London and seventeen leading clergyman, *Times,* November 18, 1924; John Simon to Herbert Morrison, May 5, 1944 (Great Britain, Home Office [HO] 45 25130).

17. Harry Frankfurt, "Equality as a Moral Ideal," in *The Importance of What We Care About* (Cambridge University Press, 1988), 134–35.

18. They are "positional goods": those "with the property that one's relative place in the distribution of the good affects one's absolute position with respect to its value": Harry Brighouse and Adam Swift, "Equality, Priority, and Positional Goods," *Ethics* 116 (2006): 471, 472.

19. The language of "zero sum" must be treated with some care because there are two possible ways in which it might be used. First, it might be used (as here) to say that there can only be one winner of the suit. Second, it might be used to describe the value of a particular resource, such as legal services: the value is sometimes said to be "zero sum" when the value of one person's holdings depends

upon the value of another's: for example, Brighouse and Swift, "Equality, Priority, and Positional Goods," 477. These senses are interrelated, but should be distinguished, hence the need for caution in this context.

20. This line of thought is developed in detail by Alan Wertheimer, "The Equalization of Legal Resources," *Philosophy and Public Affairs* 17 (1988): 303. His argument is that contracting out detracts from the maximum possible justice. That is open to question—and it is not quite the point I pursue here. The distinction is between the idea that contracting out reduces the amount of justice being done (Wertheimer's point) and the idea that it makes individual disputes unfair (mine).

21. T. M. Scanlon, "Equality of Opportunity: A Normative Anatomy," Third Uehiro Lecture (University of Oxford, 2013), 23. T. H. Marshall may have had something like this in mind with his reference to "the right to justice," which is "the right to defend and assert all one's rights on terms of equality with others and by due process of law": T. H. Marshall, *Citizenship and Social Class* (Cambridge University Press, 1950), 10–11. But it is possible that Marshall means only formal equality, with rights of access, even if those rights generate differential burdens on different individuals.

22. Scanlon, "Equality of Opportunity: A Normative Anatomy," 23. For a similar argument, see Wertheimer, "The Equalization of Legal Resources," 314.

23. Jed S. Rakoff, "Why Innocent People Plead Guilty," *New York Review of Books,* November 20, 2014.

24. Aristotle, *Politics* (circa 350 B.C.), trans. Harris Rackham, Loeb Classical Library (Harvard University Press, 1932), 4:1287b, p. 269.

25. Plato, *Laws* (circa 348 B.C.), trans. Thomas L. Pangle (University of Chicago Press, 1980), 715d, p. 102. Compare Thomas Hobbes, *Leviathan: The English and Latin Texts (ii),* The Clarendon Edition of the Works of Thomas Hobbes, vol. 5, ed. Noel Malcolm (Oxford University Press, 2012), 1094–95; first published 1668 ("it is Men, and Arms, not Words, and Promises, that make the Force and Power of the Laws. And therefore this is another Errour of Aristotles Politiques, that in a wel ordered Common-wealth, not Men should govern, but the Laws").

26. In the modern debate, which stems from Lon L. Fuller, *The Morality of Law,* rev. ed. (Yale University Press, 1969), 39, scholars usually draw up a laundry list of requirements necessary for the ideal to be met. There is quite a lot of agreement on the content of the list, though scholars disagree over whether the requirements are *moral;* scholars also disagree on whether the items on the list are criteria or desiderata. We can prescind from the bulk of this scholarly debate.

27. I am not the first to derive quite concrete provisions, such as legal aid, from the ideal: see, for example, Tom Bingham, *The Rule of Law* (Penguin, 2010), 85. But legal systems have existed without legal aid; to say that it is required by the rule of law often looks like mere assertion. We must say what the value of the rule of law is and tie any prescriptions to that value.

28. Here as elsewhere, I proceed on the simplified assumption that the law is determinate. In Chapter 8 I consider how legal institutions should be structured given the indeterminacy in the law and the fact the law is modified by courts. That question can, on certain accounts, be thought of as concerned with the rule

of law: for example, Ronald Dworkin, "Political Judges and the Rule of Law," in *A Matter of Principle* (Belknap Press of Harvard University Press, 1985).

29. Within the academic literature, this claim is most commonly associated with Joseph Raz, "The Rule of Law and Its Virtue," in *The Authority of Law: Essays on Law and Morality* (Oxford University Press, 1979), 213. It is explicit in Fuller's fifth principle; it is also implicit in a number of his other criteria, such as publicity, prospectivity, and intelligibility: Fuller, *The Morality of Law,* 39.

30. Fuller's seventh principle, for example, is that the "rules as announced" must be congruent with "their actual administration": Fuller, *The Morality of Law,* 39. This principle had special importance to him: "if the Rule of Law does not mean this, it means nothing": Fuller, *The Morality of Law,* 209–10.

31. Jeremy Waldron, "The Rule of Law and the Importance of Procedure," in *Nomos 50: Getting to the Rule of Law,* ed. James Fleming (New York University Press, 2011), 3.

32. Cassius Dio, *Roman History: Books 56–60,* vol. 7, ed. Jeffrey Henderson; trans. Earnest Cary, Loeb Classical Library (Harvard University Press, 1924), 357. Hegel made the same accusation of Dionysius the Tyrant of Syracuse: Georg Wilhelm Friedrich Hegel, *Elements of the Philosophy of Right,* ed. Allen W. Wood; trans. H. B. Nisbet (Cambridge University Press, 1991), §215; first published 1820. No historian has found any record of this action or explanation for Hegel's attribution; Allen Wood says (at page 446 of his critical edition) that this is "either obscure or misinformed." Perhaps Hegel meant the story of Caligula, which had been recently told by Blackstone: Blackstone, *Of the Rights of Persons,* 38.

33. Lord Neuberger, "Access to Justice" (Welcome address to Australian Bar Association Biennial Conference, University College, London, July 3, 2017), https://www.supremecourt.uk/ docs / speech-170703.pdf, para 6. Similar points could be made about legal judgments. Some countries, such as Australia and the United Kingdom, have measures to put judgments and statutes online; these are rarely, if ever, comprehensive. In 2017, the United Kingdom's free legal database published around 20 per cent of the judgments in the Court of Criminal Appeals.

34. Oral Argument to National Federation of Independent Business v. Sebelius 567 US 519 (2012), March 28, 2012, first part: "Mr. Kneedler, what happened to the Eighth Amendment? You really want us to go through these 2,700 pages?"

35. R v. Lang (Stephen Howard) [2005] EWCA Crim 2864, [2005] 1 WLR 2509 [153] (Rose L. J.).

36. This sentence is slightly misleading because of a somewhat technical point. Despite the way lawyers sometimes talk (and the way I suggest in this sentence), the law is never the same as meaning. These things are on a different metaphysical plane. When lawyers talk of meaning, that talk is elliptical for legal content.

37. Miranda v. State of Arizona 384 US 436 (1966).

38. This is the result of King v. Burwell 576 US (2015).

39. Ghaidan v. Godin-Mendoza [2004,] UKHL 30, [2004,] 2 AC 557.

40. The fullest treatment of this argument is David Dyzenhaus, "Normative Justifications for the Provision of Legal Aid," in *Report of the Ontario Legal Aid Review: A Blueprint for Publicly Funded Legal Services* (Ontario Government, 1997). There are some complexities that there is not space to explore. The

argument, for example, only warrants the grant of lawyers when the law in question is one which is to guide a citizen; it does not justify the grant of lawyers when the law is to guide, for example, a judge (unless the grant of lawyers to the individual is instrumentally necessary to guide the judge).

41. Raz, "The Rule of Law and Its Virtue," 217; Thomas Christiano, "The Authority of Democracy," *Journal of Political Philosophy* 12 (2004): 266, 283 ("a need for a neutral judge").

42. See De Haas and Gijsles v. Belgium (1997), 25 EHRR 1 (ECtHR), para 53; *Steel and Morris v. United Kingdom*; MGN v. United Kingdom (2011), 53 EHRR 5 (ECtHR), para 200. The point is less that judges must be guided by lawyers, more that there must be systems in place that ensure the judiciary are adequately informed of the law. This may be done in a manner that does not require lawyers' input, as in certain civilian jurisdictions.

43. Anne Burford and John Greenya, *Are You Tough Enough* (McGraw-Hill, 1986), 83–84. (Anne Gorsuch, neé Burford, is the mother of Justice Neil Gorsuch of the US Supreme Court.)

44. "Wages of Zealotry," *New York Times*, February 20, 1983, 16.

45. Hiroko Tabuchi, "What's at Stake in Trump's Proposed E.P.A. Cuts," *New York Times*, April 10, 2017, A17; Eric Lipton and Danielle Ivory, "E.P.A.'s Polluter Playbook Takes a Turn to Leniency," *New York Times*, December 10, 2017, A1.

46. John Rawls, *A Theory of Justice*, rev. ed. (Belknap Press of Harvard University Press, 1999), 208, first published 1971; H. L. A. Hart, *The Concept of Law*, ed. Joseph Raz and Penelope Bulloch, 2nd ed. (Clarendon Press, 1994), 159 ("a central element in the idea of justice").

47. Wertheimer, "The Equalization of Legal Resources," 303.

48. Wertheimer, "The Equalization of Legal Resources," 311. He actually hedges his bets: he puts forward this proposition as only "arguable." But he seems to want to make the argument.

49. Wertheimer labels his own proposal, applicable only to civil disputes, the "equalization of legal resources." That is a misnomer. He actually endorses "*whatever* regulative principle would maximize the attainment of just results": Wertheimer, "The Equalization of Legal Resources," 304. This proposal is mistaken because, like most maximising accounts, it fails to attend to distributive implications.

5. Equal Resources

1. Euripides, *Suppliant Women, Electra, Heracles* (circa 420 B.C.), ed. and trans. David Kovacs, Loeb Classical Library (Harvard University Press, 1998), 433–34, 437.

2. I am skimming lightly over some complications in legal philosophy here. There is, for example, a distinction between linguistic meaning and legal content, such that clear expression does not entail ease in ascertaining legal content: Mark Greenberg, "Legislation as Communication? Legal Interpretation and the Study of Linguistic Communication," in *Philosophical Foundations of Language in the*

Law, ed. Andrei Marmor and Scott Soames (Oxford University Press, 2011). This merely demonstrates a further claim equal justice can make, on methods of legal interpretation (i.e., on the way in which legal content is generated from social facts, such as meaning).

3. Some of the complications are helpfully explored in Rabeea Assy, "Simplifying Legal Language," in *Injustice in Person: The Right to Self-Representation* (Oxford University Press, 2015).

4. This kind of idea is not much explored in law, though it is familiar in economics. See, for example, R. G. Lipsey and Kelvin Lancaster, "The General Theory of Second Best," *Review of Economic Studies* 24 (1956): 11.

5. The difference I have in mind between unjustifiable discrimination and equal justice is this. Discrimination is about how the responsibilities of the law are allocated: whether the demands made of the poor are greater than those of the right, and so on. Equal justice concerns whether those responsibilities actually fall on the right people: whether, even if the rules are perfect in theory, the benefits and burdens of the law fall on the appropriate groups.

6. Joseph Raz's objection to egalitarian distributions of goods assumes something like this proposal: Joseph Raz, *The Morality of Freedom* (Oxford University Press, 1986), 225. Compare T. M. Scanlon, *Why Does Inequality Matter?* (Oxford University Press, 2018), 19.

7. As I explore subsequently, there are two different ways this might be done. Contracts might be made void, thus ensuring that neither party could sue the other; or the act of contracting could be made illegal, so any attempt to disrupt equality would be a criminal offence. The former is, of course, a less invasive method—but might also be less effective.

8. See Chapter 7 for a more complete discussion.

9. This is subject to the complications discussed in Chapter 9.

10. Judith Resnik, "Diffusing Disputes: The Public in the Private of Arbitration, the Private in Courts, and the Erasure of Rights," *Yale Law Journal* 124 (2015): 2804, 2806. For a similar point, see James Crawford, "International Law and the Rule of Law," *Adelaide Law Review* 24 (2003): 3, 7. It is a little misleading to say that arbitrators aim to "effectuate the intent of the parties" as it makes it sound like the employee has a say over the terms of the arbitral panel. But Resnik is far from blind to this point: she is invoking "intent of the parties" in the way contract lawyers customarily use it; the phrase does not, for contract lawyers, actually mean that any contracting party had an intention on the matter in dispute. This point is, though, far beyond the scope of this book.

11. Henry Horwitz and James Oldham, "John Locke, Lord Mansfield, and Arbitration during the Eighteenth Century," *Historical Journal* 36 (1993): 137. This was extended to all arbitration agreements by the Common Law Procedure Act, 1854, s. 17.

12. See, generally, Margaret Jane Radin, *Boilerplate: The Fine Print, Vanishing Rights, and the Rule of Law* (Princeton University Press, 2014); Resnik, "Diffusing Disputes."

13. See, for example, Family Statute Law Amendment Act, 2006, section 50.1, which limits the enforceability of arbitral awards in the family context in Ontario.

14. There are also concerns that arbitration, in practice, leads to injustice: I examine these next.

15. Tacitus, *Annals,* vol. 4, trans. John Jackson, Loeb Classical Library (Harvard University Press, 1937), 11.5–7.

16. AT&T Mobility v. Concepcion 563 US 333 (2011); American Express Co v. Italian Colors Restaurant 570 US (2013); and Epic Systems Corp v. Lewis 584 US (2018); further, Resnik, "Diffusing Disputes."

17. A thorough empirical study was conducted by David Horton and Andrea Chandrasekher, "After the Revolution: An Empirical Study of Consumer Arbitration," *Georgetown Law Journal* 104 (2015): 57. The authors found (at page 124) that "few plaintiffs pursue low-value claims and that high-level and super repeat-playing companies perform particularly well."

18. U.S. Patent No. 7797212 (filed October 31, 2006), http://www.google .com/patents/US7797212. The most complete discussion of features like these is Rory Van Loo, "Corporation as Courthouse," *Yale Journal on Regulation* 33 (2016): 547.

19. Ruth Bader Ginsburg, "In Pursuit of the Public Good: Access to Justice in the United States," *Washington University Journal of Law and Policy* 7 (2001): 1, 10.

20. Although the case of wrongful execution is the most graphic illustration, similar points can be made in the private or regulatory sphere. Some laws are concerned with the regulation of markets, for example to prevent companies from abusing their dominant positions. There is a dramatic inequality between the resources of the regulators and the most powerful of the regulated: Google has, to choose one example, much more power than any regulator. This may lead to incorrect decisions; it also affects the incidence of unjust decisions, with richer companies less likely to suffer injustice.

21. Tacitus, *Annals,* 11.5.

22. Juvenal, *Satires,* trans. Niall Rudd (Oxford University Press, 2008), 7.120, p. 65.

23. Compare James Tobin's suggestion, that "Any good second year graduate student in economics could write a short examination paper proving that voluntary transactions in votes would increase the welfare of the sellers as well as the buyers": "On Limiting the Domain of Inequality," *Journal of Law and Economics* 13 (1970): 263, 269.

24. Many regimes do have an inegalitarian distribution of judges by allocating more expensive claims to better courts. This nascent inequality does not undermine my basic point, which is that a commitment to an equal distribution of the judiciary is explicit in modern regimes.

25. I discuss these questions in greater detail in Chapters 9 and 10.

26. Arthur M. Okun, *Equality and Efficiency: The Big Tradeoff* (Brookings Institution Press, 1975), 48.

27. John Locke, *Two Treatises of Government,* ed. Peter Laslett (Cambridge University Press, 1988), 2, section 94; first published 1689. Compare Thomas Hobbes, *De Cive: The English Version,* The Clarendon Edition of the Works of Thomas Hobbes, vol. 2, ed. Howard Warrender (Oxford University Press, 2012), chap. 10; first published 1642.

28. Locke (n. 27) II, §143. For discussion, see Jeremy Waldron, *The Dignity of Legislation* (Cambridge University Press, 1999), 80; Jeremy Waldron, *Political Political Theory* (Harvard University Press, 2016), 54–55. There is a trace of Locke's thought in a saying Plutarch attributes to Solon, that the best city to live in is one "in which those who are not wronged, no less than those who are wronged, exert themselves to punish the wrongdoers": Plutarch, *Lives,* Vol. 1, trans. Bernadotte Perrin, Loeb Classical Library (Harvard University Press, 1914), 455.

29. Albert O. Hirschman, *Exit, Voice, and Loyalty: Responses to Decline in Firms, Organizations, and States* (Harvard University Press, 1970).

30. See Hirschman, *Exit, Voice, and Loyalty,* 43; and Chapter 4.

31. This is a contingent question; one of the pernicious effects of the permission is to reduce incentives to invest in the public option, which makes working in the public sphere less attractive. Problems are exacerbated when there is a global market in healthcare workers. See, generally, Robin R. Marsh and Ruth Uwaifo Oyelere, "Global Migration of Talent: Drain, Gain, and Transnational Impacts," in *International Scholarships in Higher Education: Pathways to Social Change* (Palgrave Macmillan, 2017).

32. In most countries there are push factors (the work has got a lot worse) and pull factors (arbitration pays more).

33. For this terminology see Marc Galanter, "Why the Haves Come Out Ahead: Speculations on the Limits of Legal Change," *Law and Society Review 9* (1974): 95.

34. This is the same phenomenon that leads to poor countries losing their doctors to richer countries: see the references above, at footnote 31.

35. See, for an example of this, Catherine Baksi, "Nigel Evans Rues Backing for Legal Aid Cuts," *Law Society Gazette,* April 15, 2014.

36. I discuss these considerations in more detail in Chapter 10.

6. Three Objections

1. See the law cited in Demosthenes, *Speeches,* trans. Adele C. Scafuro, 1st ed. (University of Texas Press, 2011), 46.26 (a dreadful speech Demosthenes wrote for another man to give at trial).

2. The Fundamental Constitutions of Carolina, March 1, 1669 (drawn up by John Locke), 70th clause. Professional lawyers were also forbidden in jurisdictions influenced by canon law, as, for example, England's Star Chamber: J. A. Crook, *Legal Advocacy in the Roman World* (Gerald Duckworth and Co., 1995), 14.

3. John Langbein, *The Origins of Adversary Criminal Trial* (Oxford University Press, 2005), chap. 1.

4. John Rawls says that individuals should "have a free choice of careers and occupations": John Rawls, *A Theory of Justice,* rev. ed. (Belknap Press of Harvard University Press, 1999), 241; first published 1971. This interest does not seem to be impinged upon. Rawls's remarks here are not easy to parse, though: see G. A. Cohen, *Rescuing Justice and Equality* (Harvard University Press, 2008), 197 nn. 18–19, for an attempt to reconcile them.

5. Even if some litigants do lose their freedom to choose their lawyer, in practice that freedom is lost only by a vanishingly small number. The freedom to choose a lawyer has limited value if you are unable to afford the lawyer you would like.

6. Adam Smith, *An Inquiry into the Nature and Causes of the Wealth of Nations, Volume 1,* The Glasgow Edition of the Works and Correspondence of Adam Smith, vol. 2, ed. William B. Todd (Oxford University Press, 1976), 412; first published 1776.

Condorcet, similarly, argued that free trade would avoid scarcities in grains: Marquis de Condorcet, "Sur la liberté de la circulation des subsistances," in *Oeuvres de Condorcet,* ed. François Arago and Arthur Condorcet O'Connor (Firmin Didot, 1847) 10:364; first published 1792.

7. For a recent analysis, see Elizabeth Anderson, *Private Government: How Employers Rule Our Lives (and Why We Don't Talk about It)* (Princeton University Press, 2017).

8. Compare Lucas Stanczyk, "Productive Justice," *Philosophy and Public Affairs* 40 (2012): 144.

9. For an argument of a similar form, see Liam Murphy and Thomas Nagel, *The Myth of Ownership* (Oxford University Press, 2002).

10. This "netting off" is important to show why exploited workers retain an entitlement to wages earned through an unjust labour system.

11. This argument could also be put as concerned with the holistic structure of the question of justice: see Chapter 3, note 20. Unlike the "protection" example, the response to such systemic injustice is not obviously bilateral: the lawyer's entitlement might be better than the wealthier client. But it is easier to justify imposing higher taxes on those, like the hypothetical lawyer in this example, who are not entitled to their wage. See Chapter 10; see also Michael Walzer, *Spheres of Justice* (Basic Books, 1983), 90.

12. Compare Jerry Cohen's thought that "philosophers who believe in believing in equality misname it 'slavery' only because they recoil (as I do, too: what reasonably well-heeled person with a fulfilling job would not?) at the thought of the lot that they themselves would have in a more equal society": Cohen, *Rescuing Justice and Equality,* 208.

13. Rawls, by contrast, calls these features "arbitrary from the moral point of view": see Chapter 1, note 19. Rawls's difference principle aims to justify individually undeserved distributions by their (the distributions') place in a justified holistic pattern (i.e., one benefiting the worst off). That is analogous to my own claims here: there is, I am arguing, no interpersonally just distribution of wages; the wage individuals can justifiably expect is determined by the place of their wages within a holistically justified pattern.

14. In Sam Scheffler's phrase, "the economic value of people's talents is socially determined in the sense that it depends both on the number of people with similar talents and on the needs, preferences, and choices of others": Samuel Scheffler, "Justice and Desert in Liberal Theory," in *Boundaries and Allegiances* (Oxford University Press, 2001), 191. A market price might be justified on efficiency grounds. But that is to use an argument from an institutional perspective, justified by a background theory of justice, rather than a desert criterion: see, generally,

Rawls, *A Theory of Justice,* section 48; T. M. Scanlon, "Giving Desert Its Due," *Philosophical Explorations* 16 (2013): 1, 14.

15. United States v. Gonzalez-Lopez 548 US 140, 144 (2006), (Scalia, J.). As Justice Samuel Alito points out in his dissent, this right has long been curtailed in the United States.

16. Caplin & Drysdale, Chartered v. United States 491 US 617, 624–25 (1989), (White, J).

17. Derryl Brown, *Free Market Criminal Justice: How Democracy and Laissez Faire Undermine the Rule of Law* (Oxford University Press, 2016), 85.

18. The last section considers whether there might be concerns that the abolition of this market would give the government too much control over citizens' lawyers.

19. Tamara Goriely and Alan Paterson, "Introduction: Resourcing Civil Justice," in *A Reader on Resourcing Civil Justice,* ed. Tamara Goriely and Alan Paterson (Oxford University Press, 1996) 10.

20. James Tobin, "On Limiting the Domain of Inequality," *Journal of Law and Economics* 13 (1970): 263, 264.

21. Goriely and Paterson, "Introduction: Resourcing Civil Justice," 10.

22. I am particularly grateful to Emma Saunders-Hastings, whose close attention to my claims in this section improved my account of paternalism.

23. For a defence of this characterisation, see Seana Valentine Shiffrin, "Paternalism, Unconscionability Doctrine, and Accommodation," *Philosophy and Public Affairs* 29 (2000): 205. Some argue that paternalist actions are also those made for the paternalisee's welfare. That is not necessarily true: if I try to take over your parenting of your child, it is paternalistic towards you but I do it for the sake of your children.

24. This is analogous to Mill's bridge example: John Stuart Mill, *On Liberty,* ed. David Bromwich and George Kateb (Yale University Press, 2003), 158; first published 1859.

25. I may be a lousy and moralistic dinner guest. But that is a different point.

26. An alternative analysis is to say that these two conditions define paternalism, prescinding from the question of whether the paternalistic action has a negative valence. Debating which approach is better is a sterile enterprise. The important point is to see that we must consider these two conditions and the question of whether contempt is conveyed through those actions.

27. A different kind of value-based objection, not grounded in paternalism, is found in Goriely and Paterson's claim that "a just society is much more likely to depend on the fair allocation of jobs, education, housing and income than on anything a legal aid scheme can deliver": Goriely and Paterson, "Introduction: Resourcing Civil Justice," 7. An interesting paradox of this line of thought is that the present situation, where the majority of the population fund the legal system through taxation and yet are unable to access it (because they are ineligible for legal aid and incapable of funding private legal services), is more defensible than it might first seem. Goriely and Paterson characterise legal aid as just another form of welfare payment—and most people accept these should go principally to the worst off. Compare this with more contractualist accounts, which hold that access to the court is part of the state's quid pro quo (along the lines I have

argued). The latter type of account depends upon legal services being in some sense different—and, so, is better able to say why it is a problem if many people in the middle cannot afford legal services.

28. For example, Mill, *On Liberty*, 146.

29. The "it won't work" objection also makes contestable claims about individuals' capacities. Behavioural economists have documented a dizzying array of ways in which individuals fail to make good judgements about their own interests due to cognitive biases: for example, Cass R. Sunstein and Richard H. Thaler, "Libertarian Paternalism Is Not an Oxymoron," *University of Chicago Law Review* 70 (2003): 1159, 1168; Daniel Kahneman, *Thinking, Fast and Slow* (Farrar, Straus and Giroux, 2012). Humans also sometimes suffer from *akrasia*: we sometimes drink the extra glass of wine rather than go to bed, or eat the chocolate even when we are trying to diet. In the case of legal services, we are particularly unlikely to appreciate their true value: they are only contingently valuable, contingent on some bad event happening to us. And we tend to underestimate the probabilities of such events occurring.

30. See, for example, Nicolas Cornell, "A Third Theory of Paternalism," *Michigan Law Review* 113 (2015): 1295.

31. Lord Sumption, "The Limits of Law," in *Lord Sumption and the Limits of the Law*, ed. Nicholas Barber, Richard Ekins, and Paul Yowell (Hart Publishing, 2016), 18. See, too, Goriely and Paterson, "Introduction: Resourcing Civil Justice," 7.

32. Goriely and Paterson, "Introduction: Resourcing Civil Justice," 10 ("why should the state make the decision for them?").

33. T. M. Scanlon, "Preference and Urgency," *Journal of Philosophy* 72 (1975): 655, 659–60.

34. I adapt this example from Jonathan Quong, *Liberalism without Perfection* (Oxford University Press, 2010), 79–80.

35. There are difficult questions of scope here. Insofar as the locus of objections to paternalism is in its expressive content, the case seems paternalistic: my taking your spending choices into account in this way seems to convey the same kind of insult as other instances of paternalism. I discuss this kind of claim, concerning the expressive basis of paternalism, next.

36. Joseph Raz, *Practical Reason and Norms*, reprint with new postscript (Oxford University Press, 1999), 27.

37. This strategy has a long pedigree. See, for example, John Stuart Mill, *Principles of Political Economy*, ed. Jonathan Riley (Oxford University Press, 1994), 349; first published 1848; and Gerald Dworkin, "Paternalism," *The Monist* 56 (1972): 64, 69–70; Rawls, *A Theory of Justice*, 219.

38. John of Salisbury, *Policraticus: Of the Frivolities of Courtiers and the Footprints of Philosophers*, ed. And trans. C. J. Nederman (Cambridge University Press, 1990), 28; first published 1159.

39. The 1215 charter is known as "Magna" or "the great" charter in order to distinguish it from a briefer charter of liberties issued in 1217, dealing with the royal forests. The terminology "magna" or "maior" ("great" or "greater") appeared very early and immediately stuck: A. B. White, "The Name Magna Carta," *English Historical Review* 30 (1915): 472. The historical precursors to

Magna Carta are the reason why Samuel Johnson said it was "born with a grey beard": Samuel Johnson, *A History and Defence of Magna Charta* (London, 1769), 4–5.

40. James Madison, *Federalist 47,* in Alexander Hamilton, James Madison, and John Jay, *The Federalist Papers,* ed. Lawrence Goldman (Oxford University Press, 2008), 239; first published 1788. The requirement is usually traced to Montesquieu, *The Spirit of the Laws,* ed. and trans. Anne M. Cohler, Basia C. Miller, and Harold S. Stone (Cambridge University Press, 1989), 158; first published 1748.

41. This suggests that the separation of powers has instrumental, not intrinsic, value. Whether the separation is necessary to realise the salient value is contingent. Thus there was no gain in intrinsic value when the United Kingdom's highest court was, in 2012, moved from the legislature (the House of Lords) to form a separate, judicial institution of the Supreme Court. Whether any instrumental value was realised is debatable. See, on the history of the transition, Andrew Le Sueur, "From Appellate Committee to Supreme Court: A Narrative," in *The Judicial House of Lords, 1876–2009,* ed. Louis Blom-Cooper, Brice Dickson, and Gavin Drewry (Oxford University Press, 2009).

42. The conception of liberty I have in mind here is that in the republican tradition, as developed by Philip Pettit, *Republicanism: A Theory of Freedom and Government* (Oxford University Press, 1997). But I believe that liberty as non-interference can also accommodate these concerns.

43. Philip Pettit, "Republican Freedom and Contestatory Democratization," in *Democracy's Value,* ed. Ian Shapiro and Casiano Hacker-Cordon (Cambridge University Press, 1999), 165.

44. Edward J. Dimock, "The Public Defender: A Step towards a Police State?," *American Bar Association Journal* 42 (1956): 219. See, too, Justice William Brennan, "The Community's Responsibility for Legal Aid," *Legal Aid Briefcase* 15 (1956): 75, 77.

45. Kenneth C. H. Willig, "The Bar in the Third Reich," *American Journal of Legal History* 20 (1976): 1, 14. At the start of the war, Hitler said to Rosenberg and Himmler: "Let the profession be purified, let it be employed in public service. Just as there is a Public Prosecutor, let there be only Public Defenders." Adolf Hitler, *Hitler's Table Talk, 1941–1944: His Private Conversations,* ed. Hugh Trevor-Roper; trans. Norman Cameron and R. H. Stevens, 3rd ed. (Phoenix, 2000), 132.

46. The House of Lords grew out of the House of Commons in the fourteenth century, with the first record of the House of Commons in the Good Parliament of 1376: Gerald L. Harriss, "The Formation of Parliament, 1272–1377," in *The English Parliament in the Middle Ages,* ed. R. G. Davies and J. H. Denton (Manchester University Press, 1981). The House of Lords began to exercise a regular appellate authority in the 1620s, though it was not until the late nineteenth century that it came to occupy the apex of the legal system: Patrick Polden, *The Oxford History of the Laws of England,* vol. 11 (Oxford University Press, 2010), 528–47.

47. The proper structure of either will turn partly upon different societies' legal cultures. For example, different countries have different levels of exposure to

corruption. Those with less risk of politicians exploiting their power might have more fluid structures than those with more risk. In the United Kingdom the system of judicial appointments was notably opaque for many years. Although it was not without its abuses, it was widely seen to function effectively. This is not a system that can be widely replicated with success. The replacement system, where individuals have to apply to an appointments panel, is also imperfect: causation is hard to pin down, but it is not obvious that appointees are better now than under the previous regime.

48. Those guidelines should, to conform with rule of law principles, be sufficiently general to prevent the guidelines from taking sides in particular cases.

49. United Kingdom, Rule C29, *Bar Standards Board Handbook,* 3rd ed. (November 2017).

7. The Sites of Justice

1. "London Lickpenny," in *Medieval English Political Writings,* ed. James M. Dean (Medieval Institute Publications, 1996), line 8. The precise date and authorship are a matter of dispute. It used to be attributed to John Lydgate, but his authorship is now doubted. The first three courts were all in Westminster Hall; the Court of Exchequer was in an adjoining building.

2. Eric H. Steele, "The Historical Context of Small Claims Courts," *American Bar Foundation Research Journal* 6, no. 2 (1981): 293.

3. See, for example, the courts of Eyre, discussed in Chapter 1.

4. Government of the United Kingdom, "Make a Court Claim for Money," https://www.gov.uk/make-court-claim-for-money/overview.

5. Hazel Genn, *Judging Civil Justice,* Hamlyn Lectures (Cambridge University Press, 2009), 87–126.

6. Genn, *Judging Civil Justice,* 81.

7. Genn, *Judging Civil Justice,* 117.

8. Owen Fiss, "Against Settlement," *Yale Law Journal* 93 (1984): 1073, 1076.

9. Fiss, "Against Settlement," 1075.

10. The precise date of composition is contested amongst scholars. I here follow Martin West's dating, the reasons for which he explains in M. L. West, *The Making of the Iliad: Disquisition and Analytical Commentary* (Oxford University Press, 2011), 17–20.

11. Homer, *The Iliad* (circa 1260–1180 B.C.), trans. Robert Fagles (Penguin, 1998), 484, lines 593–94.

12. Homer, *The Iliad,* 484, lines 580–94.

13. Homer, *The Iliad* (circa 1260–1180 B.C.), trans. Stephen Mitchell (Weidenfeld and Nicholson, 2011), 308, line 475. I quote Mitchell rather than Fagles because Fagles's translation does not convey the publicity with quite the same vividness.

14. Alan L. Boegehold, *The Lawcourts at Athens: Sites, Buildings, Equipment, Procedure, and Testimonia,* Athenian Agora, vol. 28 (American School of Classical Studies, 1995), 14; Alistair Blanshard, "The Birth of the Law-Court: Putting Ancient and Modern Forensic Rhetoric in Its Place," in *Oratory in Action,*

ed. Michael Edwards and Christopher Reid (Manchester University Press, 2004), 21. For the development of courts in England, see Clare Graham, *Ordering Law: The Architectural and Social History of the English Law Court to 1914* (Ashgate, 2003).

15. Blanshard, "The Birth of the Law-Court," 18.

16. We might ask similar questions about legislative buildings. The Texas legislature, for example, only meets once every two years; must it, the same logic would hold, meet there? Why not sell the capitol off and rent a few rooms every two years?

17. Demosthenes, "On the Crown," in *Speeches 18 and 19,* The Oratory of Classical Greece, vol. 9, trans. Harvey Yunis (University of Texas Press, 2005), 196. A few caveats are in order. Classical Athenians seem to have preferred private arrangements to public trials, at least in certain situations; and insofar as Athenian courts were open, they were open only for certain classes of individuals: slaves and women, for example, could not litigate in their own names: Adriaan Lanni, *Law and Justice in the Courts of Classical Athens* (Cambridge University Press, 2006), 33–35.

18. Charter or Fundamental Laws, of West New Jersey, Agreed Upon, ch. 23 (1676). Judith Resnik collects such laws together in Judith Resnik, "Bring Back Bentham: 'Open Courts,' 'Terror Trials,' and Public Sphere(s)," *Law and Ethics of Human Rights 5* (2011): 1.

19. Although I will not discuss the topic, there is also a question of whether the forum is open to the litigants themselves. Some immigration tribunals, for example, are open to lawyers with security clearance but not to the prospective immigrant. The prospective immigrant is not entitled to know the case against her.

20. See Chapters 2 through 5.

21. Whether it does so, for any token reform, is partly an empirical question. Quite a lot of discussion over reform to justice systems concerns whether some reform will further a goal or not. But you cannot sensibly ask the empirical question—about what the effects of a reform will be—unless you know what the desired consequences are.

22. Jeremy Bentham, *Draught for the Organization of Judicial Establishments,* in *The Works of Jeremy Bentham,* ed. John Bowring (William Tait, 1843), 4:316. Bentham was fond of this turn of phrase, first using it in his "Publicity of Judicature" (*Examiner,* November 21, 1820). See Jeremy Bentham, *The Correspondence of Jeremy Bentham: July 1820 to December 1821,* The Collected Works of Jeremy Bentham, vol. 10, ed. Stephen Conway (Oxford University Press, 1994), 112 n. 6 (Letter to John Bowring, 2698, 20.x.1820).

A different translation of Athena's speech in the trial of Orestes gives it a slightly different inflection from the one I consider subsequently. She says that "it helps for the whole city as well as these parties to be silent and to hear my ordinances for all time, so that the case may be well judged": Aeschylus, *Oresteia: Eumenides* (458 B.C.), trans. Christopher Collard, (Oxford University Press, 2002), 571–73. Publicity is valuable not for the watchers but the watched.

23. Jeremy Bentham, "Farming Defended," in *Writings on the Poor Laws,* The Collected Works of Jeremy Bentham, vol. 1, ed. Michael Quinn (Clarendon Press,

2001), 277 ("the more strictly we are watched, the better we behave.") Although the text was drafted in 1797, Bentham did not include it in his "Outline of a Work Entitled Pauper Management Improved." He may never have published it.

24. This is a little loose, appearing as it does to refer only to questions of quantum. I mean, slightly more formally, that a legal system is inefficient if it could comply more fully with the general principles of justice without expending greater levels of resources.

25. John Cooke, *Unum necessarium, or, The Poore Mans Case* (1648), 66. A notable lawyer, Cooke led the prosecution of King Charles I; following the Restoration, he was executed for treason.

26. Roland K. Wilson, "Lawyers' Bills—Who Should Pay Them?," *Law Quarterly Review* 12 (1896): 368, 373.

27. Oscar Wilde, "Lady Windermere's Fan," in *The Importance of Being Earnest: And Other Plays,* ed. Peter Raby (Oxford World Classics, 2008), 3.350–51; first published 1893.

28. This metaphor originates with Robert H. Mnookin and Lewis Kornhauser, "Bargaining in the Shadow of the Law: The Case of Divorce," *Yale Law Journal* 88 (1979): 950.

29. Hazel Genn and Yvette Genn, "The Effectiveness of Representation at Tribunals, Report to the Lord Chancellor" (Lord Chancellor's Department, 1989).

30. This language is taken from Jeremy Bentham, "Rationale of Judicial Evidence," in *The Works of Jeremy Bentham,* ed. John Bowring (William Tait, 1827), 6:351. See, generally, Resnik, "Bring Back Bentham."

31. The origin of a norm against mercenaries is discussed in Sarah Percy, *Mercenaries: The History of a Norm in International Relations* (Oxford University Press, 2007), chap. 3. A recent discussion is Cécile Fabre, *Cosmopolitan War* (Oxford University Press, 2012), chap. 6.

32. For a flavour of the contemporary scholarly debate, see Hazel Genn, "Why the Privatisation of Civil Justice Is a Rule of Law Issue," Thirty-Sixth F. A. Mann Lecture (British Institute of International and Comparative Law, 2012); Alon Harel, *Why Law Matters* (Oxford University Press, 2014); Judith Resnik, "Diffusing Disputes: The Public in the Private of Arbitration, the Private in Courts, and the Erasure of Rights," *Yale Law Journal* 124 (2015): 2804.

33. In the legal context it is used to ask at least three questions. Who runs the forum? Who pays for the forum? And is the forum is open to the public? These are all quite different questions, raising different concerns.

34. John Rawls, *A Theory of Justice,* rev. ed. (Belknap Press of Harvard University Press, 1999), 8; first published 1971.

35. Rawls, *A Theory of Justice,* 211.

36. Rawls, *A Theory of Justice,* 238.

37. This principle is not immutable: in cases of terrorism trials, for example, it is plausible that great risks to national security of disclosure of reasoning might trump the dignity infringement of reduced publicity.

38. Thomas Christiano, "The Authority of Democracy," *Journal of Political Philosophy* 12 (2004): 266, 271–72.

39. Aeschylus, *Oresteia: The Eumenides* (458 B.C.), ed. W. B. Stanford; trans. Robert Fagles (Penguin, 1977), 256, lines 571–75. Another translation has her

ask the Herald to "call the public to order": Aeschylus, *Oresteia: Eumenides* (458 B.C.), trans. Alan H. Sommerstein, Loeb Classical Library (Harvard University Press, 2008), 425. Different editors use different texts, which partly explains the differing translations of different editions.

40. Aeschylus, *Eumenides,* 256, lines 576–78.

41. Bruce Springsteen, "Long Walk Home," on *Magic* (Columbia Records, 2007).

42. Hannah Arendt, *The Origins of Totalitarianism* (Harcourt Brace, 1979), xxxvi.

43. Arendt, *The Origins of Totalitarianism,* xxxvii.

44. Arendt, *The Origins of Totalitarianism,* xxxvii.

8. Just Law-Making

1. Not only courts. As I have highlighted in earlier chapters, officials can be granted powers by statute to interpret and apply the law. The emergence of the administrative state has led to regulatory agencies charged with application and development of legislation. I have tried to simplify discussion in this chapter by concentrating on courts. But similar claims apply to these spheres.

2. Montesquieu, *The Spirit of the Laws,* ed. and trans. Anne M. Cohler, Basia C. Miller, and Harold S. Stone (Cambridge University Press, 1989), 163; first published 1748. Soon after, Blackstone said similar things: William Blackstone, *Of the Rights of Persons,* in *Commentaries on the Laws of England,* ed. David Lemmings (Oxford University Press, 2016), 1:52; first published 1765 (judges are "not delegated to pronounce a new law, but to maintain and expound the old one").

3. US Congress, Committee on the Judiciary, "Confirmation Hearing on the Nomination of John G. Roberts, Jr. to be Chief Justice of the United States," J-109-37, September 12–15, 2005, https://www.gpo.gov/fdsys/pkg/GPO-CHRG -ROBERTS/pdf/GPO-CHRG-ROBERTS.pdf, p. 56.

4. A hackneyed joke has three baseball umpires in a bar. "I call them the way they are," says one; "I call them the way I see them," says another. "They ain't nothing until I call them," the third says.

5. This is accepted to be the case in any common law country. It is sometimes said that countries whose legal systems are based on civil law do not permit their judges these powers. This is far from clear. Judges in civil law countries do, at any rate, affect what people—including other judges—do. Given this, many of the things I will say about common law judges apply just as much to them.

6. Sir Edward Coke, *The Third Part of the Institutes of the Lawes of England* (1644), chap. 7, p. 47: "Murder is when a man of sound memory and of the age of discretion, unlawfully killeth within any county of the realm any reasonable creature in rerum natura under the King's peace, with malice aforethought, either expressed by the party or implied by law, so as the party wounded, or hurt, etc. die of the wound or hurt, etc. within a year and a day of the same."

7. Felix Frankfurter, "Some Reflections on the Reading of Statutes," *Columbia Law Review* 47 (1947): 527, 545. The same point was made, rather more

seriously, in the Renaissance. Pierre Rebuffi wrote that "oportuit prius ius scribere et postea ex iure verborum significationes et regulas elicere" (3). (The law had first to be written and afterwards the meaning of the words of the law and the rules [*regulae*] elicited from it). *In tit. Dig. de verborum et rerum significatione commentaria* (1557), Lyons, 1586, 4. The translation is from Ian Maclean, "The Place of Interpretation: Montaigne and Humanist Jurists on Words, Intention and Meaning," in *Neo-Latin and the Vernacular in Renaissance France,* ed. Grahame Castor and Terence Cave (Clarendon Press, 1984).

8. John Austin, *Lectures on Jurisprudence,* vol. 1, ed. Robert Campbell, 4th ed. (John Murray, 1879), 642.

9. William Shakespeare, *The Comical History of the Merchant of Venice, or Otherwise Called the Jew of Venice (1596–7),* in *The Oxford Shakespeare: The Complete Works,* ed. Stanley Wells and others, 2nd ed. (Oxford University Press, 2005), 4.1.218–19; first published 1597.

10. Jeremy Bentham, *Constitutional Code,* The Collected Works of Jeremy Bentham, vol. 1, ed. J. H. Burns and F. Rosen (Oxford University Press, 1983), 434.

11. Antonin Scalia, *A Matter of Interpretation: Federal Courts and the Law,* ed. Amy Gutmann (Princeton University Press, 1997), 10.

12. It is ideas like this that Harel means to denote when he says that "some actions must be executed by public officials and ought not to be privatized": Alon Harel, *Why Law Matters* (Oxford University Press, 2014), 66. One problem that undermines Harel's treatment of privatisation is that he is imprecise on a key point: at times he seems to say that some action cannot be done by a private actor; at others (as in this quote), he seems to say that it should not be done by a private actor.

13. Jeremy Waldron, "Legislation by Assembly," in *Law and Disagreement* (Oxford University Press, 1999), 65–66; Jeremy Waldron, "Can There Be a Democratic Jurisprudence?," *Emory Law Journal* 58 (2009): 675, 700–701.

14. John Dinwiddy, *Bentham: Selected Writings of John Dinwiddy,* ed. William Twining (Stanford University Press, 2004), 63–64.

15. Austin, *Lectures on Jurisprudence,* 642.

16. The most famous is Citizens United v. Federal Election Commission 558 US 310 (2010).

17. Data released by Federal Election Commission on November 27, 2017; analysis by Center for Responsive Politics: "Donor Demographics," OpenSecretsorg, https://www.opensecrets.org/overview/donordemographics.php?cycle=2016&filter=A.

18. In the language of Marc Galanter, arguments should not be made only by the "haves": Marc Galanter, "Why the Haves Come Out Ahead: Speculations on the Limits of Legal Change," *Law and Society Review* 9 (1974): 95.

19. Waldron, "Legislation by Assembly," 65.

20. Richard Harris, *The Decision* (Dutton, 1971), 110.

21. Niko Kolodny, "Rule over None II: Social Equality and the Justification of Democracy," *Philosophy and Public Affairs* 42 (2014): 287, 319.

22. Kolodny, Rule over None II: Social Equality and the Justification of Democracy," 319.

23. Article 2 of the US Constitution.

24. The political reality in the United States is such that these hearings are rarely productive. It would be career suicide for a judge to say that she makes law or that her law-making is a political act. This is a bug, not a feature, of the appointments process: a more mature debate would permit discussion of the kinds of law-making that are thought appropriate, the proper limits of judicial powers, and so on.

25. It can also, if a legal system requires it, depend on the arguments put to those judges. A legal system might, in other words, prohibit judges from deciding according to arguments the parties to the dispute have not raised. When this is the case, it is a further reason why the quality of the lawyers matters.

26. That view is accepted by people on all sides of the political spectrum. In the United States, for example, many on the left think that *Citizens United v. Federal Election Commission*, on campaign financing, should be overturned. Many on the right think that Roe v. Wade 310 US 113 (1973), on abortion rights, should be overturned. Both groups, in other words, think that there are some precedents which should be changed.

27. See Marc Galanter, "The Vanishing Trial: An Examination of Trials and Related Matters in Federal and State Courts," *Journal of Empirical Legal Studies* 1 (2004): 459 and the other papers in the same journal.

28. Hazel Genn, "Why the Privatisation of Civil Justice is a Rule of Law Issue," Thirty-Sixth F. A. Mann Lecture (British Institute of International and Comparative Law, 2012), 1. The lecture provides the most comprehensive account of the decline in civil trials in the United Kingdom.

29. All this is to say nothing about the democratic considerations that justify a broad range of interests in court.

30. Pew Research Center, Mobile Fact Sheet, February 5, 2018, states that 95 per cent of the U.S. population owns a cell phone. The 99.9 per cent figure comes from Consumer Financial Protection Bureau, *Arbitration Study: Report to Congress 2015,* p. 8, table 1.

31. Even if those rights were known, this would not solve all the problems: as earlier chapters have stressed, a lot depends on how accessible the legal system is.

32. Ronald Coase, "The Lighthouse in Economics," *Journal of Law and Economics* 17 (1974): 357.

33. See Richard A. Posner and William M. Landes, "Adjudication as a Private Good," *Journal of Legal Studies* 8 (1979): 235, 241.

34. David Luban, "Settlements and the Erosion of the Public Realm," *Georgetown Law Journal* 83 (1995): 2619, 2622.

35. For an argument that a market system will systematically underproduce law, see Posner and Landes, "Adjudication as a Private Good."

9. The Expense of Justice

1. He followed Lyman Abbott in the order of proceedings: for Abbott's remarks, see the Introduction.

2. "Mr. Roosevelt Praises the Legal Aid Society," *New York Times,* March 24, 1901, 3.

3. William H. Taft, "The Delays of the Law," *Yale Law Journal* 18 (1908): 28, 36. Taft succeeded Teddy Roosevelt as president of the United States. After his presidency, he became chief justice of the US Supreme Court.

4. In this chapter I refer to all the expense of justice in the language of "costs." That word has a special meaning to some lawyers, a meaning I do not mean to invoke: the language of costs is simply the most natural way of talking about the expense of running a justice system.

5. Adam Smith, *An Inquiry into the Nature and Causes of the Wealth of Nations,* The Glasgow Edition of the Works and Correspondence of Adam Smith, vol. 2, ed. William B. Todd (Oxford University Press, 1976), book 5, chap. 1, part 2; first published 1776. For a helpful discussion, see Rudolf Haensch, "From Free to Fee: Judicial Fees and Other Litigation Costs during the High Empire and Late Antiquity," in *Law and Transaction Costs in the Ancient Economy,* ed. Dennis P. Kehoe, David Ratzan, and Uri Yiftach (University of Michigan Press, 2015).

6. A major comparative inquiry into the costs of the civil justice system had essentially no discussion of this question: Christopher Hodges, Stefan Vogenauer, and Magdalena Tulibacka, eds., *The Costs and Funding of Civil Litigation: A Comparative Perspective* (Hart Publishing, 2010). What statements there are in leading costs reviews are cursory at best.

7. US Office of the Attorney General, Press Release Number 18-167 (February 12, 2018); United Kingdom, Treasury, *Budget 2018* (HC 1629, 2018), 24.

8. https://www.supremecourt.gov/about/courtbuilding.pdf. Revalued to 2009 figures, for parity with the United Kingdom's court, this is $157,265,940. (I assume an average of 3.7 per cent inflation.) The United Kingdom's court cost £56m: Written Answer of the Ministry of Justice to question posed by Lord Steinberg (Col. WA102, Lords Hansard, March 26, 2008).

9. Most systems allow lawyers to charge what they like though there are attempts to regulate prices through, for example, fixed tariffs: see generally Hodges, Vogenauer, and Tulibacka, *The Costs and Funding of Civil Litigation.*

10. The exceptions are the United States of America (minus Alaska) and Lithuania.

11. Roger of Hoveden, *The Annals of Roger de Hoveden: Comprising the history of England and of other countries of Europe from A.D. 732 to A.D. 1201,* ed. and trans. Henry T. Riley (H. G. Bohn, 1853), 394. First published 1201.

12. Hoveden, *The Annals of Roger de Hoveden,* 394.

13. John Locke, *Two Treatises of Government,* ed. Peter Laslett (Cambridge University Press, 1988), 2, section 140; first published 1689.

14. The healthcare context is a possible counter-example to this; the responsibility principle is sometimes invoked. But the principle is subject to serious criticisms in that context; and, anyway, defence is a better analogy with legal services.

15. That said, how much money there is may determine the distributive principles. I will turn to this question, of what to do when there is an unjust tax system, in the next chapter.

16. Uri Gneezy and Aldo Rustichini, "A Fine Is a Price," *Journal of Legal Studies* 29 (2000): 1.

17. The precise amount consumption will decrease depends on the price elasticity of demand. Necessary and non-substitutable goods will be relatively inelastic; luxury or substitutable items will be elastic.

18. Hoveden, *The Annals of Roger de Hoveden*, 394.

19. This analysis of fees is quite conventional and has been made clearly before, for example, Reginald Heber Smith, *Justice and the Poor* (Charles Scribner, 1919), 30.

20. I have slightly hedged my bets here to leave open the possibility of some further objection to above-cost court and lawyers' fees. Some claim that profiting can be exploitative: Michael J. Sandel, *Justice: What's the Right Thing to Do?* (Farrar, Straus and Giroux, 2009), 16. It has also been said that profiting fails to treat the justice system in the appropriate way: Sir Richard Scott, Keith Tucker Lecture (Kent Law Society, March 13, 1997). I have not considered these claims in detail because they are orthogonal to my own project and because they are insufficiently developed in the literature to bring into focus.

21. Frank I. Michelman, "The Supreme Court and Litigation Access Fees: The Right to Protect One's Rights—Part II," *Duke Law Review* 3 (1974): 527, 559. The same point has been made before: Roland K. Wilson, "Lawyers' Bills—Who Should Pay Them?," *Law Quarterly Review* 12 (1896): 368; Boddie v. Connecticut 401 US 371, 381 (1971) (Harlan, J.).

22. See, for example, Nick Penzenstadler and Susan Page, "Trump's 3,500 Lawsuits Unprecedented for a Presidential Nominee," *USA Today,* June 1, 2016.

23. United Kingdom, Anti-Social Behaviour, Crime and Policing Act 2014, s 180(6).

24. This is, for reasons unexplained, said to be a "principled approach" in the leading comparative study on the topic: Hodges, Vogenauer, and Tulibacka, *The Costs and Funding of Civil Litigation,* 78. See, too, Australian Government, Attorney-General's Department, *A Strategic Framework for Access to Justice in the Federal Civil Justice System* (September 2009), which recommended full cost recovery: recommendation 9.2.

25. I discuss this question in greater detail in Frederick Wilmot-Smith, "Just Costs," in *Principles, Procedure and Justice: Essays in Honour of Adrian Zuckerman,* ed. Rabeea Assy and Andrew Higgins (Oxford University Press, 2020).

26. D.5.1.79 translated in Alan Watson, trans., *The Digest of Justinian: Books 1–15,* rev. ed. (Cambridge University Press, 1998), 174. For a collection of Roman texts on expenses, many of which contain this flavour of responsibility, see Henri Erman, *La Restitution des Frais de Procès en Droit Romain* (C. Viret-Genton, 1892), 109 nn. 2, 3.

27. For example, H. L. A. Hart, "Postscript: Responsibility and Retribution," in *Punishment and Responsibility: Essays in the Philosophy of Law,* ed. John Gardner (Oxford University Press, 2008), 211–12. Notice, in this respect, that my previous sentence spoke of the *irresponsibility* of action: responsibility can have a positive or negative valence, depending in part on whether one is responsible for a good thing or a bad thing.

28. Compare the English "criminal court charge," which I discuss in Frederick Wilmot-Smith, "Unjust and Expensive," *LRB Blog,* October 15, 2015, http://www.lrb.co.uk/blog/2015/10/15/frederick-wilmot-smith/unjust-and-expensive/.

29. Coventry v. Lawrence [2014] UKSC 13, [2014] AC 106.

30. See, however, Philippe Van Parijs and Yannick Vanderborght, *Basic Income: A Radical Proposal for a Free Society and a Sane Economy* (Harvard University Press, 2017).

31. Smith, *The Wealth of Nations,* 825. Similarly, Turgot writes that "les dépenses du gouvernement ayant pour objet l'intérêt de tous, tous touivent y contribuer; et plus on jouit des avantages de la société, plus on doit se tenir honoré d'en partages les charges": Anne-Robert-Jacques Turgot, *Oeuvres de Turgot* (Guillaumin, 1844), 183 ("the expenses of government, having for their object the interests of all, should be borne by everyone, and the more a man enjoys the advantages of society, the more he ought to hold himself honoured in contributing to these expenses"). For a more recent discussion, see Liam Murphy and Thomas Nagel, *The Myth of Ownership* (Oxford University Press, 2002), 85.

32. Immanuel Kant, *The Metaphysics of Morals,* ed. Lara Denis; trans. Mary Gregor, 2nd ed. (Cambridge University Press, 2017), section 6:326; first published 1797.

33. Jeremy Bentham, "A Protest against Law Taxes," in *Writings on Political Economy,* The Collected Works of Jeremy Bentham, vol. 1, ed. Michael Quinn (Oxford University Press, 2016), 280; first published 1795.

34. H. L. A. Hart, "Are There Any Natural Rights?," *Philosophical Review* 64 (1955): 175, 185. This has proved intensely controversial and has given rise to an enormous literature. See, for example, Robert Nozick, *Anarchy, State and Utopia* (Basic Books, 1974), 91–95; A. John Simmons, "The Principle of Fair Play," *Philosophy and Public Affairs* 8 (1979): 307; Richard J Arneson, "The Principle of Fairness and Free-Rider Problems," *Ethics* 92 (1982): 616.

35. Taylor v. Laird (1856), 25 LJ Ex 329 (Exch) 332 (Pollock CB).

36. Consumption is, in economists' parlance, "non-rivalrous" and "non-excludable."

37. I call this benefit "private" (in scare quotes) because, as I explain subsequently, it is private in a very special sense.

38. Paula Costa e Silva, *A Litigância de Má Fé* (Coimbra Editora, 2008), 282.

39. The distinction I mean to make here is between the promulgation of norms and those norms having an effect; whether norms are effective depends in part upon whether people think they will be enforced. Someone might say: judges only promulgate norms in a common law country. I doubt that, though the argument is not going to make a practical difference.

40. Bentham, "A Protest against Law Taxes," 280. See, too, Jeremy Bentham, *The Constitutional Code,* vol. 9 of *The Works of Jeremy Bentham,* ed. John Bowring (William Tait, 1843), 491, Article 20 (commenting on the expense of judges, including an explicit analogy with military and health expenses).

10. Just Injustice

1. Immanuel Kant, *Anthropology from a Pragmatic Point of View,* ed. and trans. Robert B. Louden (Cambridge University Press, 2006), 175; first published 1798.

2. See, generally, Robert Stern, "Does 'Ought' Imply 'Can'? And Did Kant Think It Does?" *Utilitas* 16 (2004): 42. The difference between Kant's claims and the contemporary understanding is that while Kant used the maxim to source our powers (if we ought to do it, we can do it), people today often run the inference the other way (if we cannot do it, it is not the case that we ought to do it).

3. James Griffin, "The Human Good and the Ambitions of Consequentialism," in *The Good Life and the Human Good,* ed. E. F. Paul, F. D. Miller, and J. Paul (Cambridge University Press, 1992), 131.

4. John Rawls, *A Theory of Justice,* rev. ed. (Belknap Press of Harvard University Press, 1999), 138; first published 1971. See, too, John Rawls, *Justice as Fairness: A Restatement,* ed. Erin I. Kelly (Belknap Press of Harvard University Press, 2001), section 5.1.

5. John Rawls, *The Law of Peoples* (Harvard University Press, 1999), 90. Compare Amartya Sen, *The Idea of Justice* (Belknap Press of Harvard University Press, 2009); Gerald Gaus, *The Tyranny of the Ideal: Justice in a Diverse Society* (Princeton University Press, 2016).

6. Rawls, *A Theory of Justice,* 8. This is part of Rawls's "ideal" theory: see pp. 8–9, 245–46.

7. I did not follow Hume's proposal that "in contriving any system of government, and fixing the several checks and controls of the constitution, every man ought to be supposed to be a knave, and to have no other end, in all his actions, than private interest": David Hume, "On the Independence of Parliament," in *Essays, Moral, Political, and Literary,* ed. Eugene F. Miller, 2nd ed. (Liberty Fund, 1987), 42; first published 1742. If there were genuinely no one intent on doing good, it would be virtually impossible to set up a justice system.

8. David Luban, "Settlements and the Erosion of the Public Realm," *Georgetown Law Journal* 83 (1995): 2619, 2647.

9. Rawls, *A Theory of Justice,* 13.

10. For example, G. A. Cohen, "Incentives, Inequality, and Community," in *The Tanner Lectures on Human Values* (University of Utah Press, 1992); G. A. Cohen, *Rescuing Justice and Equality* (Harvard University Press, 2008).

11. It could be said that these political constraints bottom out in constraints about human preferences, for political institutions are made by humans. Yet they are still a different kind of constraint and worth keeping distinct for that reason.

12. Citizens United v. Federal Election Commission 558 US 310 (2010).

13. It is always open to the opponent to argue that my principles are simply bad ones: that is a possible counterargument to any proposed principle of justice. But objections of infeasibility only arise if it is accepted (even if only *arguendo*) that the correct principles are under consideration.

14. Daron Acemoglu and James Robinson, *Why Nations Fail: The Origins of Power, Prosperity, and Poverty,* 1st ed. (Crown Business, 2012), 305–14. Their account of the rule of law stresses equality: see p. 306.

15. With respect to normative priority, we might distinguish between lexical and weight ordering. A lexical ordering would say that a principle with priority must be complied with before other goals can be pursued: Rawls, *A Theory of Justice*, 37–38. A normative ordering would say only that compliance with a principle with priority is more valuable than compliance with other candidate principles. No principle I have proposed plausibly has lexical ordering so I will assume that the second kind of priority is the only one under consideration.

16. This point is made in detail in Chapter 5.

17. For the references to the law of the European Court of Human Rights, see footnote 43 of Chapter 4.

18. Gideon v. Wainwright 372 US 335 (1964).

19. Lassiter v. Department of Social Services 452 U.S. 18 (1981), 27.

20. For discussion see David Luban, "Political Legitimacy and the Right to Legal Services," in *Lawyers and Justice: An Ethical Study* (Princeton University Press, 1988), 261.

21. Although this ranking, with criminal more important than civil, strikes most people as intuitive, that analysis is not universal. Scotland recognised a right to counsel in civil cases in 1424 (Parliament at Perth, 12th March 1424, Cap 24); it did not recognise a right to counsel in criminal cases until 1587 (29th July 1587, c.38). See, for a general account of the civil-criminal distinction, Issachar Rosen-Zvi and Talia Fisher, "Overcoming Procedural Boundaries," *Virginia Law Review* 94 (2008): 79.

22. Boddie v. Connecticut 401 US 371, 374 (1971).

23. I use the term "ethically" here in a full-blooded sense, not as the rather anaemic concept of "legal ethics"—roughly, the official code of conduct—lawyers are bound to comply with.

24. There is, however, a vast cognate literature on aggregation in ethics (especially medical ethics) that would provide fertile land for future research. A seminal paper is John M. Taurek, "Should the Numbers Count?" *Philosophy and Public Affairs* 4 (1977): 293.

25. Karl Marx, *Critique of the Gotha Programme*, ed. Robert C. Tucker, 2nd ed. (W. W. Norton, 1978), 539; first published 1875.

26. Marx, *Critique of the Gotha Programme*, 539.

27. Robert Winchelsey, *Statutes of the Court of Arches*, excerpted in James Thomas Law, *Forms of Ecclesiastical Law* (translation of the first part of Thomas Oughton's *Ordo Judiciorum*) (Saunders and Benning, 1831), 34 n. 2.

28. John Cooke, *Unum necessarium, or, The Poore Mans Case* (1648), 3.

29. Similar points can be made of the National Health Service. Why do doctors owe particular obligations, such that they might be required to work for the state, to ensure that individuals have access to healthcare?

30. Reginald Heber Smith, "Introduction," in Emery Brownell, *Legal Aid in the United States: A Study of the Availability of Lawyers' Services for Persons Unable to Pay Fees* (Lawyers Cooperative, 1951), xiii. At the most extreme, it is said that the Bar "has the responsibility—not just *a* responsibility but *the* responsibility—for a solution to the basic problem and all the underlying subsidiary problems respecting the representation of indigents in criminal cases":

E. Barrett Prettyman, "Three Modern Problems in Criminal Law," *Washington and Lee Law Review* 18 (1961): 187, 218.

31. Report of the Poor Persons Rules Committee, Cmd. 2358 (HMSO, 1925), para. 12.

32. The most sophisticated analysis in this vein is Liam Murphy, *Moral Demands in Nonideal Theory* (Oxford University Press, 2000).

33. This view is similar to the claim that we are entitled only to what we are "left with after taxes under a legitimate system, supported by legitimate taxation": Liam Murphy and Thomas Nagel, *The Myth of Ownership* (Oxford University Press, 2002), 32–33. Murphy and Nagel have a particular and controversial view of property rights that they use to justify this conclusion; we need not, however, agree with them that there are no property rights absent taxation to agree with the proposal here. For precursors to these claims, see Kenneth J Arrow, "Nozick's Entitlement Theory of Justice," *Philosophia* 7 (1978): 265, and Jeremy Waldron, "Welfare and the Images of Charity," *Philosophical Quarterly* 36 (1986): 463, 474.

34. The nature, and even the existence, of these obligations is contested: compare Robert Nozick, *Anarchy, State and Utopia* (Basic Books, 1974), 93; Daniel Butt, *Rectifying International Injustice: Principles of Compensation and Restitution between Nations* (Oxford University Press, 2009).

ACKNOWLEDGEMENTS

For help, small and large, I would like to thank Tom Adams, Rabeea Assy, Aditi Bagchi, Mitch Berman, Tim Besley, Paul Brand, Andy Burrows, Liz Chatterjee, Philip Cook, Nico Cornell, Dan Dennis, Hasan Dindjer, David Dow, David Dyzenhaus, Richard Epstein, Wolfgang Ernst, Bill Ewald, Patrick Finglass, Guy Fletcher, Sam Freeman, Brandon Garrett, Hazel Genn, Moshe Halbertal, Max Harris, Andrew Higgins, Chris Hinchcliffe, Chloë Kennedy, Sari Kisilevsky, Matt Landauer, Rick Latta, Ian Loader, Noel Malcolm, Irad Malkin, James Manwaring, Sandra Marshall, Sandy Mayson, Claudio Michelon, Cathy Morgan, Paul Myerscroft, David Neuberger, Jesse Norman, Stephen Perry, David Plunkett, Judith Resnik, Michael Rosen, Philip Sales, Kate Saunders-Hastings, Tim Scanlon, Sam Scheffler, Alice Schneider, Marco Segatti, Robert Sharpe, Lionel Smith, Sophie Smith, Amia Srinivasan, Andy Summers, Jonathan Sumption, John Vickers, Nick Vincent, Jeremy Waldron, Neil Walker, Mary Wellesley, Emily Kidd White, Claudia Wilmot-Smith, Peter Wilson, David Winterton, George Woudhuysen, Lucia Zedner, and Reinhard Zimmermann. I would also like to thank audiences at the Max-Planck-Institut in Hamburg, New York University, the University of Chicago, the University of Pennsylvania Law School, and the University of Oxford. I am also grateful to all at Harvard University Press, in particular my editor, Ian Malcolm, who commented upon a late-stage manuscript.

The first draft of the book arose out of a series of seminars I taught in Oxford on the topic. While I am grateful to all who came, I want to single out John Gardner, Les Green, Nick McBride, and Robert Stevens. They acted as commentators on various chapters; their various insights prompted innumerable changes. John deserves special thanks: he nurtured my interest in philosophy, encouraged me to pursue this project, and, despite serious discomfort through illness, gave yet another set of comments on a late-stage draft.

Edinburgh University hosted a workshop on an early draft: thanks go to all who came and commented, and to the Global Justice Academy's Innovative Initiative Fund for its financial support of the event. I am particularly grateful to Luís Duarte d'Almeida and Euan MacDonald for organising that workshop (and for their customarily penetrating comments).

A number of people read and commented on draft manuscripts. Adrian Zuckerman was an invaluable guide and critic at an early stage. Cécile Fabre was unfailingly supportive and unstintingly critical at every stage. Emma Saunders-Hastings gave numerous valuable pointers. Gabriel Roberts, a profound intellectual influence since my first day as an undergraduate, gave an extraordinarily helpful set of comments on a late draft. And my mother, Jenny Fairfax, read countless drafts: she is my most astute critic, particularly on matters of style.

Many thanks go to NYU, its Hauser Global Law School Program, and the NYU School of Law Center for Law and Philosophy for hosting me and for financial support. Aditi Bagchi, Mary Carruthers, and Anthony Gottlieb gave me rooms of my own when I lived in New York.

Finally, I would like to record my gratitude to the staff, fellows, and warden of All Souls College. My prize fellowship was a most wonderful privilege.

INDEX